Women's Economic Empowerment

Praise for this book

'Jones and Bramm's book is an authoritative point of reference for defining the concepts, terms and principles behind women's economic empowerment. It also provides a set of inspirational stories from MEDA's work that illustrate how the market systems approach can be more gender-inclusive. Highly valuable!'

Mike Albu, Director, BEAM Exchange / DCED

'This book brings together a wealth of information and experience on women's economic empowerment. It provides clear evidence from statistics and field-work on why addressing women's economic empowerment is fundamentally important to reducing poverty and achieving the SDGs. Practical examples on how to contribute to women's economic empowerment are underpinned by concise summaries of gender equality and women's empowerment theories. Each chapter is well-referenced and includes additional resources for those who want to delve deeper. The book is a valuable resource for practitioners and policy makers.'

Alexandra Miehlbradt, Director, Miehlbradt Consulting Ltd.

Women's Economic Empowerment

Transforming Systems through Development Practice

Edited by
Linda Jones and Adam Bramm

Practical
ACTION
PUBLISHING

Practical Action Publishing Ltd
27a, Albert Street, Rugby, Warwickshire, CV21 2SG, UK
www.practicalactionpublishing.org

A catalogue record for this book is available from the British Library.

A catalogue record for this book has been requested from the Library of Congress.

ISBN 978-1-78853-028-6 Paperback
ISBN 978-1-78853-027-9 Hardback
ISBN 978-1-78044-750-6 Library PDF
ISBN 978-1-78044-751-3 Ebook

Citation: Jones, L. and Bramm, A. (2019) (eds) *Women's Economic Empowerment: Transforming Systems through Development Practice*, Rugby, UK: Practical Action Publishing <http://dx.doi.org/10.3362/ 9781780447506>.

Since 1974, Practical Action Publishing has published and disseminated books and information in support of international development work throughout the world. Practical Action Publishing is a trading name of Practical Action Publishing Ltd (Company Reg. No. 1159018), the wholly owned publishing company of Practical Action. Practical Action Publishing trades only in support of its parent charity objectives and any profits are covenanted back to Practical Action (Charity Reg. No. 247257, Group VAT Registration No. 880 9924 76).

Cover photos credit: top image: Roger Reuver, bottom and middle images: Neil Palmer (CIAT)
Cover design by RCO.design
Printed on demand

Contents

http://dx.doi.org/10.3362/9781780447506.000

Figures and tables

Figures

Tables

Foreword

The 2015 Sustainable Development Goals (SDGs), endorsed by 193 nations, offered a renewed and expanded commitment to end gender inequality in all forms by 2030. At the same time, awareness and pressure were also growing as a result of the tireless efforts of women and men around the world whose work shone a light on the gender discrimination and biases that excluded women and girls from equitable participation in economic, social and political spheres. Gender equality, women's rights and the empowerment of women, girls and other excluded communities have not received sufficient resourcing to date.

Creating change requires understanding of the issues at hand and dedication to resolving inequalities. However, knowledge and commitment are not enough; change also depends on evidence-based roadmaps, frameworks, models, examples and other learning that can provide guidance to those that are striving for change. MEDA has prepared a volume that is a much needed and powerful resource for women's socio-economic empowerment through systems change. With explanations of trends, challenges and opportunities, along with numerous case studies and examples, it is a valuable reference book for practitioners, policy makers and students of development practice.

The terms, approaches and descriptions in this collection are grounded in the real lives of women and girls from developing countries in all regions of the world. It highlights the very practical concerns that they face due to social bias, inequitable access to resources, lack of community or political support, and more. Furthermore, it illustrates how women and girls can overcome such challenges, rally the support of their families, communities, business networks and government agencies, and achieve the change they seek.

Often, the desired change requires external support of local, regional and international non-governmental organizations (NGO) that are sensitive to the geographic, socio-cultural, political and economic contexts in which diverse communities of women, girls and other excluded populations live. MEDA, an international NGO, has been on the leading-edge of women's empowerment and gender equality since its work in the microfinance movement in the 1990s, followed by ongoing value chain and market systems initiatives beginning in the early 2000s, and more recently ground-breaking work in gender lens investing. As such, MEDA is ideally suited to share learning and the stories of the women and girls that they serve.

Sarah Hendriks
Director of Programme & Policy, UN Women
Formerly, Director of Gender Equality, Bill and Melinda Gates Foundation

Acknowledgements

The editors, Linda Jones and Adam Bramm, would like to acknowledge the many contributions to this volume. First, from the extensive citations, it is obvious that the hard work, experience, and expertise of many researchers, policy makers, and practitioners from around the globe have made this book possible.

We also appreciate the contributions of our Mennonite Economic Development Associates (MEDA) co-authors who have painstakingly prepared chapters from their own field experience, often stepping outside their comfort zone to share their learning with the larger development community. In particular, we would like to thank Carolyn Burns who has supported the preparation of the volume beyond her contributions as an author, as well as Clara Yoon who has provided quality control support.

As always, Practical Action Publishing – and especially the long-time Publications Manager Clare Tawney – have been wonderfully supportive and gracious colleagues. Practical Action and Clare understand that for practitioners to write a book it has to fit into a hectic schedule of fieldwork, project management, technical learning, and extensive international travel.

Finally, we thank the women who have been central to our lives for so many years – women often in the poorest of conditions who have continued to inspire us through their unflagging dignity, resilience, and commitment to creating a better life for their children and communities. We are thankful to have had the opportunity to walk with you and to learn from you, and we hope that in some small way this book recognizes your place in our hearts and minds.

Acronyms and abbreviations

AAS	aquatic agricultural systems
ADB	Asian Development Bank
AI	artificial intelligence
AKRSP	Aga Khan Rural Support Programme
AMEG	Asia and Middle East Economic Growth Best Practices
AR	augmented reality
ASI	Agribusiness Systems International
ASNA	Arab States and Northern Africa
AWID	Association for Women's Rights and Development
B2B	business-to-business
CEDAW	Convention on the Elimination of All Forms of Discrimination against Women
CGIAR	Consultative Group for International Agricultural Research
DCED	Donor Committee for Enterprise Development
DFAT	Department of Foreign Affairs and Trade (Australia)
DFID	Department for International Development
DFS	digital financial services
DIB	Educate Girls Development Impact Bond
EBRD	European Bank for Reconstruction and Development
ECDI	Economic and Community Development Institute
ESG	environmental, social, and governance
FAO	Food and Agriculture Organization of the United Nations
GALS	Gender Action Learning System
GE	gender equality
GEDI	Global Entrepreneurship Development Institute
GEM	Gender Equality Mainstreaming
GESI	Gender Equality and Social Inclusion
GLI	gender lens investing
GRB	gender-responsive budgeting
GROW	Greater Rural Opportunities for Women
GSMA	GSM Association
GSMs	gender and sexual minorities
HACCP	hazard analysis and critical control points
ICRW	International Centre for Research on Women
ICT	information and communications technology
ICT4D	information and communications technology for development

ICT4WEE	information and communications technology for women's economic empowerment
IDI	ICT Development Index
IDRC	International Development Research Centre
IDS	Institute of Development Studies
IDWF	International Domestic Workers Federation
IFAD	International Fund for Agricultural Development
IFC	International Finance Corporation
ILO	International Labour Organization
ILO-WED	International Labour Organization's Women's Entrepreneurship Development programme
IMF	International Monetary Fund
IoT	internet of things
ITU	International Telecommunications Union
IVR	interactive voice response
JICA	Japan International Cooperation Agency
LWEE	Libya Women's Economic Empowerment
M4C	Making Markets Work for the Jamuna, Padma and Teesta Chars
M4P	Making Markets Work for the Poor
MDF	Market Development Facility
MEDA	Mennonite Economic Development Associates
MENA	Middle East and North Africa
MFI	microfinance institution
MHM	menstrual hygiene management
MN	Macrosentra Niagaboga
MSD	market systems development
MSME	micro-, small-, and medium-sized enterprise
NGO	non-governmental organization
ODA	Official Development Assistance
ODI	Overseas Development Institute
OJT	on-the-job training
PNG	Papua New Guinea
PRA	participatory rural appraisal
RWEE	Joint Programme on Accelerating Progress Towards the Economic Empowerment of Rural Women
SDC	Swiss Agency for Development and Cooperation
SDGs	Sustainable Development Goals
SEWA	Self-Employed Women's Association
Sida	Swedish International Development Cooperation Agency
SMEs	small and medium enterprises
SOBA	Sierra Leone Opportunities for Business Action
STEM	science, technology, engineering, and maths
TBR Africa	TheBoardroom Africa
UN	United Nations
UNCTAD	United Nations Conference on Trade and Development

UNFPA	United Nations Population Fund
UNICEF	United Nations Children's Fund
UNIDO	United Nations Industrial Development Organization
UN OCHA	United Nations Office for the Coordination of Humanitarian Affairs
USAID	United States Agency for International Development
VR	virtual reality
VRA	Vulnerability and Risk Assessment methodology
VSLAs	village savings and loan associations
WB	World Bank
WEAI	Women's Empowerment in Agriculture Index
WEAMS	Women's Empowerment and Market Systems
WED	Women's Entrepreneurship Development
WEE	women's economic empowerment
WEF	World Economic Forum
WEOI	Women's Economic Opportunity Index
WEPs	Women's Employment Principles
WFP	World Food Programme
WIEGO	Women in Informal Employment: Globalizing and Organizing

About the contributors

Adam Bramm is the Associate Director for West Africa, Middle East, and North Africa at MEDA. He is a seasoned international development practitioner with over 15 years of experience in over 18 countries, facilitating economic development and women's economic empowerment. He serves on MEDA's Gender and Social Inclusion and Impact Investment technical areas, and on the SEEP Network's Women's Economic Empowerment Work Group Steering Committee. He has an MA in International Development from the Joseph Korbel School of International Studies.

Carolyn Burns is an impact investment researcher and practitioner, supporting the teams at MEDA, Grand Challenges Canada, and Sarona Asset Management to operationalize their respective impact investments in emerging markets. She is certified in Responsible Investing Essentials by the Principles for Responsible Investing Academy and in Fundamentals of Alternative Investments by the Charted Alternative Investment Analyst Association. Carolyn has co-authored two publications for Ivey Publishing and is a contributor to Impact Alpha. She has worked in 11 countries.

Calais Caswell is a Senior Program Manager in MEDA's Cross-Cutting Services Department, focusing on gender and environment. Her current work focuses on contributing to MEDA's thought leadership and implementation of gender and environment mainstreaming across international programmes. Prior to joining MEDA, Calais was a gender and environment specialist with an international cooperative development foundation, and a researcher and policy analyst for development programming in Canada and the Americas.

Jennifer Denomy is the Technical Director for Vulnerable Populations at MEDA. In this role, she develops and leads MEDA's strategy to promote increased economic inclusion for vulnerable populations, particularly youth, women, and rural populations. She has expertise in incorporating women and youth into markets, supporting entrepreneurship, promoting financial inclusion, and providing training and facilitation. Recently, she managed GROW (Greater Rural Opportunities for Women), a value chain project in northern Ghana impacting over 23,000 women.

Yasir Dildar is the Canadian Evaluation Society's Credentialed Evaluator and is currently working as Associate Director of Monitoring and Impact Measurement (MIM) at MEDA. He has more than 15 years of results measurement and evaluation experience with a focus on private sector development-related initiatives and women's economic empowerment (WEE). Yasir has advanced knowledge of results measurement and evaluation approaches and methodologies and hands-on experience of conducting evaluation studies. He has conducted more than 30 research and evaluation studies that involved developing methodologies, data collection, analysis, and reporting. His current responsibility involves providing advice and technical expertise to the MIM team and country offices in Africa, Asia, and Latin America in the development of strategies and systems related to results measurement.

Ann Gordon has an extensive background in international rural development and leadership in the entrepreneurial, non-profit, and government sectors, including working for MEDA, owning her own business, and six years as Executive Director for the Advanced Agricultural Leadership Program. A Canadian Nuffield Agriculture Scholar, over 25 years of experience in project-based management in various agri-food-related value chains has taken her across North America and to Afghanistan, China, Costa Rica, Ethiopia, Kenya, Pakistan, Sierra Leone, and Tanzania.

Rachel Hess has focused her work on using business transactions, enterprise support, and market systems strengthening to create opportunity for women and men who are economically marginalized. Her career has included working in fair trade, small business support programmes and, currently, directing the programmes of MEDA in eastern, southern, and central Africa. She has developed significant experience in enterprise development, facilitating market systems change, and project design and implementation in a range of international settings including Bangladesh, India, Pakistan, Egypt, Ethiopia, Kenya, Tanzania, Uganda, and Ghana.

Dr Linda Jones is Vice President, Partnerships and Innovation at MEDA, a globally recognized expert in the field of gender-inclusive private sector growth and market systems change, specializing in innovative project design and implementation, technical assistance and capacity building, and capturing and sharing learnings. Linda has contributed to the industry as a workshop facilitator, trainer, conference presenter, and author of many publications including MEDA's Gender Equality Mainstreaming Framework for impact investments, the seminal M4P WEE Framework, and the Women's Empowerment and Market Systems (WEAMS) Framework published by the BEAM Exchange. Previously the editor of the journal *Enterprise Development and Microfinance*, Linda holds an MA and a PhD in Anthropology and Linguistics.

Jennifer King has more than 20 years of experience in economic development in Asia, Africa, and Canada with a particular focus on improving women's and marginalized groups' agency and access to economic opportunities, including in post-conflict and post-disaster contexts. Jennifer has worked in the private, NGO, and government sectors in areas including market systems, entrepreneurship, trade, private sector development, and organizational capacity strengthening. Jennifer has managed or consulted on various gender and women's empowerment projects including in Myanmar, Sri Lanka, Indonesia, Nigeria, and Ghana.

Larissa Schneider is an inclusivity-oriented economic development practitioner, currently working with MEDA as a project manager, focusing on gender equality, youth and rural development, and women's economic empowerment programmes. Larissa has proven experience working with small businesses, civil society organizations, and public entities globally, to build their capacity in inclusive programming and to identify market-based strategies to inform internal policies and practices. Larissa holds a Master's degree in Global Governance from the Balsillie School of International Affairs at the University of Waterloo and an Honours degree in International Development from the University of Guelph.

Sara Seavey is Senior Program Manager for Gender at MEDA. She creates gender equality strategies for projects, develops tools, and builds the capacity of international staff and partners. Sara currently supports market system development projects in Tanzania, Myanmar, Ethiopia, Jordan, Ukraine, and Ghana. In the past, Sara has worked on mobile data for adaptive management and digital financial inclusion with USAID's Global Development Lab. She has also worked on projects covering workforce development in Morocco, women entrepreneurship in South Africa, and international exchange programmes between the US and Asia. Sara holds an MA in Social Enterprise from American University and a BA in International Development from Connecticut College.

Clara Yoon is a project manager at MEDA. She currently manages an innovation portfolio of projects testing and learning about non-traditional finance and its role in improving innovation adoption by smallholders worldwide. Her areas of interest are inclusive financial services, user-centred design, and research. Clara holds an MA in Global Governance from the University of Waterloo and a BA in Global Studies from Wilfrid Laurier University. Prior to joining MEDA in Canada, Clara interned with MEDA in Ethiopia. She has prior experience in South Korea, working with a human rights non-governmental organization.

PART 1
Introduction

Introduction

Linda Jones

Fatima lives in a conservative community in the remote mountainous district of Skardu in Gilgit-Baltistan, Pakistan. Skardu is home to K2 – the highest peak in Pakistan and the second highest in the world – a place with limited access to infrastructure, services, and markets. Families struggle to cover the costs of day-to-day needs, education, health, and productive activities. Despite social and economic challenges, Fatima has opened a small shop strategically situated near a primary school where she sells goods for women and children that are much appreciated by teachers and students alike. Fatima has a dream – if she can earn enough from her shop, she will send all five of her children to secondary school and possibly even to university.

Fatima is one of millions of women around the globe who are committed to contributing to the well-being of their families and communities. In my work that has extended to remote corners of Africa, Asia-Pacific, and Latin America, I have sat with countless women like Fatima to discuss their situations, aspirations, and solutions. Under the shade of a lone tree, in one-room houses or tents, in dusty courtyards, or in busy marketplaces women speak of their vision for a better world for themselves and their families. These women are not passive bystanders as is often portrayed, rather they are often dynamic actors who are limited by economic, social, and political circumstances and are striving to push forward despite enormous challenges.

Women everywhere know their own equality and empowerment are vital to positive economic change for their households, communities, and nations. Of course, women do not use the terms 'gender equality' or 'economic empowerment' but they talk about earning more money, connecting to markets, increasing their skills and knowledge, and obtaining needed resources and services. Moreover, women usually have solid ideas on what needs to change to attain economic goals and have suggestions on how to make that change. By understanding their specific concerns and suggestions, it is possible to arrive at long-term dynamic solutions – not quick fixes or cookie-cutter solutions that often fail over time. In short, women's economic problems are solvable, and with good listening, and the right political and social will, we can co-create a better future for all.

About this book

This book presents approaches and experiences that illustrate how development practitioners and policy makers can contribute to women's economic empowerment. It takes a systems lens, recognizing that economic issues are

http://dx.doi.org/10.3362/9781780447506.000

not isolated from political and social contexts. A systems lens, described in more depth in Chapter 2, enables practitioners and policy makers to effect change that can impact women at scale – often tens of thousands in a single initiative – by shifting systems to meet the needs of women. For example, facilitating women's access to, uptake of, and influence over a range of needed services, resources, and supports such as financial services, transportation to market, pricing information, skills development, and market linkages.

The expertise and people resources to prepare this book have been provided by Mennonite Economic Development Associates (MEDA), an organization that has been working in the field of gender equality and women's empowerment through private sector and systems lenses for decades. Our contributions over the years have included:

- A pioneering role in microfinance since the early days of the industry in Peru and Bolivia, with ongoing leadership and innovation from product development to investments in financial institutions in Zambia, Tajikistan, and Ukraine.
- Recognized innovation in women's agricultural supply chain projects in countries as diverse as Myanmar, Afghanistan, Ethiopia, and Jordan.
- Development of viable business and financial services for women in challenging environments such as Libya, Pakistan, and Nicaragua.
- A commitment to mainstreaming gender equality and women's empowerment across our programming.

The MEDA authors, noted above and identified at the beginning of each chapter, bring a range of experience in systems change and women's economic empowerment coupled with other technical areas, from inclusive finance and agricultural development to gender lens investing and digitization. Their voices and expertise are reflected in the chapters they have prepared for this volume.

Within and outside MEDA, I have been involved in women's economic empowerment for two decades. While some of you will be familiar with my work and publications in the field, I highlight two resources here that are particularly relevant to this book on women's economic empowerment and the systems thinking that underlies it. In 2011, when it had become clear that with the growth in the Making Markets Work for the Poor (M4P) programme portfolio there was a critical need to incorporate women's empowerment more explicitly into guidance documents and in practice, I researched and wrote the conceptual framework for women's economic empowerment (WEE) in M4P programmes (Jones, 2012). The M4P WEE Framework was commissioned as part of a multi-donor (SDC, DFID, and Sida) effort to strengthen the M4P approach and to lead to dialogue and consensus-building on how to prioritize and operationalize women's economic empowerment within M4P initiatives.

Since its publication, the original M4P WEE Framework has been adopted and adapted by programmes around the world; for example, Market

Development Facility in Fiji, Timor-Leste, Pakistan, Sri Lanka, and Papua New Guinea; AIP-PRISMA in Indonesia; Katalyst and M4C in Bangladesh; ALCP in Georgia; the Arab Women's Enterprise Fund in Egypt, Jordan, and Palestine; Kenya Market Trust; and Financial Sector Deepening Zambia. Building on this rich experience, I prepared a revised framework in 2016, entitled *Women's Empowerment and Market Systems (WEAMS) Framework* published by the BEAM Exchange. The WEAMS Framework is broader in scope, focused more on practice, and describes both non-negotiable dimensions of empowerment while offering the flexibility to fit with different contexts and programming approaches.

More recently, MEDA has been at the leading edge of blended finance and gender lens investing, an area that has significant implications for women engaged in business sectors as employees, managers, suppliers, owners, consumers, and industry leaders. Out of our experience has come another practical open source manual for assessing and promoting improved gender outcomes in small to medium enterprise ecosystems called the *Gender Equality Mainstreaming (GEM) Framework*. The GEM Framework is a practical toolkit for evaluating and upgrading gender equality within target companies while mainstreaming gender across environmental, social, and governance (ESG) criteria.

In short, this volume combines the expertise of MEDA and our network of consultants, partners, and donors along with that of hundreds of thousands of women with whom we have worked. We hope you find it useful and that your efforts will benefit from the experiences and approaches presented here, contributing to gender equality and women's economic empowerment in your own contexts.

We are at a time in history when gender equality and women's empowerment are daily topics of discussion among development practitioners and policy makers, as well as more widely in mainstream media and countless other public and private conversations. Bolstered by the Sustainable Development Goals, donor mandates, and more awareness in general, the time has come for us to collectively push the boulder up and over the hill, overcoming the limitations and hardships created by gender-based bias, discrimination, and exploitation. As development actors, we have a unique opportunity to contribute to this global trend, and to ensure that no one is left behind.

Contents of this book

This book is a resource for practitioners and policy makers, as well as students of development practice and policy, who have an interest in gender equality (GE) and women's economic empowerment (WEE). It is a practical volume that draws on experiences in diverse contexts to present successful programme approaches that are illustrated by examples and case studies.

The goal of the book is to support the achievement of long-term and dynamic systemic change in the economic lives of women by inspiring readers to promote GE/WEE through originality in the design and implementation of gendered solutions.

Part 1 of this book continues with an exploration of trends that are influencing the direction of WEE programming and systems change. This is followed by a discussion of key terms and concepts related to GE/WEE and systems development that underpin the book.

Part 2 consists of the core chapters of the book; that is, the specific approaches that are used to overcome systemic barriers and achieve WEE in development practice. Each chapter describes a distinct approach citing relevant literature and supported by case studies and examples. These chapters are written by different authors, and therefore reflect their unique technical expertise, programming experiences, and writing style. Each of the core chapters provides links to selected 'Useful resources' that can further readers' learning and assist in the practical application of the approaches examined herein.

Part 3 discusses the assessment of risk, and reviews monitoring and evaluation frameworks and tools as they pertain to GE/WEE. The first chapter offers guidance on how to assess and minimize risk; the second on the monitoring of project progress and the evaluation of results.

Finally, Part 4 explores emerging trends, especially in information and communications technologies and innovative finance, and offers a perspective on the future of GE/WEE in development programmes.

CHAPTER 1

Trends influencing gender equality and women's economic empowerment practice

Linda Jones

Abstract

The chapter outlines the major changes that result in increased awareness for gender equality and women's economic empowerment. The chapter then describes the work of major international donors and implementers in international development towards gender equality and women's economic empowerment practice as it relates to market systems development.

Keywords: women's economic empowerment, gender equality, inclusion, trends, international development, market systems

There are numerous trends that influence gender equality (GE) and women's economic empowerment (WEE) and the practice surrounding them. Since 2010, there has been a significant shift in these trends with growing global emphasis on GE/WEE by donors, policy makers, implementing agencies, and the public in general. During the same time period, there has been rapid growth in research, evidence, capacity, and shared experiences by implementers, consultants, civil society organizations, research institutes and other practitioners, and policy makers. The combination of these factors has created a 'perfect storm' whereby there are almost no development programmes that can ignore GE/WEE any longer. The major global trends influencing GE/WEE in development practice are discussed below.

Growing emphasis of funders on gender inclusion

After many decades of relative gender neutrality, funders are setting clear expectations and targets for GE/WEE. This section does not trace the history of gender inclusion in development aid but describes recent examples of funder actions that have contributed to significant change in the field.

As a trail blazer, the Swedish International Development Cooperation Agency (Sida) has actively pursued the promotion and evaluation of gender mainstreaming in its partner countries since the Fourth World Conference

http://dx.doi.org/10.3362/9781780447506.001

on Women, Beijing 1995 (Sida, 2002). From the early days, Sida was not just concerned with government policy and budgeting, but also assessed what was happening on the ground in terms of GE/WEE. For example, its forward-thinking 2002 evaluation stated:

> It is the intention to take the gender equality debate within development co-operation a step forward. The purpose of the evaluation is to assess gender equality, i.e. relations between women and men, and their respective roles. It will be important to assess if interventions have had (or should have had) different foci for women and men in order to contribute towards the equality goal. This involves looking at gender relations: how women and men relate, exercise power, divide work and responsibilities and make decisions (Sida, 2002: 2).

Sida continued its commitment to gender and went on to influence and financially support the first gendered market systems framework – the Making Markets Work for the Poor (M4P) WEE Framework – that integrated women's economic empowerment into market systems programming (Jones, 2012).

The government of the United Kingdom passed legislation in 2014 requiring GE reporting on the Department for International Development's (DFID) aid disbursements (Ford, 2014). As a result, DFID has adopted new annual reporting on progress towards achieving gender equality goals (DFID, 2014) and in 2018 launched a new strategic vision for gender inclusion that emphasizes bottom-up empowerment, access to opportunities, improved power relations, reductions in gender-based violence, and inclusion of all women (DFID, 2018).

Building on a strategic framework originally released in June 2014 (DFAT, 2014) the government of Australia also published a new GE and women's empowerment strategy in 2016 that identifies WEE as one of its three priorities. The strategy states that Australian aid programmes will 'integrate gender equality in our aid for trade, economic diplomacy and trade efforts, recognizing that women's economic empowerment is a driver of economic growth and prosperity' (DFAT, 2016: 9). DFAT's prioritization led to the development of Australian operational guidance, funding of market systems programmes that considered gender, and an increased sharing of lessons learned and case studies from supported programmes (for example: DFAT, 2015).

In 2017, Global Affairs Canada launched a Feminist International Assistance Policy based on the vision that GE and the empowerment of women and girls is the most effective way to reduce poverty and build a more inclusive, peaceful, and prosperous world. The approach means that Canada places GE and the empowerment of women and girls at the centre of all development efforts, prioritizing the investments, partnerships, and advocacy efforts that have the greatest potential to close gender gaps, eliminate barriers to GE, and help achieve the Sustainable Development Goals (Global Affairs Canada, 2017).

Other donors have taken similar stands and approaches to GE/WEE in recent years, which has greatly expanded budgets available for WEE projects and influenced the direction of policy and practice in development programming, including in market systems development.

Formation of UN Women in 2010

Various United Nations (UN) programmes and specialized agencies have contributed to women's empowerment over the decades. The UN has been involved in activities on the ground and landmark initiatives such as the Convention on the Elimination of All Forms of Discrimination against Women (CEDAW) and the Commission on the Status of Women. However, despite key achievements, no single agency had the mandate to drive change in gender equality across UN bodies and member states. Therefore, in 2010, the UN General Assembly took a significant step in creating the UN Entity for Gender Equality and the Empowerment of Women (UN Women) with the goal of accelerating advances in GE and women's empowerment globally.

As a UN agency, UN Women supports member states to integrate gender into policies, guidance documents, and services with a focus on five priority areas: women's leadership and participation, ending gender-based violence, engaging women in peace and security processes, enhancing women's economic empowerment, and making gender equality central to national plans and budgets (UN Women, 2018a).

Achieving the Sustainable Development Goals

Adopted by world leaders in 2015, the Sustainable Development Goals (SDGs) have influenced policy makers and practitioners, providing not only the impetus for change but also the explicit identification of development objectives including specific objectives for GE/WEE. WEE projects have tended to zero in on SDG 5 (Achieve gender equality and empower all women and girls), but the interconnection between different aspects of women's lives is increasingly recognized. Projects that promote women's economic engagement realize, for example, that access to resources for production is meaningless if women are overburdened with domestic work and subject to discrimination in marketplaces. Later sections of this book explore this relationship in greater depth.

There are nine targets for women's empowerment under SDG 5 (UN Women, 2018b):

1. End all forms of discrimination against all women and girls everywhere.
2. Eliminate all forms of violence against all women and girls in the public and private spheres, including trafficking and sexual and other types of exploitation.
3. Eliminate all harmful practices, such as child, early, and forced marriage and female genital mutilation.
4. Recognize and value unpaid care and domestic work through the provision of public services, infrastructure, and social protection policies and

the promotion of shared responsibility within the household and the family as nationally appropriate.

5. Ensure women's full and effective participation and equal opportunities for leadership at all levels of decision making in political, economic, and public life.

6. Ensure universal access to sexual and reproductive health and reproductive rights as agreed in accordance with the Programme of Action of the International Conference on Population and Development and the Beijing Platform for Action, and the outcome documents of their review conferences.

7. Undertake reforms to give women equal rights to economic resources, as well as access to ownership and control over land and other forms of property, financial services, inheritance, and natural resources, in accordance with national laws.

8. Enhance the use of enabling technology, in particular information and communications technology, to promote the empowerment of women.

9. Adopt and strengthen sound policies and enforceable legislation for the promotion of gender equality and the empowerment of all women and girls at all levels.

Changing social norms

As practitioners have become more experienced in facilitating women's empowerment, we have observed the impact that social norms have on economic advancement of women. We live in a rapidly changing world where many influences from international bodies, such as UN Women, to social media play a critical role in shifting gendered social norms. In fact, social media is taking younger women by storm, with trendsetting women communicating through Twitter, blogs, messaging apps, and sites such as Facebook. For example, Ory Okolloh Mwangi from Kenya was identified as one of the most influential people in the world by *Time Magazine* in 2014 (reported in Rogo, 2016). At the time of posting, Mwangi was the head of investment at Omidyar Network (a 'philanthropic investment firm'), the former Policy Manager in Africa for Google, and co-founder of the technology firm Ushahidi and Mzalendo (a parliamentary watchdog website). Her biggest influence is reportedly on Twitter where she sparks debates and hopes to ignite the next generation of African women leaders (Rogo, 2016). Other social media campaigns, such as the #MeToo movement, are raising viability and changing public perceptions on the role of women in society.

Recent literature on unpaid care work provides examples of shifting social norms that are particularly relevant to economic advancement of women. That is, women are traditionally the caregivers for infants, the elderly, sick, or infirm. Such unpaid care work is a significant constraint when women take on additional work outside the home and, in many instances, women leave work if a family member such as an ageing parent or parent-in-law needs care. Research conducted at the Institute of Development Studies (IDS) at the University of Sussex (Maestre and Thorpe, 2016) found that solutions are available to address problematic aspects of care provision: enabling economic change that takes care responsibilities into consideration; reduction in arduous and inefficient care tasks; or redistribution of responsibility from women to men or from the household to the community, state, or market sector. A ground-breaking private sector example is gaining traction in India – professional home healthcare that not only provides trained care for the sick and elderly, but also enables women family members, the traditional caregivers, to remain in the workforce while at the same time providing employment and skills development for disadvantaged women and youth. This example is elaborated in Chapter 6 on gender lens investing.

Climate change, resources, and environmental impacts

Our planet is going through unprecedented changes in climate and weather events, depletion of resources, and other impacts on the environment such as pollution of the oceans and air. The United Nations Office for the Coordination of Humanitarian Affairs (UN OCHA) reports that while the number of natural disasters decreased between 2015 and 2016, the actual number of people impacted doubled to 204 million in the same time period (UN OCHA, 2017a). At the same time, other negative impacts are worsening; for example, by 2025 UN OCHA predicts that 1.8 billion people will suffer from absolute water scarcity and two-thirds of the world will live with water stress (UN OCHA, 2017b).

The subsequent negative impacts disproportionately affect low-income communities that are more resource constrained, vulnerable to shocks, and likely to live in polluted or toxic environments. Among those affected most, it is widely agreed that women and girls suffer the brunt of limited resources and other environmental impacts, with their household and productive work reliant on stable environmental conditions, such as the collection of water and firewood, growing crops for household consumption, management of herds, responsibility for the health and hygiene of the family, and more. For women and girls, environmental challenges are further exacerbated by prevalent and context-specific social factors with the result that 'women face historical disadvantages, which include limited access to decision-making and economic assets that compound the challenges of climate change' (UN Women Watch, 2017).

Rural women are especially dependent on natural resources for their productive activities in agricultural sectors (e.g. crop production, livestock and dairy development, forestry, poultry, and fishing), representing over 40 per cent of agricultural labour in developing economies (FAO, 2016). In fact, every gender and development indicator for which data are available reveals that rural women fare worse than rural men or urban women and men. This disparity means that while environmental degradation and climate change are concerns for all, in terms of women's livelihoods – and particularly rural women – the impacts can be dire. Economic development programmes must facilitate women's resilience through sustainable access to knowledge, skills development, and resources, especially climate-smart and environmentally friendly technologies and practices.

Conflict and violence

The rates of death, injury, displacement, and associated harms are reaching unprecedented highs worldwide, despite optimism in the early 2000s about the emergence of a more peaceful world.

Although the number of direct deaths from armed conflict had been declining since the 1940s, there have been renewed and prolonged deadly conflicts in the 2008 to 2018 decade (Roser, 2018). The casualties, which often exceed 100,000 deaths per year, include a high percentage of civilians, with over 70 per cent in the case of explosive devices (and 92 per cent in the case of landmines) (UN OCHA, 2017a). These data points do not take into consideration related deaths from disease, famine, extrajudicial killings, and small skirmishes (Roser, 2018). For women and girls, the harm extends beyond death and injury to all forms of physical, sexual, and psychological trauma that negatively impact women's lives on multiple levels.

Displacement exacts an enormous economic toll as people flee conflict and violence; the total number of forcibly displaced persons reached a record high of 68.5 million in 2017, of which about two-thirds were internally displaced and the remainder cross-border refugees (UNHCR, 2018). Displaced women and girls are especially vulnerable to harm with lower decision-making authority and control, and reduced access to assistance, resources, and services, along with greater susceptibility to gender-based violence and discrimination. Intersectionality (see Chapter 2) comes into play as indigenous or elderly women are often doubly disadvantaged (Brookings Institution, 2014). All these factors deliver negative impacts on women's economic lives and advancement, and consequently the well-being of themselves and their families.

On a more positive note for women, post-conflict reconstruction can be an opportunity for change when country rebuilding efforts attempt to set aside past gender discrimination and to engage women as economic actors (Ruiz Abril, 2009). For example, such changes have been witnessed in Colombia (UN Women, 2018c), Eritrea (Ruiz Abril, 2009), Somalia (Abdi, 2017), and Cambodia and Guatemala (Sorensen, 1998).

Useful resources

CARE's Gender and Inclusion Toolbox (Agriculture and Climate Change):
    https://careclimatechange.org/tool-kits/gender-inclusion-toolbox/
OECD Development Co-operation Directorate: http://www.oecd.org/dac/

Oxfam's Women's Economic Empowerment Resource Guide: https://views-voices.oxfam.org.uk/wee-resources/index.html

Sida's Gender Analysis – Principles and Elements Tool: https://www.sida.se/contentassets/a3f08692e731475db106fdf84f2fb9bd/gender-tool-analysis.pdf

Sida's report, *Women's Economic Empowerment in Conflict and Post-Conflict Countries*: https://www.sida.se/contentassets/410a062d22e74371926b9c1c462b0c7d/14882.pdf

UNDG's Sustainable Development Goals Acceleration Toolkit: https://undg.org/2030-agenda/sdg-acceleration-toolkit/

UN Women Watch – Climate Change Feature: http://www.un.org/womenwatch/feature/climate_change/

World Bank's *Gender, Conflict and Development*: http://documents.worldbank.org/curated/en/514831468763468688/pdf/30494.pdf

References

Abdi, O.M. (2017) *Women Empowerment Initiatives and Socio-Economic Development: A Quest for Gender Equality in a Post Conflict Somalia* [online], CERPA Briefing Paper 2 <https://www.researchgate.net/publication/316608876_women_empowerment_initiatives_and_socio_economic_development_a_quest_for_gender_equality_in_a_post_conflict_somalia> [accessed 11 April 2019].

Brookings Institution (2014) *Improving the Protection of Internally Displaced Women* [pdf], Washington, DC: Brookings Institution <https://www.brookings.edu/wp-content/uploads/2016/06/Improving-the-Protection-of-Internally-Displacement-Women-October-10-2014.pdf> [accessed 11 April 2019].

Department of Foreign Affairs and Trade (DFAT) (2014) *Australia's New Development Policy and Performance Framework: A Summary* [pdf], Government of Australia <http://dfat.gov.au/about-us/publications/Documents/aid-policy-summary-doc.pdf> [accessed 11 April 2019].

Department for International Development (DFID) (2014) *Department for International Development: Annual Report and Accounts 2013–2014* [pdf] <https://www.gov.uk/government/uploads/system/uploads/attachment_data/file/331591/annual-report-accounts-2013-14a.pdf> [accessed 11 April 2019].

DFAT (2015) *Operational Guidance Note: Gender Equality and Women's Economic Empowerment in Agriculture* [pdf], Government of Australia <https://dfat.gov.au/about-us/publications/Documents/operational-guidance-note-gender-equality-and-womens-economic-empowerment-in-agriculture.pdf> [accessed 11 April 2019].

DFAT (2016) *Gender Equality and Women's Empowerment Strategy* [online], Government of Australia <http://dfat.gov.au/about-us/publications/Pages/gender-equality-and-womens-empowerment-strategy.aspx> [accessed 11 April 2019].

DFID (2018) *DFID Strategic Vision for Gender Equality* [pdf] <https://assets.publishing.service.gov.uk/government/uploads/system/uploads/

attachment_data/file/689939/Strategic-vision-gender-equality.pdf>
[accessed 11 April 2019].

Food and Agriculture Organization of the United Nations (FAO) (2016) *The State of Food and Agriculture: Climate Change, Agriculture and Food Security* [pdf], Rome: FAO <http://www.fao.org/3/a-i6030e.pdf> [accessed 11 April 2019].

Ford, L. (2014) 'Development bill to tackle gender inequality poised to become law', [online], *The Guardian*, 4 March 2014 <http://www.theguardian.com/global-development/2014/mar/04/development-bill-gender-equality-law> [accessed 11 April 2019].

Global Affairs Canada (2017) *Canada's Feminist International Assistance Policy* [pdf], Ottawa: Global Affairs Canada <http://international.gc.ca/world-monde/assets/pdfs/iap2-eng.pdf> [accessed 11 April 2019].

Jones, L. (2012) *"Discussion Paper for an M4P WEE Framework: How can the Making Markets Work for the Poor Framework work for poor women and for poor men?"* [pdf], Springfield Center, DFID/SDC <http://springfieldcentre.com/wp-content/uploads/2012/11/M4P_WEE_Framework_Final.pdf> [accessed 20 May 2019].

Maestre, M. and Thorpe, J. (2016) *Unpaid Care Work – Facilitating Change towards Women's Economic Empowerment when Market Systems Care* [pdf], IDS, Oxfam, the BEAM Exchange <https://beamexchange.org/uploads/filer_public/fa/73/fa73f0e0-f2de-4913-b409-fb6d575dbaad/unpaid_carework.pdf> [accessed 11 April 2019].

Rogo, P. (2016) '15 African women you absolutely need on your timeline', [online], *Essence*, 18 August 2016 <https://www.essence.com/essence-africa/african-women-tastemakers-to-follow-social-media#993197> [accessed 11 April 2019].

Roser, M. (2018) 'War and peace', *Our World in Data* [online] <https://ourworldindata.org/war-and-peace> [accessed 11 April 2019].

Ruiz Abril, M.E. (2009) *Women's Economic Empowerment in Conflict and Post-Conflict Countries* [pdf], Stockholm: Sida <https://www.sida.se/contentassets/a7f86b2b8a774b0dacb7bce5f689dae5/14881.pdf> [accessed 11 April 2019].

Sida (2002) *Mainstreaming Gender Equality*, UTV Working Paper 2002:1 [pdf] <https://www.sida.se/contentassets/836ce29b2d3942a5b632ebf60803302f/20021-mainstreaming-gender-equality_1894.pdf> [accessed 11 April 2019].

Sorensen, B. (1998) *Women and Post-Conflict Reconstruction*, WSP Occasional Paper, June 1998 [pdf], Geneva: UNRISD <http://www.unrisd.org/80256B3C005BCCF9%2F(httpAuxPages)%2F631060B93EC1119EC1256D120043E600%2F%24file%2Fopw3.pdf> [accessed 11 April 2019].

UNHCR (2018) *Global Trends: Forced Displacement in 2017* [pdf], Geneva: UNHCR <https://www.unhcr.org/5b27be547.pdf> [accessed 11 April 2019].

UN OCHA (2017a) *World Humanitarian Data and Trends (WHDT) 2017* [online] <http://interactive.unocha.org/publication/datatrends2017/> [accessed 11 April 2019].

UN OCHA (2017b) *World Humanitarian Data and Trends 2017: Global Landscape* [pdf] <http://interactive.unocha.org/publication/datatrends2017/resources/WHDT2017_Global%20Landscape_final.pdf> [accessed 11 April 2019].

UN Women (2018a) 'About UN Women' [online] <http://www.unwomen.org/en/about-us/about-un-women> [accessed 11 April 2019].

UN Women (2018b) 'SDG 5: Achieve gender equality and empower all women and girls' [online] <http://www.unwomen.org/en/news/in-focus/women-and-the-sdgs/sdg-5-gender-equality#sthash.sY6dW3zE.dpuf> [accessed 11 April 2019].

UN Women (2018c) 'From where I stand: "It's not just men who can do business"', [online], 7 May 2018 <http://www.unwomen.org/en/news/stories/2018/5/from-where-i-stand-deyanira-cordoba> [accessed 11 April 2019].

UN Women Watch (2017) *Women, Gender Equality and Climate Change Fact Sheet* [pdf] <http://www.un.org/womenwatch/feature/climate_change/downloads/Women_and_Climate_Change_Factsheet.pdf> [accessed 11 April 2019].

CHAPTER 2

Concepts and terms

Linda Jones

Abstract

This chapter describes the major concepts and terms in gender equality and women's economic empowerment practice within a market systems development approach.

Keywords: gender equality, market systems, gender mainstreaming, gender blind, gender neutral, intersectionality

Certain concepts and terms are essential to the discourse on gender equality (GE) and women's economic empowerment (WEE). The overarching approach to development adopted by this book – market systems development (MSD) – is underpinned by another equally important set of concepts and terms. As in any field of practice, concepts and terms vary in usage and may even be under hot debate. Since GE and WEE come together as two areas of practice come together in this book and are elaborated by multiple authors, the authors have agreed to limit use of jargon and to harmonize our use of the key concepts and terms as much as possible. Terms and concepts that are used throughout are explained in this chapter. Where concepts or terms are specific to a chapter, they are clarified in that chapter.

Gender equality and women's economic empowerment

Gender equality and *women's (economic) empowerment* are often spoken in the same breath – but not always with a clear distinction of meaning. *Gender equality* refers to an egalitarian situation between women and men in which both genders enjoy the same opportunities, status, rights, and responsibilities. *Women's economic empowerment* describes a process through which women achieve improved access, agency, control, and power. Thus, GE is a desired outcome to which WEE interventions may contribute.

When adopting a systems lens, we aim to empower women through activities that shift market systems to be more favourable for women. As we facilitate increased empowerment of women by implementing gender-inclusive approaches, this contributes to greater gender equality (Jones, 2016). For example, in Mennonite Economic Development Associates' (MEDA) programming

http://dx.doi.org/10.3362/9781780447506.002

in Pakistan over the past two decades, we have worked across rural sectors enabling women to access inputs, improve the quality of production, reach markets, and realize greater leadership roles and decision-making authority in their households and communities. Over the five-year span of one of MEDA's initiatives in Pakistan, USAID reported a 147 per cent increase in income for women in the project who exhibited improved skills, better capacity to manage their businesses, and greater control over related income (IDS, 2014). Nevertheless, while considerable economic empowerment has been achieved across key indicators along with shifts in target sectors, equality is still far from being achieved for many women in rural sectors in Pakistan (Center of Gender and Policy Studies, 2018).

Market systems

The *market systems* or *market systems development (MSD)* field of practice builds on the ground breaking work of The Springfield Centre and the Making Markets Work for the Poor (M4P) approach (The Springfield Centre, 2015). In current usage, the term *market system* applies to a range of economic and non-economic sectors such as education, health, and finance, or to more narrow segments such as agricultural sectors or enterprise ecosystems. The word *market* in the phrase *market systems* can sometimes be confusing as it might be understood to reference only the buying and selling function. However, in MSD the term *market* is applied more broadly to both economic and non-economic sectors.

A market system encompasses the transactions at the heart of a sector as well as local, national, and international supporting functions, rules and regulations, and actors. Thus, a market system can be broken down into three main components that are shaped and/or carried out by a range of market actors (The Springfield Centre, 2015):

- *Core functions* are the central set of transactions between the demand and supply side of a market system, such as buying and selling of goods and services.
- *Supporting functions* incorporate the entities and activities (e.g. information, infrastructure, capacity building, products and services) that exist around the core exchange and affect the way the market system operates.
- *Rules* include both formal rules (e.g. laws, regulations, standards) and informal rules (e.g. social norms, gender biases, traditional practices) that govern participation and behaviour in market systems.
- *Market actors* represent a wide range of individuals and institutions from private, public, and civil society sectors that are (or could be) active or influential in a market system.

MSD approaches have evolved and differentiated over the years, with notable shifts when organizations and projects strive to be more inclusive of vulnerable and excluded populations such as disadvantaged women (e.g. World Vision, 2017; Bekkers et al., 2015). MEDA's successful approach to WEE is based on facilitating systemic change by influencing the rules, attitudes, and actions of relevant market actors and supporting women to develop capacities to participate in markets. For example, in an economic sector dominated by men, inclusive systems change should not only lead to greater empowerment for women in existing roles, but also result in the advancement of women as suppliers, buyers, service providers, business leaders, and consumers on their own terms. At the systems level, this means reducing or eliminating underlying formal and informal barriers to ensure equal access to resources and opportunities while building the agency of women so that they can fully engage in market systems. When an initiative integrates a gender lens across its research, implementation, and monitoring and evaluation, then we can call this *gender-inclusive market systems development.*

Note that in this volume, we often use just the word *system* (rather than the entire phrase *market system*), particularly when it is used as an adjective as in *systems lens* or *systems/systemic change*. We also employ the terms *ecosystem* and *sector*, which are analogous in our usage herein.

Gender-inclusive market systems development

Inclusion is a process that promotes the fair and equal participation of every person in a market system, adapting that system as needed to allow all to contribute and benefit, regardless of sex, age, ethnicity, religion, disability, and so on. *Gender inclusion* emphasizes equal participation of women and men across all dimensions of empowerment. This involves not only equal access to products, services, and opportunities, but also the agency needed for equal participation such as decision-making power, leadership roles, and balanced workloads. Ideally, inclusive systems change occurs at all levels and in all spheres of the system. While earlier the term *integration* was the goal of GE/WEE programming, *inclusion* has now been adopted to connote a much deeper shift for GE/WEE. That is, *integration* supported the adaptation of the individual to an existing system, while *inclusion* emphasizes changes in the system to meet the needs and situation of excluded groups.

This book adapts an early definition of *gender mainstreaming* by SDC (2003) that identified a three-prong approach that is still relevant today. *Inclusion* requires gender to be a theme in all planning phases and processes of a project and is a minimum requirement for gender inclusion. It incorporates a gendered approach into each step of research, analysis, planning, implementation, and monitoring and evaluation. *Targeting* focuses on women and is best employed alongside strategies that aim for gender inclusion. The intent is not to separate women from the mainstream economy, but to utilize targeted strategies to enhance inclusion efforts over the longer term. *Dialogue* involves discussion at all levels of society, from households and communities to national, regional, and international venues. Dialogue contributes to a gender perspective being understood and internalized by individuals, communities, implementing organizations, and other stakeholders including lawmakers and regulators. All three – integration, targeting, and dialogue – can be incorporated into a single project with various interventions taking different tacks, with the ultimate goal of shifting a system to be gender inclusive.

Making Markets Work for the Jamuna, Padma and Teesta Chars (Making Markets Work for the Chars, or more simply M4C), a five-year project implemented by Swisscontact and Practical Action in Bangladesh, aimed to reduce poverty and vulnerability of *char* (alluvial islands that may disappear completely during flooding) households in 10 districts of northern Bangladesh by facilitating market systems that enhance opportunities for employment and income generation for women and men. M4C utilized a three-prong approach to gender programming:

- M4C emphasized inclusion of women in grass-roots producer groups as well as in subcontracting relationships with buyers, ensuring both women and men had the opportunity to develop skills, access information, and be more productive in selected sectors.
- The project also targeted women in the handicraft sector by facilitating capacity building and income creation for women in partnership with handicraft companies that train women, offer inputs, and build market linkages.
- Finally, M4C promoted dialogue at multiple levels among public and private partners and service providers through seminars, workshops, and sharing learning papers and cases.

This multi-pronged approach enabled M4C to rapidly achieve change at scale for *char* women (M4C, n.d.).

Gender blind and gender neutral

According to UN Women (n.d.), being *gender blind* refers to the lack of recognition that the roles and responsibilities assigned to women and men are determined by sociocultural norms and political and economic contexts. As such, gender-blind programmes do not consider the diverse needs of women and men resulting from these assigned roles, and do not attempt to change the status quo. *Gender neutral* originally referred to language that could be more inclusive by not giving prominence to the male gender, thus changing *mankind* to *humankind, all men are created equal* to *all people are created equal,* and so on. Sometimes in development, policy makers and practitioners refer to their work as gender neutral, implying that they do not give preference to one gender over the other (which is meant to be interpreted positively like when we use gender-neutral language). However, in development practice, *gender neutral* is de facto *gender blind*. That is, in programming, gender neutral does not acknowledge that economies, sectors, business relationships, and communities are usually male dominated or have long been skewed towards men's roles and place in society. In order not to favour men nor further disadvantage women, programme activities must be gender inclusive, recognizing the different situations and needs of women and men, rather than widening the gender equality gap.

Sustainable and dynamic systems change

Sustainable change is achieved in MSD when the needed resources and services continue to be offered to and consumed by a target group beyond the period of an intervention (The Springfield Centre, 2015). This is a feat in and of itself. However, for the change to be dynamic and adaptive over time, power structures must be shifted, with all market actors having not only access to but also influence or control over opportunities, resources, and services. A sustainable system must itself change by having the structure and processes that allow it to adapt to market demand and other externalities with all participants empowered to contribute to and benefit from shifts in the systems. For dynamism and adaptation to be gender inclusive, initiatives must ultimately facilitate women's influence and control over their involvement in a system. Hence, a market system needs to be understood from a gender perspective, and the right interventions piloted and scaled up in order to achieve equitable change over the long term.

CARE's role in the coffee industry in Papua New Guinea (PNG) provides an interesting example of how women's roles can be enhanced not only to their benefit but for the long-term well-being of a sector. Even though conditions existed to produce one of the highest quality coffees in the world, most smallholder coffee producers in PNG were living in poverty. CARE had worked in the coffee industry for some time when it concluded that gender inequality was one of the reasons why the coffee industry had not taken off. With the support of the Australian Government, CARE started the Coffee Industry Support Programme in 2013 that aimed to redress gender biases in coffee production that had previously compromised productivity and quality. To create sustainable change in the coffee industry in PNG, CARE needed the right partners who would be long-term players in the sector. Despite structural constraints in the industry, CARE convinced the main coffee traders in PNG, the coffee government agency (the Coffee Industry Corporation), and leading civil society organizations that there was a need to invest in extension services for women to strengthen the sector. The coffee traders' extension officers began delivering inclusive training to coffee smallholder households that combined elements of financial management, business management, and household gender equality, with benefits to women and to the sector as a whole. As a result of these efforts, most of the extension services in the country have now become accessible to women, making both gender equality and the coffee industry more sustainable (Nardi, 2015).

Access and agency

Women's *access* and *agency* are key concepts that are used to define WEE in market systems programmes. The International Centre for Research on Women (ICRW) (Golla et al., 2011) builds on earlier empowerment literature (i.e. Kabeer, 1999) to streamline the definition of WEE into two distinct areas. That is, 'a woman is economically empowered when she has both the ability to succeed and advance economically and the power to make and act on economic decisions' (Golla et al, 2011: 4). Today, these two sets of capacities are commonly referred to as *access* and *agency*. Women's access represents a wide range of external resources, services, and opportunities that are required by women for economic advancement: from land title to financial services to market information. Women's agency is concerned with internal characteristics that contribute to and result from participation and leadership, such as confidence, aspiration, voice, decision-making authority, and financial autonomy (Jones, 2016).

The Market Development Facility (MDF), a flagship private sector development programme of the Government of Australia, offers an interesting example of how access and agency considerations play out in their interventions. MDF stimulates investment, business innovation, and regulatory reform to create jobs and increase income for disadvantaged women and men in rural and urban areas in the Indo-Pacific region. As a market systems programme that partners with the private sector, MDF is primarily concerned with better access to a wider variety of improved products and services for all. However, MDF realizes that while increasing access to a service, asset, or skill specifically for women, the market systems programme must consider how their objectives fit into a woman's overall situation and whether she has the agency to make decisions, manage her workload, and navigate other social norms and expectations. Without considerations of agency, the sustainability of the increased access comes into question. That is, a woman may not have the means to continue to use the service if she has limited control over how she interacts with it or benefits from it (Bekkers et al., 2015).

Non-negotiable dimensions of WEE

In the section above on GE/WEE, WEE is defined as *a process through which women achieve improved access, agency, control, and power*. This is what we aim to achieve in inclusive market systems programming.

Based on a review of the empowerment literature and an analysis of the M4P approach, the original M4P WEE Framework (Jones, 2012) suggested relevant dimensions of WEE for MSD programmes. That is, a tightly worded definition was not offered, but rather a summary of the key dimensions that could guide programmes in achieving and measuring women's empowerment outcomes that were compatible with a market systems approach. These dimensions have been implemented across multiple projects and have resulted in the solidification of five non-negotiable WEE dimensions. Case examples include the Market Development Facility in Fiji, Timor-Leste, Pakistan, Sri Lanka, and Papua New Guinea; AIP-PRISMA in Indonesia; Katalyst and M4C in Bangladesh; Alliances Lower Caucasus Programme in Georgia; Ukraine Horticulture Business Development Program; Arab Women's Enterprise Fund in Egypt, Jordan, and Palestine; Jordan Valley Links Project; Kenya Market Trust; and Financial Sector Deepening Zambia, among others. The five non-negotiable WEE dimensions are (Jones, 2016):

- Economic advancement resulting in increased income and return on labour.
- Access to opportunities and life chances such as skills development or job openings.
- Access to assets, services, and needed supports to advance economically.
- Agency in decision-making authority in different spheres including household finances.
- Agency in control over manageable workloads for women.

That is, without improved access to resources, decision-making authority, and the agency to manage workloads, increased incomes do not contribute to women's empowerment.

These WEE dimensions are not intended to be dogmatic or static but are flexible and can be nuanced or expanded to fit a programme's strategy and vision for change. In fact, adaptation and expansion are encouraged since GE/WEE are context specific, and our experiences and knowledge should enable us to continually strive for refinements and improvements.

For example, there has been considerable attention paid to gender-based violence and WEE. Hughes et al. (2015) describe Oxfam's approach that incorporates both economic dimensions as well as self-worth, equal rights to men, freedom from domination in the household, and domestic violence. For Oxfam, when analysing initiatives, it is important to consider more holistic empowerment and the potential of economic empowerment to shift social norms. Although WEE can contribute to negative outcomes such as gender-based violence, Oxfam cautions us not to be deterred in our WEE work but to be aware of and mitigate risks:

> Recognition that women's economic empowerment programming can potentially increase violence should not call women's economic empowerment into question; it is clearly in women's interests to raise incomes and promote gender equality, and many women are keen to be involved in these programmes. Therefore, as we argue in this article, interventions aimed at economically empowering women must incorporate strategies to minimise unintended negative impacts on women, including risks of increased domestic violence, and promote the empowerment of women from a holistic perspective (Hughes et al., 2015).

In addition to the five non-negotiable WEE dimensions, programmes should reflect on their own context and determine what other aspects of empowerment (economic and non-economic) are relevant, important, or pressing.

Intersectionality of identities

Intersectionality theory, first coined by Kimberlé Crenshaw (Crenshaw, 1989), refers to the way a combination of identities (e.g. race, gender, ethnicity, and class) combine to lead not only to complex identity but also to multiple layers of bias and discrimination. Due to intersectional identities, a woman's status and agency, as well as her ability to access resources, opportunities, and services, can be compromised or, conversely, improved. This concept was brought from academic discourse to international practice when the Association for Women's Rights and Development (AWID) published *Intersectionality: a tool for analysis, advocacy and policy development* (AWID, 2004) that offers insights on multiple identities and how different sets of identities impact women's rights and opportunities.

In MEDA's work around the globe, we have often observed that women's power vis-à-vis that of men is dependent on other aspects of their identity, and gender alone is not always the pivotal differentiator in power relationships. For example, depending on context, educated middle-class women are normally accorded higher status than uneducated, low-income men; or, middle-class women of an ethnic minority often face heightened discrimination compared with lower-income men of the ethnic majority. Women who are excluded across multiple identities – for example, a low-income ethnic minority woman who is illiterate and does not practise a mainstream religion – usually exist within a community with the same multiple identities that contribute to the powerlessness of the entire community. However, women have the added disadvantage of their gender identity, which can make them so powerless as to be invisible across society's various systems (education, healthcare, political participation, economic sectors, and so on) and therefore vulnerable to all kinds of discrimination and abuse.

Push–pull in market systems development

MSD has come under fire in terms of whether the approach can reach and integrate vulnerable populations into market systems, including but not limited to low-income women and youth, post-conflict communities, and ethnic minorities. Various methodologies (e.g. cash transfers, training, subsidized events) have been implemented to prepare such populations for mainstreaming into market systems. Drawing from private sector terminology, this approach has been labelled *push–pull* (Garloch, 2015): the *push* in a system prepares individuals, households, and communities to participate in markets; the *pull* references the activities of other market actors to integrate those individuals, households, and communities into the market system. Garloch states that the push–pull approach responds to the need 'not only to facilitate more competitive systems, but more inclusive and resilient systems as well' (Garloch, 2015: 1). While some MSD programmes embrace push–pull, others adhere to a stricter version of MSD that relies more exclusively on a pull strategy by private sector actors.

In many countries, MEDA has found that challenges for women exist in pervasive, negative social, legal, and cultural barriers that inhibit their participation in the productive sphere and particularly their entry into market systems. The experiences of MEDA in Ghana along with its partners ECDI in Pakistan and Zardozi in Afghanistan have demonstrated the importance of 'push' strategies to help women overcome gender-based discrimination and deficits in skills, confidence, capital, linkages, resources, and so on. 'Push' interventions can be utilized to empower women and enable them to overcome these deficits. For example, in Afghanistan, Zardozi supported the development of neighbourhood skills centres that were managed by women in their homes and where training and networking could take place in the community. The training and networking provided women with the skills, confidence, and connections they needed to engage directly with other market actors such as shopkeepers, traders, and input suppliers (Faveri et al., 2015).

Development actors

This book references an array of individuals or organizations that are actors in the field of international development and whose roles can be distinct or overlapping. This section offers a brief description of the roles of key categories of development actors as used in this volume and does not represent a full mapping of the current system of aid and development.

Policy makers

Policy makers are institutions (or the individuals in those institutions) that develop and implement formal laws, rules, and standards. Policy makers exist at multiple levels – international, national, local, and sectoral – and although usually associated with government agencies may also be civil society bodies such as business or industry associations. In addition to developing regulatory frameworks, policy makers may also provide guidance documents, certification, enforcement, and related activities. Policy makers may also conduct media campaigns, training, and awareness-raising around existing or changing policies.

The United Nations (UN) system

The UN system consists of both the main international body known as the UN as well as numerous funds, programmes, and specialized agencies that function under its umbrella. The UN Entity for Gender Equality and the Empowerment of Women (UN Women) is one of the programmes in the UN system and has the greatest relevance to this book. There are also a number of specialized agencies operating independently that target poverty alleviation and equal opportunity: for example, the International Labour Organization (ILO), the Food and Agriculture Organization (FAO), the United Nations Industrial Development Organization (UNIDO), and the World Bank (WB). These are also called multilateral organizations as they execute projects across multiple sovereign countries.

Funders

Official Development Assistance (ODA) incorporates both development aid, which supports the advancement of countries and their citizens (the focus of this book), and humanitarian assistance, which responds to crises from natural disasters to disease outbreaks and the impacts of conflict. The providers of ODA are the 'bilateral' government donor agencies, such as the Japan International Cooperation Agency (JICA), Global Affairs Canada (Global Affairs), United States Agency for International Development (USAID), Swiss Agency for Development and Cooperation (SDC), and Australia's Department of Foreign Affairs and Trade (DFAT), among many others. Bilateral donors provide funding direct to governments, to multilateral organizations – usually UN bodies such as UN Women and the WB – or to projects carried out by implementing agencies.

ODA is complemented by financing from family and corporate foundations, individual donors, investors, and businesses. Given the current funding gap of US$2.5 tn which is needed to achieve the Sustainable Development Goals (SDGs) by 2030 (Wilson, 2016), these other sources of funding will be critical to achieving gender inclusion and women's economic empowerment. This book illustrates, through a market systems approach, how it is possible to engage private sector partners, including investors, to leverage these important contributions.

Implementing agencies

International and local non-governmental organizations (I/NGOs), private sector contractors, research institutes, civil society networks, and other institutions implement development projects around the world, often in partnership with other agencies or in large consortia. UN bodies, local governments, and, in some cases, bilateral donors can also act as implementing agencies.

Useful resources

The Springfield Centre's *The Operational Guide for the Making Markets Work for the Poor (M4P) Approach*, 2nd edition: http://www.springfieldcentre. com/wp-content/uploads/2014/09/2014-09-M4P-Operational-Guide-with-watermark1.pdf

"*Discussion Paper for an M4P WEE Framework: How can the Making Markets Work for the Poor Framework work for poor women and for poor men?*"

http://springfieldcentre.com/wp-content/uploads/2012/11/M4P_WEE_
Framework_Final.pdf

The WEAMS framework: women's empowerment and markets systems concepts:
https://beamexchange.org/resources/794/

ICRW's *Understanding and Measuring Women's Economic Empowerment: Definition,
Framework and Indicators:* https://www.icrw.org/wp-content/uploads/2016/10/
Understanding-measuring-womens-economic-empowerment.pdf

DCED publications on Women's Economic Empowerment: https://www.
enterprise-development.org/implementing-psd/womens-economic-
empowerment/

The SEEP Network Thematic Area on Women's Economic Empowerment: https://
seepnetwork.org/Thematic-Areas-Womens-Economic-Empowerment

References

Association for Women's Rights and Development (AWID) (2004)
'Intersectionality: A Tool for Gender and Economic Justice' [online] https://
www.awid.org/publications/intersectionality-tool-gender-and-econom-
ic-justice [accessed 29 July 2019].

Bekkers, H., Carter, V. and Jones, L. (2015) *Women's Economic Empowerment:
How Women Contribute to and Benefit from Growth* [pdf], Market
Development Facility <http://marketdevelopmentfacility.org/wp-content/
uploads/2015/09/Womens-Economic-Empowerment.pdf> [accessed 11
April 2019].

Center of Gender and Policy Studies (2018) *Rural Women in Pakistan: Status Report
2018* [pdf], Islamabad, Pakistan: UN Women <http://www2.unwomen.
org/-/media/field%20office%20eseasia/docs/publications/2018/08/status-
of-the-rural-women-in-pakistan-report.pdf?la=enandvs=3739> [accessed
12 April 2019].

Crenshaw, K. (1989) 'Demarginalizing the intersection of race and sex: a black
feminist critique of antidiscrimination doctrine, feminist theory and anti-
racist politics' [online], University of Chicago Legal Forum, Special Issue:
Feminism in the Law: Theory, Practice and Criticism, University of Chicago Law
School: 139–168 <http://heinonline.org/HOL/LandingPage?handle=hein.
journals/uchclf1989anddiv=10> [accessed 11 April 2019].

Faveri, C., Shaikh, P. and Wilson, K. (2015) 'Making markets work for women:
how push and pull strategies can support women's economic empowerment', in L. Jones (ed.), *Financial and Market Integration of Vulnerable People:
Lessons from Development Programmes*, Rugby: Practical Action Publishing
https://doi.org/10.3362/1755-1986.2015.003.

Garloch, A. (2015) *A Framework for a Push/Pull Approach to Inclusive Market
Systems Development* [online], ACDI/VOCA and USAID – Leveraging
Economic Opportunities <https://www.marketlinks.org/library/framework-
pushpull-approach-inclusive-market-systems-development> [accessed 11
April 2019].

Golla, A., Malhotra, A., Nanda, P., and Mehra, R. (2011) *Understanding and
Measuring Women's Economic Empowerment: Definition, Framework and
Indicators* [pdf], Washington, DC: International Centre for Research on Women
<https://www.icrw.org/wp-content/uploads/2016/10/Understanding-

measuring-womens-economic-empowerment.pdf> [accessed 11 April 2019].

Hughes, C., Bolis, M., Fries, R. and Finigan, S. (2015) 'Women's economic inequality and domestic violence: exploring the links and empowering women', *Gender and Development* 23(2): 279–97 <https://dx.doi.org/10.108 0/13552074.2015.1053216>.

Innovative Development Strategies (IDS) (2014) *Performance Evaluation/Impact Assessment: USAID Entrepreneurs Project* [online], Islamabad, Pakistan: IDS <https://www.meda.org/news/publications-main/gender-equality-and-so-cial-inclusion/pakistan/12-performance-evaluation-impact-assess-ment-of-usaid-entrepreneurs/file> [accessed 29 July 2019].

Jones, L. (2012) *Women's Economic Empowerment Framework for M4P Programs* [pdf], M4P Hub paper, DFID/SDC <http://springfieldcentre.com/wp-content/uploads/2012/11/M4P_WEE_Framework_Final.pdf> [accessed 20 May 2019].

Jones, L. (2016) *The WEAMS framework: women's empowerment and markets systems concepts* [online], BEAM Exchange <https://beamexchange.org/resources/794/> [accessed 12 April 2019].

Kabeer, N. (1999) 'Resources, agency, achievements: reflections on the mea-surement of women's empowerment', *Development and Change* 30: 435–64 <https://doi.org/10.1111/1467-7660.00125>.

M4C (no date) *Making Markets Work for the Jamuna, Padma and Teesta Chars* [pdf] <https://www.enterprise-development.org/wp-content/uploads/M4C_Project_Overview.pdf> [accessed 12 April 2019].

Nardi, G. (2015) 'Can more gender equality boost the competitiveness of the PNG coffee industry?' [blog], 24 March 2015, CARE Insights <http://insights.careinternational.org.uk/development-blog/private-sector-engage-ment/can-more-gender-equality-boost-the-competitiveness-of-png-cof-fee-industry> [accessed 12 April 2019].

Swiss Agency for Development and Cooperation (SDC) (2003) *Gender Toolkit* sheets 1-10 [online], Bern: SDC/FDA (Federal Department of Foreign Affairs) <https://www.eda.admin.ch/deza/en/home/themes-sdc/gender-equality/instruments-gender-mainstreaming/gender-tool-kit.html> [accessed 12 April 2019].

The Springfield Centre (2015) *The Operational Guide for the Making Markets Work for the Poor (M4P) Approach*, 2nd edn [pdf], SDC and DFID <http://www.springfieldcentre.com/wp-content/uploads/2014/09/2014-09-M4P-Opera-tional-Guide-with-watermark1.pdf> [accessed 12 April 2019].

UN Women (no date) 'Gender equality glossary' [online] <https://training centre.unwomen.org/mod/glossary/view.php?id=36andmode=letterand hook=Gandsortkey=andsortorder=andfullsearch=0andpage=-1> [accessed 12 April 2019].

Wilson, G. (2016) 'There's a $2.5 trillion development investment gap. Blended finance could plug it' [online], World Economic Forum <https://www.weforum.org/agenda/2016/07/blended-finance-sustainable-development-goals/> [accessed 12 April 2019].

World Vision (2017) *Integrating Extremely Poor Producers into Markets: Field Guide*, 4th edn [pdf] <https://www.agrilinks.org/sites/default/files/field_guide_iv_0.pdf> [accessed 12 April 2019].

PART 2
Key approaches for women's economic empowerment

Part 2 presents proven approaches for achieving gender equality and women's economic empowerment (GE/WEE) in programming with a systems lens. Each chapter describes strategies and methods that are elucidated with examples and case studies. Please note that the names and unique characteristics of people in the case studies have been changed to protect their identities.

CHAPTER 3

Regulatory and sociocultural enabling environments

Jennifer King and Larissa Schneider

Abstract

This chapter discusses the complex regulatory and sociocultural barriers that enable or constrain gender equality and women's economic empowerment and outlines solutions for practitioners to increase economic inclusion for women within a market systems approach.

Keywords: gender equality, enabling environment, market systems, awareness raising, gender sensitization, unpaid care work

Introduction

Once Kapetha started menstruating she was banished from her household to the *chhaupadi*, an isolated shed outside of her village in rural Nepal, until she finished bleeding. This was due to the prevailing cultural belief that women and girls are impure during menstruation. While in the shed, Kapetha was unable to be with her family; was denied nutritious food; prohibited from bathing and accessing water used by other villagers; and prevented from attending school, going to work, or to the marketplace. Kapetha's experience is not hers alone. Many women and girls in the far- and mid-western regions of Nepal experience *chhaupadi*. During this time of isolation, they are exposed to extreme weather conditions, are at a higher risk of sexual violence and animal attacks, and their social and economic rights are physically and symbolically curtailed (UN Women, 2016).

The Supreme Court of Nepal banned the *chhaupadi* practice in 2010 and the *Nepalese National Plan of Action Against Gender-Based Violence 2017–2021* (SEM, 2017) recognizes it as a form of violence against women. However, the practice persists, fuelled by 'myths and ignorance' (UN Women, 2017). UN Women, in partnership with international and local non-governmental organizations, has been working to eliminate *chhaupadi* in four districts of the country through education and community stakeholder support (UN Women, 2017). Moreover, advocates in Nepal have pushed for the criminalization of *chhaupadi* at the household level and for officials to address the banishment

http://dx.doi.org/10.3362/9781780447506.003

of women from other public places during menstruation. As a result, on 9 August 2017, Nepal's parliament passed a bill criminalizing the banishment of women during menstruation and to sentence anyone who forces a woman into a menstrual hut to prison or a fine (Pokharel and Gurung, 2017). At the time of writing this chapter, the law is relatively new, so data are not yet available on the outcomes for women.

Unfortunately, women and girls' lives around the world are negatively impacted on economic, social, and political levels by discriminatory practices that exclude and shame women. To shift harmful, gendered social norms and practices such as *chhaupadi*, policy makers and practitioners must take a multidimensional approach in creating an enabling environment that promotes women's empowerment, economic inclusion, and well-being. Laws must be implemented and enforced, along with shifting the mindsets and behaviours of those at the household, community, and public levels who customarily support such disempowering practices.

For women to flourish as economic actors in society, a supportive enabling environment is essential to combat the formal and informal drivers of gender inequality, and to address the social, economic, and political factors that directly and indirectly influence women's equal access to and control over economic resources (Hunt and Samman, 2016). The enabling environment must also strengthen women's agency, power, and choice through the elimination of biases found in social and political institutions (Hunt and Samman, 2016).

When designing and facilitating gender-inclusive initiatives, market systems development (MSD) practitioners need to understand how various factors in the enabling environment affect women's participation and advancement in business and markets. Practitioners must consider how laws and regulations may restrict women from participating in the economic opportunities that are commonly available to men, while also considering the constraints and opportunities that gendered social norms present in the upgrading of women's contributions and the concomitant business and market growth. Engaging a variety of stakeholders at multiple levels, early in the design phase of MSD projects, ensures that the multidimensional factors of the enabling environment are strengthened to holistically tackle gender disparities and promote WEE beyond the life of the project.

The enabling environment for women's economic empowerment

In this paper, the *enabling environment* refers to two interconnected spheres of influence – regulatory and sociocultural – that can either promote or discourage women's economic engagement within a market system.

As illustrated in Figure 3.1, the first sphere centres on regulatory frameworks and legal systems that are largely informed and maintained by government bodies but can also be advanced by the private sector through the

Women's economic empowerment	
↑ *Can promote and discourage* ↑	
Regulatory	**Sociocultural**
Legal systems	Cultural norms
Regulatory frameworks	Customs and practices
Good governance	Women's collective voice
Government and private sector policies	Partnerships

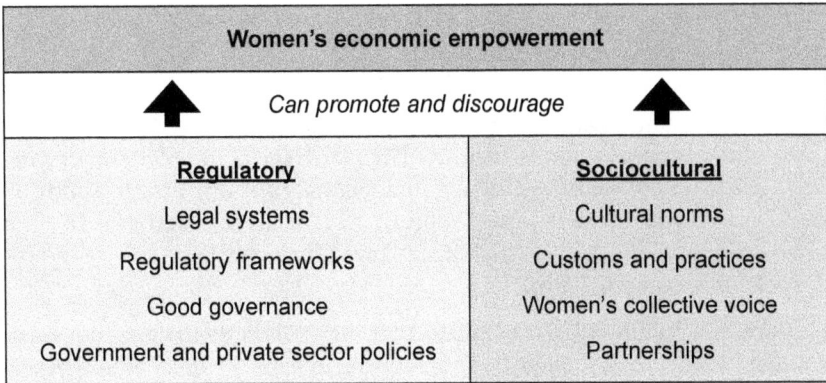

Figure 3.1 Interconnected enabling environment for women's economic empowerment

implementation of company or industry policies and incentives (for example, women's hours of work and maternity leave).

The second sphere involves sociocultural norms, customs, and practices that are informed and enforced by individual and collective perceptions and behaviours at the household, community, business, and government levels (UN High-Level Panel on Women's Economic Empowerment, 2016). The sociocultural context is multifaceted, with systemic gender biases and inequalities that shape the way women function within a market system. Empowerment is a process that cannot be done 'for' or 'to' women; women themselves must be actively involved in their empowerment (O'Neil et al., 2014) and, when organized, they can be tireless advocates and drivers of regulatory change in the absence of government commitment to reform, as further described below.

These two interconnected areas, which include both formal and informal rules and spheres of influence, can support and reinforce each other to create an environment that has the potential to enable the advancement of GE/WEE in market systems. Alternatively, these spheres can be at odds with one another. For example, a woman may not be able to fully realize the economic benefit of business ownership, even when new reforms legalize that ownership, due to deeply entrenched social norms regarding women's work and women's business ownership.

The enabling environment has been described in various ways by different organizations. The United Nations (UN), the Overseas Development Institute (ODI), and The Springfield Centre – key influencers in the field of WEE and market systems – offer three definitions that provide a useful overview.

The UN High-Level Panel on Women's Economic Empowerment, a multi-sectoral group appointed by the UN Secretary-General to develop a global agenda and call to action for WEE in support of the Sustainable Development Goals (SDGs), defined a supportive enabling environment as follows:

> An enabling environment is characterized by the implementation of policies and legal reforms that remove structural barriers, challenge discriminatory norms, ensure adequate social protection, expand access to crucial infrastructure and facilitate the organization and collective voice and representation of women to set the terms of their economic engagement (UN High-Level Panel on Women's Economic Empowerment, 2016: 3).

Hunt and Samman (2016) explain that the ODI views the enabling environment more broadly, identifying and characterizing 10 direct or underlying factors (known in MSD as root causes), both of which can enable or constrain WEE. Direct factors are linked to the individual or collective experiences of women and underlying factors are the 'wider structural conditions that determine women's individual or collective lived experiences' (Hunt and Samman, 2016: 11). These underlying factors, listed in Table 3.1, shape the trajectory for women's economic participation formally through laws and policies and informally through social norms and customs that influence behaviour and perpetuate gender stereotypes.

Market systems approaches, developed originally by The Springfield Centre and explained in the introduction to this book, define the enabling environment as the 'rules' that govern the market system. These rules include standards, regulations, laws, informal rules, and norms which all differentially impact the transactions of low-income women and men within a market system (The Springfield Centre, 2015).

For development practitioners, an enabling environment approach to achieving WEE requires an integrated strategy to tackle the systemic gender imbalances that inform and result from laws and regulations, as well as societal behaviours and attitudes. And while governments are primarily responsible for engendering WEE within the regulatory environment by supporting policies and regulations that improve economic inclusion, private sector and

Table 3.1 Factors that enable or constrain WEE

Direct factors	Education, skills development, and training
	Access to good quality, decent paid work
	Unpaid care and work burdens
	Access to property, assets, and financial services
	Collective action and leadership
	Social protection
Underlying factors	Labour market characteristics
	Fiscal policy
	Legal regulatory and policy framework
	Gender norms and discriminatory social norms

Source: Hunt and Samman (2016)

civil society organizations are also important partners in influencing policy makers and designing programmes that promote the advancement of women.

Enabling environments and market systems change

> Political changes without fundamental changes in moral and social norms remain temporary victories (Dr Amany Asfour, Egypt).

Consistent in the literature and among practitioners is the recognition that economic interventions alone are insufficient to achieve lasting WEE. Even the best designed and executed programmes can be hindered by the absence of laws, weak policies, restrictive social norms, and other factors. Conversely, having laws that respond to gender inequality does not ensure that there is sufficient institutional will or capacity to apply the law; having sound mechanisms and tools for implementation and appropriate budgetary commitments for the uptake and enforcement of laws matters when advancing legal reform (World Bank Group, 2018).

Programmatic integration of enabling environment approaches is key to the sustainable and effective functioning of market systems, shifting the focus upward from bottom or production-level interventions to longer-term systems-level change (Markel and Jones, 2014). Utilizing a market systems perspective is fundamental to understanding the underlying enabling environment factors that can inhibit market function and determining approaches that can be taken to overcome barriers and achieve desired outcomes. At the same time, a strengthened regulatory environment supports systemic change and bolsters women's empowerment in market systems. A supportive enabling environment can also accelerate the pace of change, foster the movement of women from informal to formal economic activity, and encourage the start-up of women-owned businesses (UN High-Level Panel on Women's Economic Empowerment, 2016).

A strong enabling environment for WEE is key to achieving the SDGs, most notably the stand-alone gender goal SDG 5, 'achieve gender equality and empower all women and girls', and its pertinent targets, including:

> 5.A: undertake reforms to give women equal rights to economic resources, as well as access to ownership and control over land and other forms of property, financial services, inheritance and natural resources, in accordance with national laws; and

> 5.C: adopt and strengthen sound policies and enforceable legislation for the promotion of gender equality and the empowerment of all women and girls at all levels (United Nations, 2015: 18).

The absence of an effective regulatory environment negatively impacts how women interact in a market system and ultimately limits a country's economic growth potential. Laws, policies, rules, and customary laws can reinforce power differentials between men and women and directly and indirectly discriminate against women, preventing women from full economic participation (UN High-Level Panel on Women's Economic Empowerment, 2016). This can include: property laws that limit a woman's ability to own land that in turn reduces her access to finance; agricultural policies that fail to recognize the contributions and needs of women; and labour laws (for example, 104 countries restrict the types of occupations that women can undertake, thereby limiting their access to employment) (World Bank Group, 2018).

> Bringing women to the workplace...reduces inequality because one of the major inequalities is the fact that women are left out, underutilized, over exploited, generally underpaid, and quite often in the informal sector. If you improve on all those counts, you reduce inequality (Christine Lagarde, Managing Director, International Monetary Fund).

In the Russian Federation, for example, women are restricted from working in hazardous, arduous, or 'morally inappropriate' occupations or industries, and are often disallowed from performing certain tasks in other industries (World Bank Group, 2018). A study on the differences in earnings between Russian men and women reported that 'job segregation by gender accounted for about three quarters of gender earnings differentials' (Donor Committee for Enterprise Development (DCED), 2016: 32). Yet around the world, if women's wages were equal to men's, countries would experience higher rates of economic growth. Research conducted by the McKinsey Global Institute concluded that if all women were able to participate in market systems identically to men, global GDP would jump by a remarkable 26 per cent by 2025 (McKinsey Global Institute, 2015).

Challenges to strengthening enabling environments for women

Incorporating an enabling environment approach into WEE programming is complex, requiring the involvement of multiple actors and stakeholders, many of whom will be part of institutions that lack capacity. Achieving sustainable systems change also requires longer timeframes to assess, design, implement, monitor, adapt, and learn. Strengthening institutional capacity and changing social norms takes even longer. Yet, many MSD projects are too short to achieve meaningful change in the enabling environment. A 2016 review of 240 of USAID's Feed the Future investments in enabling environment reform found that many projects were concerned that 'the nature of policy reform work is often at odds with the typical USAID program design and lifecycle', adding that 'a regular lack of sufficient resources and capacity for policy formulation and implementation has frequently made policy objectives unattainable within five years' (USAID, 2016: 3).

Other challenges to implementing an enabling environment approach are scarcity of high-quality or relevant data (including sex-disaggregated data), insufficient monitoring and evaluation, difficulty generating stakeholder buy-in for reform, weak coordination between various levels of government in a country, lack of flexibility in project design, low levels of participation from women themselves in the governments and institutions tasked with reform, and entrenched attitudes and social norms.

Enabling environment approaches that focus primarily on reform and policy changes often fail to consider that laws cannot solely change deep-rooted gender norms. Even when laws are in place, their implementation, awareness, and enforcement can be challenging. In 143 countries around the world, constitutions and other legal frameworks guarantee equal treatment for women and men (UN Women, 2016). However, the lack of understanding, capacity, and resources among policy makers, and even among women themselves, limits implementation and enforcement and the ability to counter social norms and customary laws that constrain a woman's ability to become economically productive (DCED, 2016). For example, in a study on the business environment for women in Tanzania, more than 50 per cent of women survey respondents said that they require consent from their husbands to start a business, even though women are legally permitted to start and register businesses (Equality for Growth, 2009). Universal conventions, such as the Convention on the Elimination of All Forms of Discrimination against Women (CEDAW), also require significant advocacy from local NGOs and the CEDAW Committee to ensure that signatory countries comply with the convention (Byrnes and Freeman, 2012).

Solutions for strengthening enabling environments

Designing and implementing projects that support an enabling environment for WEE requires practitioners to work with a variety of stakeholders to understand how policies, laws, customs, and practices affect the transactions that women and men make within a market system. Projects and programmes rarely focus solely on one area of the enabling environment, as all factors, whether formal or informal, are interconnected. As such, projects that work on strengthening the enabling environment for WEE vary in scope. They can range from a light-touch 'pull' approach – for example, shifting biases and raising awareness of business partners on the value of being gender inclusive – to a more intensive 'push' approach, such as actively engaging government departments to strengthen institutional capacity or working with men and boys as community gender champions. In any context, practitioners should consider both the interconnected nature of the various aspects and actors in the enabling environment as well as the long-term sustainability of systems change when designing and implementing an initiative to increase WEE outcomes.

Regulatory context solutions

Laws and regulations define the scope of women's participation in the economy and in society (UN High-Level Panel on Women's Economic Empowerment, 2016). The structures and processes in the regulatory environment design and enforce the formal rules that governments implement (Markel and Jones, 2014).

Laws and regulations can be designed to engender WEE if policy makers take into consideration the differential impact that their decisions can have on women and men. The biennial World Bank publication *Women, Business and the Law* (World Bank Group, 2018) measures how regulations and laws in economies around the world limit women's economic participation. The reports capture data on laws that provide rights for women and men in accessing institutions, using property, gaining employment, equal pay and incentives, building credit, going to court, and protecting women from violence. The report's 2018 data revealed continued progress, with 87 reforms implemented in 65 countries in the two years since the report's 2016 edition. However, there are still 59 countries that have no laws on sexual harassment in the workplace, and 18 countries where husbands can legally prevent their wives from working (World Bank Group, 2018).

In promoting a regulatory environment that supports WEE, it is crucial to understand that the 'equality of opportunity' impacts the choices that women can make for themselves and their families. When there are legal restrictions on a woman's ability to engage in economic activities, this extends and impacts the woman's ability to engage in other spheres of life. For example, the World Bank found that:

> Disparities in outcomes can persist throughout a woman's life: where there are more legal gender differences, not only is she less likely to go to secondary school, she is also less likely to be employed or run a business, and if she does manage to do either she is likely to earn less than a man would (World Bank Group, 2015: 5).

Women's control over resources is consistently restrained by discriminatory laws, which are often reinforced by patriarchal social norms and practices (Hunt and Samman, 2016). For example, in levels of land ownership, women constitute only 15 per cent of agricultural landholders globally, with much smaller plot sizes than those of men (FAO, 2018). Land ownership reforms must consider local tenure systems that are often rooted in customary practices pertaining to inheritance rights, marital, and divorce laws (Hunt and Samman, 2016: 19). Ensuring that women have equal access to resources under the law is crucial to advancing WEE, along with having government support and capacity to guarantee that discriminatory practices are actively eliminated in markets, public institutions, and within households. Working through an enabling environment approach, practitioners need to leverage the advocacy of civil society groups to enhance the government's understanding of the regulatory frameworks that limit a woman's ability to access, own, and control land, finances, and other economic assets and productive resources (Global Affairs Canada, 2017).

In 2007, the government of Ghana initiated gender-responsive budgeting (GRB) to ensure that policies and budgets were not gender blind but rather identified and targeted the different needs and interests of women and men, boys and girls. For example, a gender-responsive budget might address the educational attainment gap between boys and girls by allocating budgets accordingly and thereby levelling the gender playing field. By dedicating budgets to gender programming, Ghanaian policy makers and government departments worked to mainstream the issue to avoid 'policy evaporation' and ensure the full adoption and implementation of GRB (SIANI, 2013).

Making the case for legal reform can be housed in other international protocols (such as the SDGs) and supported by data (such as global gender indices) that point to the correlation between discriminatory legal regulations and policies and gender disparities in development outcomes (World Bank Group, 2018). International conventions, namely CEDAW, were leveraged in Latin America to reform inheritance laws and practices leading to positive impacts in women's levels of land ownership (Deere and Leon, 2001). In the Philippines, the Global Affairs Canada-funded GREAT Project leveraged national action plans to help create an enabling environment for WEE at national and local levels by mainstreaming gender responsiveness into the country's overarching National Action Plan for Women, and by dedicating budget towards support for women micro-entrepreneurs (Philippine Commission on Women, 2014).

When governments fail to incorporate gender into their regulatory frameworks, as was reported in a 2016 study the UK's Department for International Development (DFID), not only is gender too often neglected in interventions in general, but it represents a significant missed opportunity for delivering systemic change.

Sociocultural context solutions

Social norms are the 'rules and accompanying behaviours that govern social behaviour and expectations' (Markel et al., 2016: 6). In MSD there are both informal rules, which dictate and reinforce social norms, and formal rules, which become entrenched in laws and policies that solidify and moderate the ways that people and businesses can legally function in society. Gendered social norms reflect the societal expectations for women and men and underpin why the genders are treated differently (Markel et al., 2016). When social norms uphold the 'power relations which limit women's access to and agency over economic opportunities' (DCED, 2017: 36), it is crucial that practitioners understand how social norms impact the possibilities of gender transformation in MSD when engaging actors at multiple levels within the enabling environment.

A 2013 MSD pilot funded by DFID entitled the Sierra Leone Opportunities for Business Action (SOBA) Project assessed the impact of social norms in influencing women's empowerment in market systems (Markel and Miller, 2016). SOBA was not a WEE project but sought to increase the net income of men and women living in poverty through a sectoral approach, particularly in agriculture, to increase market linkages and partnerships for smallholder farmers (Markel and Miller, 2016). The SOBA pilot highlights the importance of assessing social norms at the outset of a project to develop an understanding of the 'gendered roles, obstacles and opportunities for women within different areas of the market system, [which] is useful for identifying appropriate entry-points' (Markel and Miller, 2016: 11). For example, research revealed that SOBA programme participants feared sanctions (e.g. teasing, shunning) from their communities for shifting their commonly accepted gender roles. In creating an enabling environment for WEE, it is important to consider the social constraints women face in upgrading their status in the market based on sanctions and beliefs that shape gender norms resulting in stymied economic growth (Markel et al., 2016).

In Zambia, a 2011 Consultative Group for International Agricultural Research (CGIAR)-funded research project took a multidimensional approach to understanding the constraints impacting poverty and food security for men and women involved in aquatic agricultural systems (AAS) (SIANI, 2013). Rather than solely focusing on the productive assets to measure gender disparities in AAS, the project built its contextual knowledge of the systemic factors of gender inequality that contribute to asset disparities, such as social norms and customary traditions that shaped women's opportunities. Like the SOBA case, cultural sanctions influenced the participants' perceptions of risk and the likelihood of taking on new roles within the market system.

Partnerships for effective solutions

Given the complexity of the enabling environment, effective implementation typically requires working across sectors and with multiple partners. The Joint Programme on Accelerating Progress Towards the Economic Empowerment of Rural Women (RWEE), implemented by the Food and Agriculture Organization of the United Nations (FAO), the International Fund for Agricultural Development (IFAD), the World Food Programme (WFP), and UN Women in Ethiopia, Guatemala, Kyrgyzstan, Liberia, Nepal, Niger, and Rwanda, has achieved notable results with its partnership approach. In Liberia, a partnership with the National Rural Women Structure and the Association of Women in Cross-Border Trade has given voice to rural women in government initiatives – including the constitutional reform process. In Nepal, RWEE has been instrumental in ensuring that the importance of safeguarding rural women farmers' access to and control over agricultural resources and services is included in the draft Gender Equality and Social Inclusion (GESI) strategy of the Agriculture Development Strategy (Joint Programme on Accelerating Progress Towards the Economic Empowerment of Rural Women, 2017).

Civil society actors are key contributors to effective enabling environments around the world, often pushing for and participating in reform, and filling voids left by weak institutions, lax laws, and discriminatory policies. Civil society organizations – whether informal networks, business associations, savings groups, cooperatives, trade unions, or self-help groups – are structures through which women can exercise agency and have influence over market systems. In this dimension of the enabling environment, women themselves are the agents of their empowerment and can exercise power in groups to achieve common goals (also referred to as 'power with' in various frameworks). Such civil society groups can facilitate access to resources, services, and information that can strengthen women's economic decision making, while also working to increase women's political leadership and the profile of women as economic actors.

Civil society organizations can also represent the needs of women in consultative processes and fora, enable women to advocate for themselves, partner with the private and public sector, play a critical role in making legal challenges of discriminatory practices, increase awareness of existing rights and regulations and of plans and available support, and support the visibility, confidence, and progression of women in industry. For example, in many African countries, Women in Mining network chapters support the advancement of women working in the mining industry through access to education, skills, mentorship, advocating for licensing of women miners, and women's representation (BSR, 2017). Women in Mining Nigeria has been a particularly strong advocate for women's voices in mining decision-making processes, pushing against a mining industry that is governed by gender-blind laws and developing action plans to help ensure that gender is mainstreamed into the Nigerian mining industry.

Trade unions are a type of civil society network that has often played a role in WEE advancements. In India, for example, the Self-Employed Women's Association (SEWA) is a union for women in the informal economy that started as a grass roots movement in 1972. Of the female labour force in India, more than 94 per cent are in the informal sector (SEWA, 2015). SEWA's main goal is to organize women to achieve secure employment and self-reliance. Core to the SEWA movement are campaigns that push for awareness and change of policies that negatively impact its 1.4 million informal women workers, many of whom live in poverty. Its collective action and influence have led to informal workers receiving business licences and inclusion in labour statistics and research. SEWA is an excellent example of a sustainable civil society entity with multiple components and income streams.

> Through WIEGO's [Women in Informal Employment: Globalizing and Organizing] work with (member-based organizations) of informal workers, they have learned that increased access to resources without the ability to influence broader external factors will not necessarily translate into more secure and remunerative livelihoods. Existing policies, regulations, and institutions are not designed to meet the needs of these women's lives (and, therefore, offer little real choice); improved outcomes are often not sustainable without the ongoing ability to significantly influence the wider environment (Women's Economic Empowerment: WIEGO Position and Approach, 2016).

The support of WIEGO for the International Domestic Workers Federation (IDWF) through the Securing Economic Rights for Informal Women Workers Programme was deemed to be instrumental in the growth and recognition of the federation, the 'achievement of legal rights and protection for domestic workers in 15 countries, and (an) increase in income due to securing minimum wages and strengthened women's leadership among domestic worker organizations' (WIEGO, 2016: 31).

Private sector partnerships are also emerging as an increasingly effective force for change given businesses' ability to adopt new policies, steer sector rules and certifications, and be champions of women's contributions to business and sector growth. The Women's Employment Principles (WEPs), launched in 2010, emphasize the business case for corporate action to promote gender equality and women's empowerment and have led global business leaders to commit to gender equality in business. Companies such as IKEA, which has committed to the principles, can act as role models within the business sector and apply peer pressure to other companies. For example, IKEA Switzerland and its CEO, Simona Scarpaleggia, have convinced 40 CEOs of Swiss companies to 'commit to concrete actions to advance the WEE agenda' (Wahlén, 2017).

Donor governments can play a critical role in supporting the development of a stronger enabling environment for WEE in a target country. Donor governments can ensure that trade agreements do not negatively impact women, and they can provide technical assistance to governments to strengthen processes such as procurement and to bolster women entrepreneurs' ability to compete. Donor frameworks often specify enabling environment objectives in development efforts, and donors can incentivize governments receiving funds by incorporating strategies and plans that promote legislative and policy change. For example, the US Department of State Strategy for WEE is guided by a three-pronged action framework for: legal, regulatory, and policy reform; gender-inclusive economic development; and institutional and individual skills and capacity building. The framework has resulted in the creation of inclusive trade agreements and other policy tools that boost women's economic engagement (US Department of State, 2016).

Capacity development and institutional strengthening

For an enabling environment to be effective, strengthening the capacity of organizations, institutions, and the people that run them is critical for reinforcing the structures and processes that will endure over the long term (Asian Development Bank, 2016).

> Involving women in training and capacity-building activities, enabling them to build stronger social networks through group membership structures, and facilitating their access to income-generating opportunities are important ways of promoting women's economic advancement, power and agency. In themselves, they are not enough to bring about the structural changes in formal and informal institutions required to create an enabling environment to facilitate and sustain advances in women's economic empowerment over the longer term (CARE Australia, n.d.: 3).

In Indonesia, a bilateral partnership between the Australian (DFAT) and Indonesian governments is working with a series of gender-interested civil society organizations through the MAMPU programme (MAMPU, 2018) to improve the access of disadvantaged women to essential services and other government programmes. To increase access to services, a core focus of the programme is building the capacity of the local civil society partners to enable women to advocate directly with government agencies by increasing their voice and influence. For example, 12 significant government policy decisions were taken between May 2016 and March 2017 as a result of the input from MAMPU civil society partners and the women they support (MAMPU, 2018).

DFID's Civil Society Challenge Fund directly supported women's empowerment projects as part of a focus on the creation and development of an enabling environment. Results included an improved capacity of civil society to: participate in local decision making (100 per cent); participate in national decision making (65 per cent); and provide innovative service delivery (44 per cent). Common results factors included: organizational clarity of vision and goals; moving from individual to group empowerment; working with men, boys, and other stakeholders; access to information and the ability to use it; and flexibility in adapting a project to on-the-ground realities (DFID, 2015).

The International Labour Organization's Women's Entrepreneurship Development programme (ILO-WED) in South Africa has developed the enabling environment for women entrepreneurs in the KwaZulu Natal tourism sector by supporting the institutional capacity in government offices to 'redress existing gender imbalances in enterprise development through approaches and activities aimed specifically at women and small enterprise initiatives that are gender sensitive' (ILO, 2010: 5). Activities included initiatives such as analysing women's roles and barriers in the sector and promoting women entrepreneurs at the policy level through dialogue and increasing awareness of business women's needs.

Awareness raising and gender sensitization

When it comes to sociocultural norms, awareness raising and gender sensitization can support women and shift the attitudes of men and boys around women's engagement in market systems. If a few men and boys shift their behaviours towards WEE, others will follow by recognizing the benefits to their households.

The Aga Khan Rural Support Programme (AKRSP) in Pakistan, working in some of the country's most conservative mountainous areas, supports women to become economically empowered through multiple approaches. Two innovations that combine to achieve high impact are gender sensitization for men and establishment of women's markets. Male staff members of AKRSP engage with the male community and household members on gender issues, often bringing in local religious leaders to legitimize dialogue around women's issues. In these remote communities, and with support of male family members, AKRSP has facilitated the development of women's markets (often near the main market), providing women with the opportunity to be self-employed outside the home in a way that is culturally acceptable. The existence of women's marketplaces has led to gender advancement in other areas – for example, women opening neighbourhood shops, socializing and networking within the marketplace, and even some men's shops in or beside women's markets – breaking down cultural barriers and contributing to women's entrepreneurship development (Markel and Jones, 2014).

Overcoming the traditional burden of unpaid work

Women are often constrained in their ability to take part in the paid 'productive' economy (informal or formal) by their unpaid and traditionally sanctioned 'reproductive' work. While this is closely connected to sociocultural norms, other factors such as level of poverty and enabling environment issues (i.e. availability of day care and paid maternity leave) also undermine women's situation. Women are usually responsible for caring for the family (children, elderly, sick, less abled), for community work, for the household (including organizing fuel and water), and for tending kitchen gardens or working in the fields as unpaid family workers. In fact, it is estimated that women's unpaid work would constitute between 10 per cent and 39 per cent of GDP if it were given a monetary value. Because of this contribution by women, if mechanisms are not in place to reduce their workload, unpaid contributions to the community and household inhibit them from participating at a more beneficial level of the economy (i.e. full-time business operation), limits their choice of employment opportunities, and impairs access to training and educational opportunities (Chopra, 2014).

Case study: Nepal – shifting the enabling environment for women's empowerment

In Nepal, rural women, ethnic minorities, and those considered low caste face disproportionate levels of poverty and social exclusion. To address this, the Asian Development Bank (ADB) and the government of Nepal through the Department of Women and Children implemented the Gender Equality and Empowerment of Women Project (ADB, 2016) with the goal of reducing poverty by empowering rural and marginalized women. Begun in 2003, this eight-year project took an integrative approach to tackling socio-economic empowerment, with strong regulatory and sociocultural themes.

The economic empowerment component focused on improving access to training and finance to increase incomes and on increasing women's agency through improved decision making and increased self-esteem. For social empowerment, the project took a multifaceted approach to ultimately shift internal (self) and external (community) perceptions of women's roles and capabilities, while also creating physical spaces and community decision-making processes.

The project also aimed to raise awareness of women's legal rights and obligations while building an enabling environment to enforce women's rights. The project successfully worked with village groups, involving both men and women, as well as other stakeholder groups such as professional audiences, including judges, prosecutors, and female police personnel to further embed an understanding of women's legal rights at various levels. The project also leveraged support from complementary international initiatives working in the country to increase women's visibility in Nepal by working with UNICEF on their women's paralegal programme.

Lastly, the project strengthened the Department of Women and Children's ability to mainstream gender throughout central and local gender offices. Gender audits and capacity-building activities were completed while promoting interagency cooperation. Ultimately, strengthening local institutions' ability to deliver women's empowerment programming promotes sustainability of gender equality beyond the life of the project.

The broad and intersectional range of activities of this project lent to its success in achieving specific gender equality targeted outcomes. Through this multidimensional and mutually reinforcing approach, the project was able to positively impact the enabling environment for women's economic development, effectively increasing incomes for programme clients, while also increasing women's ability to understand their legal rights and confidently seek redress, at credible, gender-sensitive government agencies.

This case exemplifies the importance of integrating multidimensional aspects of poverty alleviation and empowerment into a project's design to alter the entrenched socio-economic norms that dictate gender roles and expectations (ADB, 2016).

Useful resources

DCED's Business Environment Reform and Gender report https://www.enterprise-development.org/wp-content/uploads/BEWG-DCED-Technical-Paper-Gender-and-BER.pdf

DCED's Synthesis Document: How to Integrate Gender and Women's Economic Empowerment into Private Sector Development Programmes report https://www.enterprise-development.org/wp-content/uploads/DCED-WEEWG-How-to-integrate-gender-into-PSD-programmes.pdf

ODI's Women's Economic Empowerment: Navigating Enablers and Constraints report https://www.odi.org/sites/odi.org.uk/files/resource-documents/10683.pdf

UN Secretary-General's High-Level Panel on Women's Economic Empowerment Toolkit: How to change norms in support of women's economic empowerment http://www2.unwomen.org/-/media/hlp%20wee/attachments/reports-toolkits/hlp-wee-toolkit-driver-1-en.pdf?la=enandvs=5507

UN Secretary-General's High-Level Panel on Women's Economic Empowerment Toolkit: How to ensure legal protections and reform discriminatory laws and regulations http://www2.unwomen.org/-/media/hlp%20wee/attachments/reports-toolkits/hlp-wee-toolkit-driver-2-en.pdf?la=enandvs=5412

USAID's Women's Economic Empowerment and Equality (WE3) Dashboard
https://idea.usaid.gov/women-e3

References

Asian Development Bank (2016) *Gender Equality Results Case Study: Nepal Gender Equality and Empowerment of Women Project*, Mandaluyong City, Philippines: Asian Development Bank.

BSR (2017) *Women's Economic Empowerment in Sub-Saharan Africa* [pdf] <https://www.bsr.org/reports/BSR_Womens_Empowerment_Africa_Main_Report.pdf> [accessed 21 May 2019].

Byrnes, A. and Freeman, M. (2012) *The Impact of the CEDAW Convention: Paths to Equality*, Sydney: University of New South Wales.

CARE Australia (no date) *Promoting Women's Economic Empowerment with Ethnic Groups in the Mekong: A Vietnam Case Study* [pdf] <https://www.care.org.au/wp-content/uploads/2016/08/000203_WEEEM_Vietnam-Summary-Report.pdf> [accessed 15 July 2019].

Chopra, D. (2014) *Unpaid Care Work and Empowerment of Women and Girls* [pdf], United Nations Research Institute for Social Development (UNRISD) <www.unrisd.org/80256B3C005BCCF9/(httpAuxPages)/D502EE1053BF3C8DC1257D080042B9B8/$file/Chopra%20slides.pdf> [accessed 17 July 2019].

Donor Committee for Enterprise Development (DCED) (2016) *Business Environment Reform and Gender* [pdf] <https://www.enterprise-development.org/wp-content/uploads/BEWG-DCED-Technical-Paper-Gender-and-BER.pdf> [accessed 21 May 2019].

DCED (2017) *Synthesis Document: How to Integrate Gender and Women's Economic Empowerment into Private Sector Development Programmes* [pdf], Women's Economic Empowerment Working Group, DCED <https://www.enterprise-development.org/wp-content/uploads/DCED-WEEWG-How-to-integrate-gender-into-PSD-programmes.pdf> [accessed 21 May 2019].

Deere, C. and Leon, M. (2001) *Empowering Women: Land and Property Rights in Latin America*, Chicago, IL: Bibliovault OAI Repository, University of Chicago Press.

Department for International Development (DFID) (2015) *DFID Civil Society Challenge Fund, Final Evaluation* [pdf], Sheffield: IOD PARC <https://assets.publishing.service.gov.uk/government/uploads/system/uploads/attachment_data/file/496983/Evaluation-Civil-Society-Challenge-Fund.pdf> [accessed 12 April 2019].

"Economically empowering women is 'macrocritical' — IMF chief Christine Lagarde" By Sophie Edwards // 08 March 2017 https://www.devex.com/news/economically-empowering-women-is-macrocritical-imf-chief-christine-lagarde-89786 [accessed 15 July 2019]

Equality for Growth (2009) *Equality for Growth: Baseline Survey of Female Entrepreneurs*, United Republic of Tanzania: Equality for Growth.

Food and Agriculture Organization of the United Nations (FAO) (2018) *The Gender Gap in Land Rights* [pdf] <http://www.fao.org/3/I8796EN/i8796en.pdf> [accessed 12 April 2019].

Global Affairs Canada (2017) *Women's Economic Empowerment: Guidance Note* [online] <http://international.gc.ca/world-monde/

issues_development-enjeux_developpement/priorities-priorites/women-femmes.aspx?lang=eng#a5_1_1> [accessed 12 April 2019].

Hunt, A. and Samman, E. (2016) *Women's Economic Empowerment: Navigating Enablers and Constraints*, London: Overseas Development Institute <https://www.odi.org/sites/odi.org.uk/files/resource-documents/10683.pdf> [accessed 15 July 2019].

International Labour Organization (ILO) (2010) *The Kwa Zulu Natal Tourism Sector: Selected Perspectives on the Enabling Environment for Women's Entrepreneurs* [online] <http://www.ilo.org/empent/Publications/WCMS_184782/lang--en/index.htm> [accessed 12 April 2019].

Joint Programme on Accelerating Progress towards the Economic Empowerment of Rural Women (2017) *The JPRWEE Pathway to Women's Empowerment* [online] <https://www.ifad.org/documents/38714170/39148759/Five+years+of+the+AAF%E2%80%99S+technical+assistance+facility/de6fa0c4-1398-4b0c-acdc-c9e227d73439> [accessed 21 May 2019].

McKinsey Global Institute (2015) *The Power of Parity: How Advancing Women's Equality Can Add $12 Trillion to Global Growth* [pdf], McKinsey & Company <https://www.mckinsey.com/featured-insights/employment-and-growth/how-advancing-womens-equality-can-add-12-trillion-to-global-growth> [accessed 29 May 2019].

MAMPU (2018) *MAMPU Program* [online] <http://www.mampu.or.id/en/mampu-program> [accessed 12 April 2019].

Markel, E. and Jones, L. (2014) *Women's Economic Empowerment: Pushing the Frontiers of Inclusive Market Development* [pdf], LEO Brief, Washington, DC: USAID <https://www.enterprise-development.org/wp-content/uploads/WEE_in_Market_Systems_Framework_final.pdf> [accessed 21 May 2019].

Markel, E. and Miller, E. (2016) *Gendered Social Norms for Programme Design: Sierra Leone Opportunities for Business Action (SOBA)*, London: The BEAM Exchange <https://beamexchange.org/uploads/filer_public/ca/ca/caca2590-5067-4579-83a9-be2ebeb30237/social_norms_factor_report.pdf> [accessed 15 July 2019].

Markel, E., Gettliffe, E., Jones, L., Miller, L., and Kim, L. (2016) *The Social Norms Factor: How Gendered Social Norms Influence How We Empower Women in Market Systems*, London: The BEAM Exchange.

O'Neil, T., Domingo, P., and Valters, C. (2014) *Progress on Women's Empowerment: From Technical Fixes to Political Action*, London: Overseas Development Institute.

"President of Egyptian Business Women Association (EBWA) Member Of FCEM President of Business and Professional Women –Egypt (BPW-Egypt) Africa Coordinator" slide 19, https://slideplayer.com/slide/7594952/ [accessed 15 July 2019]

Philippine Commission on Women (2014) *The GREAT Women Project 2* [online] <https://www.pcw.gov.ph/gwp2> [accessed 12 April 2019].

Pokharel, S. and Gurung, D. (2017) 'Nepal outlaws menstruation huts, but what will take their place?' [online], *CNN*, 27 August 2017 <http://www.cnn.com/2017/08/25/health/nepal-menstruation-huts-chhaupadi-ban/index.html> [accessed 12 April 2019].

SEM (2017) *National Action Plan on Gender-Based Violence 2017–2021* [online], UN Women Asia and the Pacific <http://asiapacific.unwomen.org/en/

digital-library/publications/2017/10/national-action-plan-on-gender-based-violence-2017-2021> [accessed 12 April 2019].

Self-Employed Women's Association (SEWA) (2015) *SEWA Annual Report*, New Delhi, India: SEWA.

Swedish International Agricultural Network Initiative (SIANI) (2013) 'Transforming the enabling environment', in C. Farnworth, M. Fones Sundell, A. Nzioki, V. Shivutse, and M. Davis (eds), *Transforming Gender Relations in Agriculture in Sub-Saharan Africa*, [pdf], pp. 20–32, Stockholm: SIANI <https://www.siani.se/wp-content/uploads/2013/09/siani-2013-transforming-gender-relations-agriculture-africa.pdf> [accessed 12 April 2019].

The Springfield Centre (2015) *The Operational Guide for the Making Markets Work for the Poor (M4P) Approach*, 2nd edition [pdf] <https://www.enterprise-development.org/wp-content/uploads/m4pguide2015.pdf> [accessed 21 May 2019].

United Nations (UN) (2015) *Transforming Our World: the 2030 Agenda for Sustainable Development*, New York, NY: UN.

UN High-Level Panel on Women's Economic Empowerment (2016) *Leave No One Behind: A Call to Action for Gender Equality and Women's Economic Empowerment* [pdf] <http://www2.unwomen.org/-/media/hlp%20wee/attachments/reports-toolkits/hlp-wee-report-2016-09-call-to-action-en.pdf?la=en&vs=1028> [accessed 21 May 2019].

UN Women (2016) *Women and Sustainable Development Goals*, Nairobi: UN Women Eastern and Southern Africa Regional Office.

UN Women (2017) 'Abolishing chhaupadi, breaking the stigma of menstruation in rural Nepal', [online], 6 April 2017 <http://www2.unwomen.org/-/media/hlp%20wee/attachments/reports-toolkits/hlp-wee-report-2017-03-taking-action-en.pdf?la=en&vs=5226> [accessed 15 July 2019].

United States Agency for International Development (USAID) (2016) *Review of Feed the Future Investments in Enabling Environment Reform*, Washington, DC: USAID.

US Department of State (2016) 'U.S. Department Strategy for Women's Economic Empowerment', [online], 14 June 2016 <https://2009-2017.state.gov/documents/organization/258680.pdf> [accessed 15 July 2019].

Wahlén, C.B. (2017) 'High-level event urges action on women's empowerment; EU-UN launch spotlight initiative on VAWG', [online], 21 September 2017, IISD SDG Knowledge Hub <http://sdg.iisd.org/news/high-level-event-urges-action-on-womens-empowerment-eu-un-launch-spotlight-initiative-on-vawg/> [accessed November 2017].

Women in Informal Employment: Globalizing and Organizing (WIEGO) (2016) *Economic and Employment Rights: Advancing Domestic Workers' Leadership*, Manchester: WIEGO <https://www.wiego.org/sites/default/files/resources/files/DomesticWorkers-Economic%20and%20Employment%20Rights-JDave-CaseStudy-Nov2016.pdf> [accessed 15 July 2019].

WIEGO (no date) <http://www.wiego.org/organizing/organizing-organizations> [accessed on 15 July 2019]

World Bank Group (2015) *Women, Business and the Law*, Washington, DC: World Bank.

World Bank Group (2018) *Women, Business and the Law*, Washington, DC: World Bank.

CHAPTER 4

Sector development: focus on agriculture

Ann Gordon and Rachel Hess

Abstract

This chapter discusses the challenges of increasing gender equality and women's economic inclusion in agricultural market systems and provides evidence for practitioners in facilitating systems change.

Keywords: gender equality, women's economic empowerment, agriculture, market systems, lead firms

Introduction

When her husband died, Damata became the sole support for her seven children in an impoverished region of northern Ghana. Her family joined the ranks of the world's most vulnerable population as a woman-headed rural household. Despite this, her hopes of an education for each of her children motivated her to work hard to increase her income. The chance arose to develop her small subsistence farm into a business by planting a new crop, soybeans, and it seemed like a good prospect to Damata (MEDA, 2017). Adopting new agronomic practices, Damata planted 2 acres (0.8 ha) of soybeans. After a successful year of soybean production, Damata chose to attend a workshop that encouraged her to diversify her farm income by becoming a soybean sales agent (trader) – a big step for a woman in her community. At the workshop, she learned basic business management and record keeping skills that she lacked due to a low level of education. She used these skills as she built her business that aggregates harvested soybeans from neighbours and sells them to a larger-scale aggregator in the nearby town. Damata was also linked to potential soybean buyers, making it easier to establish business contacts. As a trusted sales agent, she provides the critical first link among a network of remote, small-scale farmers, many of them women, and the nearest market town. Her neighbours save time and money on transporting their harvest individually, and the town-based aggregator values the opportunity to buy larger quantities of soybeans. Damata's service earns a small commission on each bag. In 2017 her combined income from sales and farming was US$684,

http://dx.doi.org/10.3362/9781780447506.004

nearly four times her earnings of $172 from farming alone (MEDA, 2018). As a sales agent, Damata has successfully negotiated prices and delivery terms with her male buyer, creating positive impact for the women from whom she buys soybeans. With more income, Damata has a broader range of options for use of these resources, and she is now building a house and saving to buy a three-wheeled motorcycle to make transportation of her soybeans easier (MEDA, 2017).

Around the world, women like Damata play a vital role in producing the world's food but are often under-resourced and disempowered (FAO, 2013). While women are engaged in many aspects of agricultural production and marketing, the systemic barriers that they face are deepened by gender-based challenges in accessing information, resources, market linkages, negotiating power, and financing that are needed to upgrade productivity. If women have access to resources equal to men, their productivity can increase by as much as 30 per cent (FAO, 2013); in fact, Armstrong (2014) makes the case that closing the gender gap and engaging women in equitable economic will go a long way to breaking the cycle of poverty and contribute to more competitive and prosperous national economies.

With different motivations, governments, non-governmental agencies, private businesses, local communities, and women have launched many initiatives to overcome market failures in agricultural sectors such as those faced by Damata, leading to more inclusive market systems and a resulting increase in both women's contribution and benefit.

Women face similar constraints in access, agency, and labour burdens around the world; however, the complexity of the situation is unique to each specific market system and its context. Therefore, change can best be supported when the gendered dynamics of a targeted agricultural sector as well as the relationships among men and women and the communities in which they live are well understood. While there is no one-size-fits-all solution, patterns are emerging that reveal the most effective approaches and entry points for the advancement of gender equality and women's economic empowerment (GE/WEE) in agricultural systems.

In a comprehensive analysis of more than 30 development initiatives that has stood the test of time, Doss et al. (2012) note that the most successful projects demonstrate a basic principle for WEE in agricultural sectors; that is, an integrated approach. Such an approach combines interventions that facilitate change so that women are able to gain and use new skills, accumulate assets, and link other actors in the market system. Moreover, Doss et al. (2012) found that winning projects frequently engage men as well as women, particularly spouses and community leaders, building male support for women's empowerment. Market systems projects that address gender directly help both men and women understand the benefits of increased equality and pave the way for project success (Heilman and Meyers, 2016).

Challenges to advancing women's economic empowerment in agriculture

While there have been advances in recent years in women's inclusion in market systems development (MSD) programmes, challenges remain. Women still face higher barriers than their male counterparts in accessing business financing, inputs, information, markets, and other resources and supports. Additionally, women continue to carry a disproportionate share of unpaid care and housework, and lack access to quality education and skills building opportunities. Interventions designed to specifically address economic 'productive' needs, and household work or 'reproductive' support can assist women in becoming successful market actors, contributing to more sustainable growth.

In a recent study of East African countries by Graca Machel Trust, over half of the female entrepreneur respondents, including smallholder farmers, indicated that access to finance and to markets are still their main barriers (Chakava et al., 2017). Collateral requirements and prohibitive interest rates were identified as key constraints on the finance side, with the recommendation that financial institutions need to create customized products and services that appeal to and cater for women entrepreneurs. On the demand side, capacity building programmes that help women better prepare for financing options are highlighted, along with more marketing opportunities and access to trade (Chakava et al., 2017).

Research and statistics show that women can be instrumental in improving the economic performance of communities and nations; sadly this data falls on deaf ears (Armstrong, 2014). Projects and publicity can boost visibility of the roles women are playing in agriculture, as women are frequently regarded as unpaid labour on the family farm. As the MEDA Greater Rural Opportunities for Women (GROW) project in which Damata participated was launched, one government official stated, 'There are no women farmers in northern Ghana', and yet, in 2016, 24 GROW participants won awards in Ghana's annual Farmer's Day celebrations. These included a woman farmer who was named Best Soybean Farmer in Upper West Region. Others were recognized as Best Soybean Aggregator, Best Conservation Agriculture Farmer, and Best Soybean Farmer at the District Level (MEDA, 2017).

The lack of adequate services and supports is further reinforced by recent research by the Donor Committee for Enterprise Development (DCED) that shows persistent gaps, ranging from 4 per cent to 25 per cent, between men and women who remain in labour participation and land productivity in the agriculture sector. This is primarily due to unequal access to agricultural inputs such as land, labour, machinery, knowledge, fertilizer, improved seeds, and credit (DCED, 2017).

An underlying challenge curbing women's participation in agricultural market systems is the fact that they carry a heavy responsibility for family care. The multifaceted workload typical of women has implications for her family's food security and limits her ability to produce for the market (Grassi et al., 2015). MSD interventions seeking to advance WEE through greater participation in agricultural markets must recognize this extra labour burden and incorporate considerations of the disparate workloads of women and men into gendered market systems analysis so that causes are understood and opportunities for change identified. Maestre and Thorpe have assembled a set of tools that support this analysis and identification of solutions. Such solutions must be context-specific and can include promotion of affordable labour-saving technologies and products, redistribution of care more equally within the family, and fostering women's expanded agency and ability to negotiate (Maestre and Thorpe, 2016).

The multiple responsibilities women carry can limit their ability to fully benefit from newly available economic opportunities. Women coffee growers in Oaxaca, Mexico, saw their incomes rise as they joined organically certified coffee organizations. They also reported high levels of household decision making and control over the income from coffee production. However, their disproportionate responsibility for family care limited their participation in the coffee organization, which meant there were few women leaders within the organization and women did not fully benefit from membership (Lyon et al., 2016).

Limited experience with business transactions and negotiating can also put women at a disadvantage in dealing with other market actors, who are frequently men. As Damata's experience illustrates, initiatives that incorporate training in leadership can provide opportunities for women to practise these skills in new roles and prepare them for greater success in the market (MEDA, 2017).

Solutions for facilitating inclusive agricultural sector development

Based on an understanding of how markets work and recognizing the importance of assessing gender in each context, this chapter outlines several entry points for facilitating gendered change through inclusive MSD approaches in agricultural systems.

A gendered market systems analysis is a fundamental first step to ensuring the design of effective interventions that can advance the participation of women in agricultural systems. It is necessary to understand underlying social norms, power dynamics in male/female and value chain relationships, differences in and barriers to access to resources, services, opportunities, and information, as well as the incentives at play within the market system (Jones, 2016). Interventions intending to promote WEE run the risk of failing to facilitate new opportunities for women or worsening conditions through unintended consequences (Humphrey, 2014).

The following strategies elaborate selected ways to address disorganized or biased market systems, overcome market failures, and consequently promote expanded economic activity, increased income, and greater access and agency among women.

Interventions that change vertical and horizontal relationships in agricultural systems

Vertical relationships in MSD are those that occur among buyers and sellers of products along the value chain – input suppliers to farmers, farmers to aggregators, aggregators to larger buyers, and possibly several other layers before reaching the final consumer. Horizontal relationships exist within groups or collectives, or among businesses that cooperate to achieve market advantages (i.e. joint promotion). Understanding women's relationships with other actors in a market system, and inherent power structures within those relationships, is a crucial consideration for transforming women's engagement in agricultural sectors (Coffey International Development, 2013). By building on the foundation of a gender-informed analysis, understanding the roles and issues faced by women, and analysing the dynamics of the targeted system, stronger vertical and horizontal linkages can be fostered to overcome market barriers.

Strengthening women's vertical relationships in market systems

Business relationships are shaped by business interest, power inequalities, and social norms (Markel et al., 2016). To create enduring systemic change that benefits women, market actors must see the business potential of working with women. In some cases, business partners will need initial support to catalyse behaviour change and learning.

In the GROW project in Ghana, MEDA recognized two sets of business actors who would benefit from enhanced engagement with women as suppliers or consumers: soybean buyers were interested in securing adequate volume for their processing plants and suppliers wished to expand their customer base for products and services. The GROW project promoted stronger integration of women into agricultural value chains by facilitating meetings and information sharing with input suppliers and soybean buyers. When each of these sets of market actors experienced the benefit of working together with women, the vertical relationships were strengthened.

> In the past we worked with men and they ran away with our money; since then we have been working with women and we have never experienced such problems, they are supportive of our business and we appreciate their effort. Women want to pay right away and if they are buying products they want you to pick up the money right away (Manager, Input Supply, Wa, Ghana, April 2018).

Along with information and introductions, many development programmes share the risk that businesses take when extending their backward supply chains or services to reach women – often in the form of cost-sharing or other incentives. One such example in the GROW project was technical and financial support provided to an entrepreneur to start the first soy milk processing business in northern Ghana, providing a nearby market for women soybean farmers who had been selling to processors in the south. Identifying a new role for women in Ghana also enhanced vertical relationships and the benefit to women. Antika, an input supply company, recruited women farmers into its sales agent network in order to reach remote rural communities. Antika and other businesses were glad of the opportunity to reach women cost-effectively through a local sales agent model as women farmers are valued as trustworthy clients who are likely to be repeat customers.

Strengthening women's horizontal relationships in market systems

Groups can take many forms and serve a range of purposes. Farmer groups are formed to deliver information and training or as a mechanism to strengthen links to other actors in the market system. Community-managed production or aggregation of outputs by women's groups can create new opportunities for women. Formation of savings and loan groups have proven to be a powerful method for women to save small amounts of capital for productive investment, to cover household costs, or hedge against economic shocks. In these new horizontal structures, women create value addition, take on tasks that were previously the domain of men, develop leadership skills, and coordinate with other women to become more visible to other market actors such as buyers, input suppliers, and service providers.

The Sunhara Walmart project in Uttar Pradesh, India, implemented by Agribusiness Systems International (ASI), brought women together in farmer groups headed by a lead farmer as a mechanism to collectively expand economic opportunities for women. Bulk buying of inputs and aggregating harvest for group transport and selling has saved women time and money, and motivated businesses to view women as beneficial customers and suppliers. This group structure has also allowed women to address other constraints, allowing them to access individual bank accounts, and to gain greater mobility as family and community members recognize the value of the training and group activities in which they participate.

Groups also provide an opportunity for women to discuss their common experience and challenges. Women commonly report this as an empowering opportunity – as Sally Armstrong points out in her book documenting women's movement towards empowerment, 'Talking to other women was key for Western women in the 60's/70's and the best step toward change for women seeking change today' (Armstrong, 2014). In the ASI project, group leaders were given gender and leadership training and the opportunity to participate in exposure visits to agricultural universities and farmer field days hosted by more advanced farms to learn about new business models and market opportunities. Not only have women seen increases in their income, they report greater control over the use of this income. A gender impact assessment following the project period confirmed that participation in the project had significantly increased women's control over income as well as their mobility and control over production and marketing (Caro et al., 2013). Many of the stories of change collected by the researchers mention new and stronger relationships between women as a result of working together in groups.

Interventions that support women moving into new roles in the market system

While facilitating change that allows women to earn more from their traditional roles, women can also be encouraged to take on new roles, thus expanding their choices and prospects. In some cases, such change emerges from the work that women have traditionally done. Women livestock health workers, trained and supported by CARE Bangladesh, have moved beyond their traditional role of caring for livestock on the homestead to offering a sustainable business service to others. Trained to diagnose and treat common livestock illnesses, these women open local shops providing training to others in livestock husbandry, selling vaccines and medicines, and making farm calls to treat sick animals (KIT et al., 2012).

Women intermediaries or sales agents are often new roles for women within a value chain. Sales agents aggregate farm produce from other women farmers and on sell to larger buyers in the value chain, thereby earning a small commission on sales. Sales agents also deliver value addition services such as grading and/or packaging or bulk purchase of higher quality inputs. For example, MEDA successfully trained and supported sales agents to link women backyard seedling growers with commercial nurseries in northern Pakistan (Hoffman and Dohad, 2012).

Some women take on new roles in market systems such as that of lead farmer. When adopting this role – usually facilitated through a funded project – women lead farmers gain knowledge, develop linkages to goods and services, and bring critical information and services to other excluded women farmers. The lead farmer approach has been widely adopted and shows evidence that it indeed contributes to women's empowerment in agriculture by increasing women's participation in household- and community-level agriculture production and providing access to markets. Kalagho's (2013) analysis of women lead farmers in Malawi shows that increased capacity building, including access to market information within the value chain, leads to asset accumulation and decision-making power.

> Women already do much of the work in many male-dominated value chains. By making their contributions explicit, women gain opportunities and are able to improve their abilities and practices (KIT et al., 2012: 116).

In other situations, women take on roles in sectors that were previously reserved for men. In Ethiopia, honey collection and processing has traditionally been carried out by men. Travelling long distances from home and climbing trees to collect the honey was seen as inappropriate work for women. Oxfam, working with Zembaba, a beekeepers' union in Amhara Region of Ethiopia, identified an opportunity for women to be trained on beekeeping with improved hives that could be located near their homes. Women beekeepers have now organized self-help groups through which they can continue to improve their skills. Collection centres set up by Zembaba's member cooperatives make it easy for women to deliver their honeycomb. The combined introduction of improved hives and support for women to participate in honey production has increased productivity of the entire value chain. Improvements in quality have resulted in price increases for both men and women beekeepers (KIT et al., 2012).

Interventions focused on firm upgrading

Improvements in business performance and competitiveness at all levels of the market system can expand economic opportunities for women. Interventions that support such growth stimulate system-wide change that, while advancing WEE, also benefits the whole sector. Upgrading firm performance can focus on a range of business opportunities, including increased production efficiency, improved product quality or value, or changes in function that allow a firm or group to capture more value by moving into new positions in the value chain (Marketlinks, 2018). A business may enter new markets or build upon current expertise to develop new business capacity. The sections below focus on two approaches to business upgrades that have the potential to advance WEE.

Sustainability certifications and women's economic empowerment. Farm enterprises can reach higher value markets by meeting standards such as GLOBALG.A.P. (Good Agricultural Practices), Rainforest Alliance certification, HACCP (hazard analysis and critical control points) for food safety, and gaining production and processing certification that allows them to export to European markets. However, a review of initiatives to promote a range of sustainability certifications, including organic, Fair Trade, and Rainforest Alliance, found that gaining such certifications does not universally result in an increased benefit to women.

On the one hand, a study of Fair Trade and organic certified coffee producers in Guatemala and Mexico provides evidence that the Fair Trade requirements for women's participation has meant that women are more involved in village and regional organizations and as a result have access to a greater range of services and benefits (Bray and Neilson, 2017). Moreover, organic certification requirements resulted in more land being registered by women, and women having a more prominent role in coffee production. The combination of Fair Trade and organic certifications means that both women and men receive higher prices. While the quality requirements of these certifications can increase women's workload – since they are typically performing the laborious processing tasks that are key to quality – cooperatives with these certifications are more likely to have access to mechanization that can reduce women's labour.

On the other hand, an evaluation of Fair Trade certified banana and coffee producers in Peru, Costa Rica, and Ghana (Ruben, 2008) found evidence that women's contribution to household income and participation in decisions about use of resources declined as a result of certification processes. This may be because gender dynamics within the household were not directly considered in the certification process, thus reinforcing existing inequities and male capture of opportunities such as training and market linkages. Kasente (2012), in her research of the gender impact of Fair Trade and organic certification of coffee growers in Uganda, observed that because certifications intend to address social issues, there may be an assumption that everyone participating in the process benefits from it. She warns that if gender roles and power relations are overlooked, life may become more challenging for women. Initiatives committed to supporting producers to secure such certification do well to begin with a thorough analysis of existing gender relationships to identify gender-based barriers to greater economic opportunity for women and to design interventions that use the procedures and regulations of the certification process to ensure positive outcomes for women as well as men.

Lead firms as a vehicle for improving gender equity. Promoting inclusive lead firm models can be an important force in advancing WEE by enabling these businesses to exert positive influence on other firms in the sector through demonstrating new ways of doing business. Targeted lead firms typically have a significant number of vertical and horizontal commercial linkages, which position them to encourage more opportunities for women in their own business as well as to model the way for others, thereby stimulating industry competitiveness and sustainability (Action for Enterprise, 2014). Supporting growth of these firms, through access to finance, business development services, new technology, or new markets, can create expanded opportunity throughout a lead firm's supply chain and distribution networks.

Moreover, when the lead firm itself has women in senior leadership positions, this is not just an example for others in the value chain, but also sets a course for improved financial performance in the business. The International Monetary Fund (IMF) reports in a recent study of over 2 million firms across 34 countries that there is a strong positive correlation between the share of women in senior leadership positions and a corporate return on assets (Christiansen et al., 2016). This evidence reinforces the link between gender diversity in senior positions of a business and firm performance.

Interventions involving men in solutions

Gender norms shape attitudes, behaviour, and opportunities for men as well as women. Advancing WEE cannot be accomplished without deep understanding of the intertwined nature of expectations and constraints placed on both women and men by the society in which they live and work. This section focuses on the imperative to thoughtfully engage men in efforts to increase GE and advance WEE in agricultural market systems, while gender norms are dealt with more extensively in Chapter 3 on the enabling environment.

Failure to engage men in women's advancement in agriculture runs the risk of unintended consequences such as deterioration of women's position in the community, an increase in gender-based violence, or moves by men to take over the resources or assets women have newly gained.

Developed initially in 2008 by Oxfam, the Gender Action Learning System (GALS) is a participatory process for engaging women and men in reflecting on their lives, the power relationships within their households and communities, and opportunities for greater equality (GALS, 2018). This process is designed to build the capacity of marginalized groups of women and men to help them identify ways to improve their economic opportunities, and at the same time to engage more powerful players in the market system to understand gender inequality and the business case and human rights rationale for equitable change. In Zimbabwe, women and men using the GALS framework came to see that a more equitable division of housework made economic sense for the family unit. Shifting the dialogue to a focus on poverty reduction rather than on gendered social norms stimulated new mindsets regarding the ability and contribution of both men and women. Over time, the GALS methodology helped these same households to address ownership and control of assets as well as gender-based violence, polygamy, and alcohol abuse (Reemer et al., 2015).

In the Sunhara project in India described above, women-only and men-only groups were initially formed. However, as the project evolved, interaction between women and men emerged in ways that were not anticipated. In one project area, a woman extension agent began her outreach by contacting men's groups to build their understanding of why she would be targeting women. While men initially were sceptical about women's ability to learn new practices, they soon saw results from the training, and the extension agent began receiving calls from men asking for assistance for themselves. At the same time, women in the group requested that she provide training to the men as well (Caro et al., 2013).

In Honduras, where machismo attitudes shape the way both men and women think about masculinity, Fintrac found that male support and engagement was essential for sustained gains in WEE. Fintrac launched a series of workshops for men addressing gender, masculinity, and the causes of domestic violence. The workshops not only provided space for men to reflect on their own gender conditioning but also tools and guidance to break harmful patterns (Wessels, 2016).

Case study: advancing inclusive market systems in Ghana

The GROW project was launched in 2012 to address market system failures in the soybean sector in northern Ghana, with the ultimate objective of achieving increased income and food security for 20,000 farming families. Funded by Global Affairs Canada and implemented by Mennonite Economic Development Associates (MEDA), it sought to improve market linkages with buyers, enhance productivity, and facilitate access to needed inputs and services. With high market demand from soybean buyers, market gaps such as insufficient extension services, poor market linkages, and lack of needed inputs and services could be addressed sustainably at scale. The project facilitated market systems change through:

- Strengthening input supply chains by facilitating access to improved seeds and appropriate equipment from commercial suppliers.
- Catalysing the supply of productive finance by forging linkages and incentivizing financial institutions through credit guarantees.
- Connecting farmers to downstream market actors that are linked to higher value markets: processors, wholesalers, traders, and warehouse facility operators.
- Facilitating access of women farmers to market information and extension services.

GROW's MSD project mechanisms included:

- *Market research for crop selection.* Soybean was selected as the core crop because of the strong demand by small- to medium-scale oil processors who could not source adequate raw materials. Customarily, men cultivate grains for household staples and to sell in the market; however, this was not the case with soybeans. This meant that the project promoted this crop as both a cash opportunity for women farmers and an important addition to the household diet.
- *Lead farmers as agents of change.* Only about a quarter of women in the region had received agriculture training prior to the project. GROW identified lead farmers in each community to address this void. Selected women lead farmers were not only trained on soybean agronomic practices but also linked to sources of quality seed and other inputs and services. Four years later, over 1,000 farmer groups were formed, each with a trained lead farmer who provided a critical market system role of giving information and guidance to the group. A total of 22,449 women farmers cultivated 19,347 acres (7,829 ha) of soybeans during the 2016 season.
- *Promotion of savings groups.* Women typically did not have resources for farming; therefore, the project promoted the formation of village savings and loan associations (VSLAs) that could be leveraged for financial inclusion. More than half of the VSLAs were linked to financial institutions through which women could access a broader range of financial services.
- *Equipping women with basic business skills.* The GROW project provided training in basic production budgeting for women farmers. As women adopted this practice it enabled them to plan what crops they planted and the inputs and labour they needed, well in advance of the rainy season. It also allowed them to decide whether to save the money they needed for production or whether to secure a loan.

Results

A mid-term project evaluation found a doubling, on average, in annual income of women farmers from all sources ($120 to $243). The income increase was attributed to soybean cultivation and expanded dry season economic activities, also promoted by the project. Women farmers indicated more engagement in making family farm and household decisions. Male community members observed that women made more economic contributions to their households, saw an increase in food for the family, and were better able to pay school fees. Furthermore, 60 per cent more women farmers reported selling soybean than at the beginning of the project, showing better connections to markets. Additionally, the increased soybean production by women farmers fostered new businesses offering a broader range of services to farmers and additional markets for soybeans.

Useful resources

BEAM Exchange WEAMS Framework: https://beamexchange.org/resources/794/

FAO's *Developing Gender-Sensitive Value Chains: A Guiding Framework*: http://www.fao.org/3/a-i6462e.pdf%3E

Marketlinks Value Chain Wiki, 'Key constraints and promising strategies in applying the value chain approach with women': https://www.marketlinks.org/good-practice-center/value-chain-wiki/key-constraints-and-promising-strategies-applying-value-chai-0

Mercy Corps' *Gender and Market Development*: https://www.mercycorps.org/sites/default/files/Gender%20and%20Market%20Development_Mercy%20Corps.pdf

Oxfam Novib, *Gender Action Learning System: Practical Guide for Transforming Gender and Unequal Power Relations in Value Chains*: https://www.oxfamnovib.nl/Redactie/Downloads/English/publications/150115_Practical%20guide%20GALS%20summary%20Phase%201-2%20lr.pdf

Promundo and CARE International, *Journeys of Transformation: A Training Manual for Engaging Men as Allies in Women's Economic Empowerment*: http://promundoglobal.org/wp-content/uploads/2014/12/Journeys-of-Transformation.pdf

References

Action for Enterprise (2014) *Tools and Methodologies for Collaborating with Lead Firms: A Practitioner's Manual* [pdf] <http://www.actionforenterprise.org/lf-manual.pdf> [accessed 15 April 2019].

Armstrong, S. (2014) *Ascent of Women*, Toronto: Vintage Canada.

Bray, J. and Neilson, J. (2017) 'Reviewing the impacts of coffee certification programmes on smallholder livelihoods', *International Journal of Biodiversity Science, Ecosystem Services and Management* 13(1): 216–32 <http://dx.doi.org/10.1080/21513732.2017.1316520>.

Caro, D., Pangare, V. and Manfre, C. (2013) *Gender Impact Assessment of the ASI Sunhara India Project* [pdf], Bethesda, MD: Cultural Practice, LLC <http://www.culturalpractice.com/wp-content/uploads/2014/02/Gender-Impact-Assessment-of-the-ASI-Sunhara-India-Project.pdf> [accessed May 2019].

Chakava, A., Mworia, M., Moshe, M., Mbinya J., Magaga, S. and Gachoki, L. (2017) *Survey to Explore Growth Barriers Faced by Female Entrepreneurs in East Africa* [online], Graça Machel Trust <https://d3n8a8pro7vhmx.cloudfront.net/eatradehub/pages/3137/attachments/original/1489042773/Graca_Machel.pdf?1489042773> [accessed May 2019].

Christiansen, L., Lin, H., Pereira, J., Topalova, P. and Turk, R. (2016) *Gender Diversity in Senior Positions and Firm Performance: Evidence from Europe* [pdf], International Monetary Fund <https://www.imf.org/external/pubs/ft/wp/2016/wp1650.pdf> [accessed 15 April 2019].

Coffey International Development (2013) *Mainstreaming Women's Economic Empowerment in Market-Systems Development: Practitioner Guidelines* [pdf] <https://beamexchange.org/uploads/filer_public/d3/5f/d35f410a-2064-46f9-8f04-7044a8a32c70/mainstreamingwomenseconomicdevelopment 2013.pdf> [accessed 15 April 2019].

Donor Committee for Enterprise Development (DCED) (2017) *Latest Research and Evidence on PSD* [pdf], DCED <https://www.enterprise-development.org/wp-content/uploads/DCED_LatestResearchandEvidenceonPSD_SpecialFeatureWEE_2017.pdf> [accessed 15 April 2019].

Doss, C., Bockius-Suwyn, Z. and D'Souza, S. (2012) *Women's Economic Empowerment in Agriculture: Supporting Women Farmers* [pdf], UN Foundation <http://www.womenconroadmap.org/sites/default/files/Doss%20Bockius-Suwyn%20and%20DSouza_Supporting%20Women%20Farmers.pdf> [accessed 20 July 2017].

Food and Agriculture Organization of the United Nations (FAO) (2013) 'Equal access to resources and power for food security in the face of climate change' [online] <http://www.fao.org/resources/infographics/infographics-details/en/c/180754/> [accessed 15 April 2019].

Gender Action Learning System (GALS) (2018) 'What is GALS at scale?' [online] <http://www.galsatscale.net/index.html> [accessed 15 April 2019].

Grassi, F., Landberg, J. and Huyer, S. (2015) *Running Out of Time* [pdf], Rome: FAO <http://www.fao.org/3/a-i4741e.pdf> [accessed 15 April 2019].

Heilman, B. and Meyers, L. (2016) *Engaging and Working with Men: Program Insights and Key Considerations for the Agriculture Sector* [pdf], USAID <https://banyanglobal.com/wp-content/uploads/2017/06/LEO_SEEP_Brief_2_-_Engaging_Men_FINAL.logos_.pdf> [accessed May 2019].

Hoffman, P. and Dohad, R. (2012) 'Pathways and pursestrings; enhancing market access for women producers in Pakistan', Global Affairs Canada, unpublished final report for project evaluation.

Humphrey, J. (2014) *Market Systems Approaches: A Literature Review* [pdf], London: The BEAM Exchange <https://beamexchange.org/uploads/filer_public/b2/3a/b23a3505-e3f1-4f63-8c0c-aeb35a763f91/beamliteraturereview.pdf> [accessed 15 April 2019].

Jones, L. (2016) *The WEAMS Framework – Women's Empowerment and Market Systems: Concepts, Practical Guidance and Tools* [pdf], London: The BEAM Exchange <https://beamexchange.org/uploads/filer_public/0d/50/0d5009be-

faea-4b8c-b191-c40c6bde5394/weams_framework.pdf> [accessed May 2019].

Kalagho, K.G. (2013) 'The contributions of lead farmer concept towards women lead farmers' empowerment in agriculture: Case studies from Kasungu district, Malawi', [online], Master's thesis, Van Hall Larenstein University of Applied Sciences, The Netherlands <http://edepot.wur.nl/279065> [accessed 15 April 2019].

Kasente, D. (2012) 'Fair Trade and organic certification in value chains: lessons from a gender analysis from coffee exporting in Uganda', *Gender and Development* 20(1): 111–27 <http://dx.doi.org/10.1080/13552074.2012.663627>.

Lyon, S., Mutersbaugh, T. and Worthen, H. (2016) 'The triple burden: the impact of time poverty on women's participation in coffee producer organizational governance in Mexico', *Agriculture and Human Values* 34(2): 317–31 <http://dx.doi.org/10.1007/s10460-016-9716-1>.

Maestre, M. and Thorpe, J. (2016) *Understanding Unpaid Care Work to Empower Women in Market Systems Approaches* [online], London: BEAM Exchange <https://beamexchange.org/resources/761/> [accessed 15 April 2019].

Markel, E. Gettliffe, E., Jones, L., Miller, E. and Kim, L. (2016) *The Social Norms Factor: How Gendered Social Norms Influence How We Empower Women in Market Systems Development* [pdf], London: The BEAM Exchange <https://beamexchange.org/uploads/filer_public/3c/a9/3ca93f29-ceaf-4172-9edc-738676c1a7ab/social_norms_factor_report_compressed.pdf> [accessed May 2019].

Marketlinks (2018) 'In-depth concepts for VC project managers and technical staff: types of upgrading value chain wiki' [online] <https://www.marketlinks.org/good-practice-center/value-chain-wiki/types-upgrading> [accessed 15 April 2019].

Mennonite Economic Development Associates (MEDA) (2017) *Greater Rural Opportunities for Women: A Market Actor Case Study* [online] <https://www.meda.org/news/publications-main/gender-equality-and-social-inclusion/grow-greater-rural-opportunities-for-women/336-greater-rural-opportunities-for-women-market-actor-case-study-february-2017/file> [accessed 15 April 2019].

Mennonite Economic Development Associates (MEDA) (2018) 'Greater Rural Opportunities for Women (GROW) annual report', prepared for Global Affairs Canada, unpublished report.

Royal Tropical Institute (KIT), Agri-ProFocus and IIRR (2012) *Challenging Chains to Change: Gender Equity in Agricultural Value Chain Development* [pdf], Amsterdam: KIT Publishers, Royal Tropical Institute <https://www.cordaid.org/en/wp-content/uploads/sites/3/2013/02/Challenging_chains_to_change.pdf> [accessed 15 April 2019].

Ruben, R. (2008) 'Final report fair trade programme evaluation: impact assessment of fair trade programmes for coffee and bananas in Peru, Costa Rica and Ghana' [online] <http://hdl.handle.net/2066/73192> [accessed May 2019].

Wessels, S. (2016) 'Enlisting men to empower women in Honduras' [blog], 30 April 2016, SEEP <https://seepnetwork.org/Blog-Post/Enlisting-Men-to-Empower-Women-in-Honduras> [accessed May 2019].

CHAPTER 5

Financial inclusion: challenges and opportunities

Linda Jones, Carolyn Burns, and Clara Yoon

Abstract

This chapter discusses the gap in financial services for women and women-owned small businesses and provides approaches, strategies, and tools for closing that gap within a market systems approach.

Keywords: gender equality, women's economic empowerment, financial inclusion, financial gender gap, digital finance, savings groups

Introduction

Agathe is a farmer in Kabwe, Zambia. Agathe not only grows her own crops but also has a business that sells agricultural inputs to 3,000 female and male smallholder farmers in her district. Agathe further supports these smallholder farmers with training to ensure that agrochemicals are properly applied, resulting in improved quality and increased volume. Agathe has self-financed the development of her business, incrementally expanding her reach to more farmers as capital allows. Yet, despite her business growth year-on-year, she is unable to get a bank loan to develop her business due to lack of collateral and perceived risk by lenders. Ironically, Agathe has learned to manage collateral and risk issues, investing her own capital into providing inputs on credit to farmers and taking payment on the sale of their harvest. In her small dusty shop on the main road in Kabwe, Agathe keeps sacks of inputs and customer files – a single piece of paper for each customer that received inputs on credit that season. The records itemize the quantity and price of inputs received and the collateral offered – goats, farm equipment, other crops – and include the signature of both buyer and seller. Despite her lack of access to finance, Agathe has done what many larger suppliers and development projects have been unable to do; she has reached disadvantaged farming households with needed inputs based on a sustainable and commercial approach. Agathe stands out as an exception as many of the financially excluded cannot manage cyclical cash flow challenges. However, Agathe is the norm when it comes to being unable to access finance from mainstream financial institutions.

http://dx.doi.org/10.3362/9781780447506.005

Financial inclusion can be a game changer for low-income people, enabling one to start a microenterprise, take a growing business to the next level, or upgrade production through better inputs and equipment. However, financial exclusion remains a widespread constraint in emerging economies, and women are especially challenged in accessing finance. The latest Findex (Demirguc-Kunt et al., 2017) reports that 1.7 billion people remain unbanked (without an account at a formal financial institution or through a mobile money vendor), and that less than half of women are banked. While financial exclusion is not inherently a gender issue, women are disproportionately over-represented in the financially excluded, lagging behind men's access to account ownership by a global average of 9 per cent (Demirguc-Kunt et al., 2017). The severity of this account gender gap varies across regions, with women in South Asia having the lowest account uptake, at 37 per cent for women and 55 per cent for men (Nel de Koker, 2015). By enabling women to save, invest, borrow, and insure their lives and businesses, they can participate in the formal economy and contribute to economic growth and prosperity (Women's World Banking, 2016).

This chapter discusses women's financial inclusion in general with specific insights into the largest group of working women worldwide – smallholder farmers – who are also the most financially excluded. A women's agricultural finance case from Zambia is featured throughout this chapter, while other examples are used to further illustrate statements on financial inclusion.

Challenges to women's financial inclusion

Although our knowledge of the 'gender gap' in financial inclusion is growing, the 2013 findings of Demirguc-Kunt et al. indicate that we have a weak understanding of the specific barriers that limit access to finance for women, which remains true today. In general terms, we know that there are systemic barriers to women's access at multiple levels of a financial system whether rural or urban; that is, enabling environment, sociocultural rules and norms, infrastructure, support services, and issues of supply and demand in financial markets. While some of these barriers overlap with men's (i.e. low-income rural men are less included than more affluent urban women and men), it has been repeatedly documented that constraints are deeper for women, often relating to women's status and power in society and their own households. One example of this is the misalignment between collateral requirements and women's borrowing needs. In Rwanda and in many developing economies, individual loans currently offered by banks require collateral such as a land or house title; however, the value of such assets is typically much larger than required loan sizes of women, as women tend to seek smaller loans (Women's World Banking, 2017).

Women's financial exclusion often stems from two sources – gendered bias and poverty; but gender and poverty are complex constructs that have contextual implications. For example, women who live on less than US$2 per day are, on average, 28 per cent less likely than men to have a bank account (Bin-Humam, 2017). But the reality is more nuanced when we consider the rural–urban and gender divide. Low-income people often live far from services and earn their income from agriculture. For example, in Zambia, although rural women can access finance for about half of their needs, this is largely informal finance, and their total financial inclusion still lags behind other groups: 8 per cent less than rural male counterparts, 22 per cent behind urban women, and 40 per cent lower than urban men (Jones and Grundling, 2016a).

Since socially and economically vulnerable women are more likely to be excluded from the formal banking system (as in the Zambia case), this causes them to default to cash to handle their financial transactions. While cash offers women some elements of financial independence, it largely limits their financial capacity. For instance, cash's liquidity can make women a target for theft, vulnerable to exploitation by family members, and without formalized account records, affecting access to financial services for their businesses. Furthermore, a cash-based economy requires women to always have their money on-hand, which may not be feasible or secure. In the case of women farmers, cash flow is irregular, dependent on a range of factors including the agricultural cycle, regular expenses such as children's schooling, unexpected expenses, and their almost complete reliance on informal finance (Jones and Grundling, 2016b). Finally, relying on cash can constrain women's ability to save for higher-value purchases by being more prone to impulse spending and demands from family members and neighbours when cash is in hand. A cash-based economy can, therefore, leave women unable to rise above their current financial status.

Other barriers impede women's financial inclusion. For example, the requirement to present identification when establishing a bank account or taking a loan discriminates against women who often do not have such paperwork. For example, Pakistani women are 11 per cent less likely than men to have a national identity card (Nel de Koker, 2015), while women farmers in Zambia are required to have both an identity card and proof of address (e.g. a utility bill), with very few able to present the latter (Jones and Grundling, 2016a). Mobility constraints can also limit women's access to finance, often exacerbated by women's heavy workload within and outside the home. In addition, even when mobility and time permit, women may be curtailed by limited transportation options such as prohibitions against women drivers (e.g. in Turkmenistan; AKI Press, 2018).

Socio-economic and cultural norms and biases also cause limitations on uptake of other formalized financial services by women. Understanding how and why social norms prevent approximately 1.1 billion women and girls worldwide from participating in the formal financial system is critical to reducing the financial gender gap in women's financial inclusion (Bin-Humam and Ayes, 2017). For example, women in conservative cultures typically have limited interactions with men outside the family, which reduces exposure to or information about formal financial services, while other social norms may restrict women's control and decision making on how their income is spent (Bin-Humam and Ayes, 2017). As stated in G20 Insights (Robino et al., 2018):

> For financial inclusion to have an impact on women's economic empow-
> erment, livelihoods and broader welfare effects, social norms need to
> be considered and acted upon. While social norms change is complex,
> financial services and products design and roll out can have a role to
> play' (Robino et al., 2018).

Women's World Banking (2016) reports that financial institutions are typically unaware of barriers women face in using their services and the missed business opportunity if these barriers are not addressed. In addition, women customers often experience biases from loan officers and report 'feeling uncomfortable and that they do not belong in bank branches' (Women's World Banking, 2016: 3). These points highlight the breadth of factors limiting women's abilities to access and use appropriate services and products, and they are often disadvantaged compared with their male counterparts.

Financial inclusion strategies

Financial inclusion requires access to a range of appropriate and affordable financial products and services along with the capacity to uptake and use these products and services. Gender-sensitive or gender-inclusive financial interventions present an opportunity for women to take greater ownership over their financial positioning and redefine gender-biased socio-economic and cultural norms. For instance, women's enrolment in a formalized savings programme can help them transfer their unprotected cash into secure savings that may even offer interest through loans made to other group members. Women's savings groups have historically played an important role in addressing or changing gender norms by building confidence, transferring knowledge, and promoting a greater sense of self-esteem (Burjorjee et al., 2017). Women who can financially provide for themselves and their families boast higher rates of economic empowerment (Siddik, 2017).

Increasing the rate of women's financial inclusion can lead to positive changes at the household, community, and ecosystem levels, promoting more equitable prosperity. Women's access to and use of financial services is linked with greater financial stability, financial integrity, and consumer protection (Sahay et al., 2015). In addition, one global study found that 90 per cent of women are interested in applying their increased wealth to improve society (Hewlett et al., 2014), demonstrating that women are likely to use their wealth for good. Finally, promoting greater women's financial inclusion aligns with a broader development agenda as laid out in the Sustainable Development Goals 1, 4, 5, 8, 10, and 16, the Universal Declaration of Human Rights, and the G20 Platform for Financial Inclusion (Sahay et al., 2015).

In terms of specific financial responsibilities and corresponding needs, there are also notable gender differences that will impact selected strategies (Napier et al., 2013). Women are often assigned responsibility for household expenditures – maintaining the family with food, clothing, schoolbooks, and other day-to-day necessities – while men may focus on productive resources and access to jobs. It is common, for example, for rural women to be concerned about cash flow-smoothing to ensure household well-being, using methods such as informal savings or borrowing to make ends meet. On the other hand, male members of the household may be more likely to use formal financial services such as loans for inputs or leases for equipment.

In this section, we expand upon strategies for financial inclusion and organize financial solutions around four main topics: financial literacy, microfinance (credit and savings), microinsurance, and digital financial services.

Financial literacy

Financial literacy is an important skill as it enables one to be a competitive economic actor. Financial literacy can be defined as 'the ability to use knowledge and skills to manage financial resources effectively for a lifetime of financial well-being' (President's Advisory Council, 2009: 7). It is often measured via the testing of basic financial principles (e.g. numeracy, compound interest, inflation, and risk diversification) (Hasler and Lusardi, 2017). Financial illiteracy is a global phenomenon, affecting 35 per cent of men and 30 per cent of women worldwide (Hasler and Lusardi, 2017), with the rates highest in South Asia (Klapper et al., 2015). Among women, those most likely to be financially illiterate include young women, elderly widows, the poorly educated, and low-income earners (OECD, 2013). Women's unique role as primary caregivers causes financially illiterate women to pose a high risk of transmitting poor financial decision-making practices on to their children (OECD, 2013), with the spillover effect that both women and their families are unable to rise above their economic circumstances.

Financial literacy programmes targeting women can help them to gain greater control over their finances and increase their sphere of financial influence within the household. Programmes that respond to women's unique financial needs can help to reinforce women's interest in financial management topics. Likewise, financial literacy programmes that emphasize decision making can help women to overcome potential discomfort with financial matters. The success of the International Finance Corporation (IFC)-funded Training Women In SolTuna programme in the Solomon Islands demonstrates this (IFC, 2016). The project sought to overcome SolTuna's employees' low literacy and numeracy by teaching 300 production workers, of which 225 were women, financial literacy, life skills, and gender awareness. The training led to significant improvements in workers' cash flow management and savings and helped many women workers to gain greater confidence in speaking with their families about financial matters. One SolTuna employee was able to convince her husband to save alongside her towards the purchase of a family home, providing evidence that a gender-sensitive financial literacy programme can empower women to become more involved in household financial decision-making activities (IFC, 2016).

Women's participation in financial literacy training can lead to economic and sociocultural gains felt throughout the larger financial ecosystem. In one study of financial literacy, 77 per cent of women participants stated they had shared their learnings with other women and 59 per cent indicated that they had encouraged their children to save (Kc and Tiwari, 2015). In addition, greater numbers of financially literate women can craft a new narrative around women's capacity to internalize financial information and help redefine sociocultural norms around money management.

Microfinance: credit and savings

Access to basic credit and savings products is critical to the development of economically sustainable livelihoods. Yet, traditional banks find it unprofitable to service high volumes of customers who engage in small transactions and have low account balances. This has contributed to the fact that only 63 per cent of adults in developing economies have access to bank accounts and has created a 9 per cent gender gap that has left many more women unbanked (Demirguc-Kunt et al., 2017). Women over age 15 in sub-Saharan Africa have the lowest rates of account ownership with only 27 per cent uptake (Demirguc-Kunt et al., 2017). While access to credit and savings products can facilitate increased economic opportunities for women, and bank accounts can be a gateway to the use of additional financial services, the financial inclusion community recognizes access alone is insufficient, especially for women. As Blake and Propson state, 'prosperity is not directly derived from the standalone ownership of bank accounts, but from their appropriate and consistent use' (Blake and Propson, 2018: 6). The theme of moving beyond access to usage is an ongoing challenge and opportunity for providers of microfinance, to enable clients to utilize appropriate and affordable financial products to progress towards financial health, which is the ability to build resilience from shocks and create opportunities to pursue one's aspirations (Blake and Propson, 2018).

By the end of 2017, microfinance institutions (MFIs) reached an estimated 139 million low-income and underserved clients, 83 per cent of which were female and 17 per cent were male (Convergences, 2018). With such a large share of women clients, microfinance is often associated with women's empowerment due to its poverty alleviation outcomes, yet research is yielding conflicting evidence (Robinson, 2019). Anecdotal evidence suggests microfinance has had a positive impact on women's empowerment. For example, in a survey of 100 women who received group loans from an Indian MFI, 92 per cent experienced improved standard of living; 91 per cent increased self-confidence; 65 per cent became more involved in household decision making before receiving the loan; and 74 per cent said they were consulted for advice by other women interested in loans (Ahmed-Karim and Alders-Sheya,

2017). On one hand, such positive outcomes and changes demonstrate benefits beyond financial ones, such as improving household dynamics, self-confidence, and community leadership. However, microfinance loans alone cannot facilitate structural transformation and social norms change; nor does improving women's financial situations always result in greater gender equality. While the aim of microfinance is to alleviate poverty and, in most cases, to empower women, increasing women's economic empowerment 'can also challenge established gender roles and power hierarchies, causing conflict in the home and even domestic violence' (Niner, 2018). The promise of microfinance in the 1980s and 1990s was hailed as a way to end poverty and promote women's empowerment; however, more recently others have criticized and condemned it as a disaster for the poor (Pomeranz, 2014) with risks and consequences of over-indebtedness (Blake and Propson, 2018).

According to the Consultative Group to Assist the Poor (CGAP), the role of microfinance as an industry and an 'anti-poverty tool' has evolved significantly in recent decades. Experience and research have revealed the limits of microcredit and 'led to recognition that low-income households require access to a full range of financial services, not only to generate income, but also to build assets, smooth consumption, and manage risks' (CGAP, n.d.). Lensink et al. (2017) build on existing research that providing only microcredit as a solution to poverty is inadequate, and that low-income households typically benefit from a bundle of services, rather than the simple provision of credit. In addition, since 'poverty is multidimensional, poor people need access to a coordinated combination of both financial and nonfinancial services (e.g. business trainings) to overcome poverty' (Lensink et al., 2017).

Another mechanism critical to facilitating financial inclusion for women is savings: 'affording the ability to store value of money safely with the added capability to retrieve or use it whenever required' (Blake and Propson, 2018: 7). A recent study found that women prefer savings more than men do for business development or expansion (Buvinic and Jaluka, 2018). Savings accounts that women can use privately and securely present multiple benefits including increased decision-making power and economic independence, and decreased pressure to share income or spend the funds right away (Buvinic and Jaluka, 2018). In the Philippines, the success of the Green Bank of Caraga's commitment savings product illustrates this (Ashraf et al., 2010). This product prevented women clients from accessing their funds until a predetermined savings goal was achieved, or a certain date passed (e.g. school term fees were due, or Christmas). This enabled women to reduce the risk that their savings would be appropriated by others and allowed women to earmark their savings towards self-determined purchases (Ashraf et al., 2010). In doing so, women were able to establish new household norms regarding the earmarking of funds for certain purposes (Ashraf et al., 2010). The commitment savings product also offered women the option to keep their savings in a locked box at their home for which only the bank had a key (Ashraf et al., 2010). By reducing women's financial liquidity, locked box users were able to better prioritize their expenditures while also achieving financial privacy (Ashraf et al., 2010). While this example demonstrates how a gender-sensitive product can coach women into implementing practices that enhance their financial well-being, savings accounts are not always appropriate. For very poor rural women or those in very traditional settings, savings may need to be part of a bundle of productively oriented interventions (Buvinic and Jaluka, 2018).

Women's uptake of savings and credit products can lead to economic and sociocultural gains felt throughout the larger financial ecosystem. For instance, women may use their strengthened economic position to employ other women in their businesses and in doing so, unlock new sources of labour. This can have a ripple effect throughout the economy as women gain employment. The success of women's businesses may also crowd-in additional economic activities (e.g. hospitality services, real estate services) and expand value chains to support their business growth. In addition, greater numbers of financially independent women can help to redefine socio-economic and cultural norms regarding women's financial capabilities, particularly in terms of their ability to operate successful businesses.

Microinsurance

Access to microinsurance helps mitigate financial exposure to unexpected events and subsequently to prevent individuals, households, and businesses from falling into poverty or becoming impoverished (IFC, 2015). Microinsurance typically refers to 'insurance services offered primarily to clients with low income and limited access to mainstream insurance services and other means of effectively coping with risk' (Microinsurance Network, 2015). Microinsurance is a means of protecting low-income clients from specific risks in exchange for a regular payment of premiums whose amount is proportional to the likelihood and cost of the relevant risk (Microinsurance Network, 2015). Unlike traditional insurance providers that build a cushion against many types of economic shocks, microinsurance has been successful in providing more selective coverage for services (e.g. health insurance, life protection, agriculture/property, job loss, and catastrophes; IFC, 2015). This enables a focus on 'low-income customers with income of $2 to $8 per day and provide annual coverage that ranges in cost from $5 to $6 per person' (IFC, 2015: 42). While the total market potential for microinsurance is roughly 2.3 billion consumers (IFC, 2015), only 3 per cent of low-income people in the world's 100 poorest countries have access to a microinsurance product (Banithia et al., 2009).

Most people who lack microinsurance are women as 'only a handful [of banks] have actually implemented insurance solutions for women' (Global Banking Alliance for Women, 2018: 1). Women's limited access to microinsurance can cause them to be ill-prepared to handle financial crises, with a reliance on traditional risk management and coping measures leaving them financially unsecured and unable to improve their economic positioning

(Banithia et al., 2009). For instance, women may invest in several low risk, low return business opportunities (e.g. planting a variety of crops, raising different types of animals, working a second job) to diversify their income-generating activities and reduce risk (Banithia et al., 2009). Women who pursue this 'horizontal investment' strategy may not be able to gain enough to increase their standard of living (Banithia et al., 2009).

When available, gender-sensitive microinsurance products present an opportunity for women to manage their unique financial risks and apply their savings more productively. Microinsurance products that provide coverage for the risks that mostly affect women (i.e. health risks associated with maternal and child health) can reinforce women's interest in such protections (Banithia et al., 2009). Likewise, women's low literacy and education, as well as their overall unfamiliarity with microinsurance, mean that they value simple plans (IFC, 2015). Gender-sensitive microinsurance products that provide high-quality customer service to help women understand payment terms and exemptions are poised to see high demand by women (IFC, 2015). The success of La Equidad's long-standing Amparar life microinsurance programme in Colombia showcases this by supporting Colombian women's efforts to reduce the economic shocks of death on their families, protecting children with monthly benefits that can be used towards their children's education in the first two years following a parent's death, and for food for up to one year following a parent's death (Banithia et al., 2009). The programme's uptake by 30,000 clients is evidence that microinsurance can empower women to lead more financially secure lives knowing that their affairs are in order (Banithia et al., 2009).

Women's use of microinsurance can also lead to economic and sociocultural gains felt throughout the larger financial ecosystem. For example, the IFC reports that women across China, Mexico, and Nigeria are willing to spend up to 20 per cent of their income to protect against risks in the future and play an important role in scaling the insurance market (IFC, 2015). Finally, women entrepreneurs' preference for insurance can also lead to ripple effects throughout the economy. If women's businesses are better protected, women will be able to take more calculated risks and grow their enterprises. Again, this can support macroeconomic growth and stability. In addition, high numbers of financially protected women can help to redefine socio-economic and cultural norms regarding women's risk tolerance levels, especially with regard to their interest and ability to take on business risks.

Digital financial services

The Global Findex shows great progress for financial access – and also great opportunities for policymakers and the private sector to increase usage and to expand inclusion among women, farmers and the poor. Digital financial services were the key to our recent progress and will continue to be essential as we seek to achieve universal financial inclusion

(H.M. Queen Máxima of the Netherlands, the United Nations Secretary-
General's Special Advocate for Inclusive Finance for Development).

Beginning in the early 2000s, digital financial services (DFS) have enabled
transformative product and service design innovations in the payments
space by tackling traditional barriers to financial inclusion, from reduced
transaction costs to time saved in travelling to and from branches, to added
privacy and trust (Holloway et al., 2017). Of the 1.7 billion unbanked adults,
two-thirds own a mobile phone, presenting significant opportunities for
increasing financial inclusion through innovative digital financial platforms
and technologies such as mobile money (GSMA, 2015; World Bank, 2018).
Access to mobile phones has enabled the acceleration of financial inclusion,
yet because of a persistent digital divide, men are 10 percentage points more
likely to report owning a phone than women (Klapper, 2019). In addition, a
2016 Gallup World Poll provided more insight into women's mobile phone
ownership across over 140 countries, revealing trends and gender differences
across countries and population segments (Burjorjee and Bin-Humam, 2018).
The data revealed that women lag behind men in mobile phone ownership,
and that promoting mobile phone ownership does not always equate to usage
of digital financial services for a variety of reasons such as cost and affordability,
technical literacy and confidence, mistrust of agents or operators, legal/
regulatory and basic infrastructure requirements, and sociocultural norms
(Burjorjee and Bin-Humam, 2018).

The 2017 Findex report outlines opportunities to expand financial
inclusion through digital technology and shifting payments from cash into
accounts for the overarching benefits of improving efficiency, reducing
costs, enhancing security, increasing transparency, and reducing corruption
(Demirguc-Kunt et al., 2017). The story of Safaricom, Kenya's largest mobile
operator, which launched M-Pesa in 2007 ('m-money' in Swahili), is well
known and documented. M-Pesa revolutionized the way Kenyans use mobile
phones for payments and money transfers and currently has 21 million
active users, which represents over 50 per cent of Kenya's population (Miriri,
2018). Recent research indicates that M-Pesa contributed to increased per
capita consumption levels and lifted 194,000 households (i.e. 2 per cent of
Kenyan households) out of poverty, with pronounced impacts for female-
headed households, enabling financial behaviour change, increased financial
resilience and savings, and opportunities for occupational choice to move out
of agriculture and into business (Suri and Jack, 2016).

The emergence of digital technologies and DFS has started to level the playing
field for women. Marie Kyle from insurance provider BIMA states, 'provided
you have access to a mobile phone, you can access the same services as male
counterparts who are more likely to be banked' (Women's World Banking,
2018). However, access to technology is one side of the picture, as mobile
phones and the internet can only drive financial inclusion if the necessary
infrastructure is in place (physical infrastructure such as reliable electricity

and mobile networks; and financial infrastructure including adequate payment systems and a physical network to deliver payments in rural and urban places) along with agent networks or automated teller machines (ATMs) with sufficient liquidity (Demirguc-Kunt et al., 2017). Even with the necessary technology and infrastructure in place, governments play a significant role in ensuring that appropriate regulations and consumer protection safeguards are in place, especially tailored to the needs of disadvantaged groups such as women, low-income people, first-time users, and those with low literacy and numeracy skills (Demirguc-Kunt et al., 2017).

To tackle the financial inclusion gender gap, the role of technology to unlock payment systems and financial products and services that can benefit and work for women has enormous potential and benefits. We need more data that informs women's behaviour and needs and to ask better questions and provide customer-centric product and service design that will result in transformative systems change. Klapper (2019) argues:

> we need to better identify the underlying causes of digital exclusion, such as social norms ... but it's not just technology – we need more data on how women experience financial inclusion broadly. We'd be in a position to close the gender gap if we had more data.

In addition to more data, improved policy frameworks that address and dismantle legal barriers women often face, such as obtaining an ID, is also critical for women to benefit from DFS (Ferracuti, 2018). If the promise of DFS is improved efficiency, reduced costs, enhanced security, and the acceleration of financial inclusion for the unbanked or underbanked, financial service providers (including financial technology 'FinTech' companies), governments, implementers, and civil society actors need to ensure women are not left behind. The above opportunities and challenges demonstrate the interconnections with other topics covered in this book including enabling environments (regulatory and sociocultural spheres); enterprise development and labour force participation; and women's access to and empowerment from information and communications technology (ICT4WEE).

Case study: risks for women farmers' access to financial services in Zambia

Women smallholder farmers in Zambia face multiple barriers in managing their financial lives and in advancing economically. These constraints include but are not limited to: low levels of financial literacy, lack of awareness around the benefits of formal financial services, perceived distance from services, appropriateness and affordability of available services, fear of inability to repay loans, and so on. The resulting financial exclusion affects women farmers' ability to manage day-to-day expenses, deal with emergencies, and invest in assets and productive activities that would enable them to build healthier lives for themselves, their families, and their communities.

Credit and savings – usually from informal sources – are the two main strategies for women farmers in Zambia to manage cash flow, unanticipated expenses, and longer-term investments (as described above). However, even utilizing these fairly basic financial strategies, the process of financial inclusion for women farmers in Zambia is not straightforward. The following list illustrates that even savings groups can be complicated, resulting in no benefits and sometimes a negative impact on women. Some examples of additional challenges for savings groups are listed below:

- An NGO started a 'pay-it-forward' type of savings group in Mulola, Chongwe involving goats and sewing machines. Women formed a group to keep savings, but the NGO did not return to support the approach and women ended up paying the savings out to members rather than purchasing assets.
- A rotating savings and credit association initiated by an NGO in Upper Kaleya, Chikankata district started a 20-woman group to save for assets, production, and day-to-day needs, but some women did not continue participating or stopped contributing once they had received their own payout.
- Women in Upper Kaleya also explained that an attempt had been made in a nearby town to start a savings and loan group, but nobody joined since the monthly contribution was set at ZMW200 ($16), which was not affordable.
- Five women joined a savings group in Mudenda, Pemba district with various outcomes. Of the five, three borrowed to start enterprises of which two failed, and the women lost money but still had to pay back the savings loan.

These examples highlight the complications of achieving financial inclusion of low-income women farmers in a country such as Zambia. Other risks that contribute to this extreme situation, where women farmers have almost no formal financial inclusion, are as follows:

- Savings groups are normally a relatively low-risk financial service. However, as we saw in the examples above, women who borrow from their savings group may lose money (e.g. if undertaking an economic activity that is not viable) and poorly structured groups that do not fit the needs of the group/community can lead to failure.
- With crop insurance there is still a risk that crops could completely fail and although insurance would cover the cost of inputs, women's time, opportunity cost, and loss of anticipated revenue would leave women financially stretched and further indebted. Also, women may not have adequate knowledge, may not be able to access agrochemicals in a timely manner, could become overburdened during certain seasons of the year, or be unable to sell their outputs due to distant, glutted, or fickle markets.
- Livestock loans would appear to be an easy choice given the role livestock play in women's financial lives. However, due to potential death, illness,

or low productivity of livestock, financial institutions would need to consider what other types of non-financial services would be required to prevent animal loss or poor performance. For example, do women have access to information on animal management, can they acquire appropriate inputs such as feeds and supplements, and are veterinary services available for basic vaccines and unexpected illness?

- Small business loans are often suggested by women. However, small businesses can have a high failure rate if markets and costing/pricing are not well understood. Women with no advice (or even bad advice) can choose options that are risky and result in indebtedness. NGOs sometimes take on the role of the adviser, but this does not always lead to good outcomes as NGOs often do not understand business either. Small business development would have to be undertaken with considerable caution and would benefit from multiple partnerships with financial institutions and civil society.

- Technology loans could benefit women in areas such as micro-irrigation. The greatest risk is that the investment of capital is not fit for purpose and women would be unable to repay loans and make good use of the technology. As it is not often the lender's responsibility to provide this type of expert advice, then other sources of information such as extension officers, retailers, and distributors would have to be consulted.

Useful resources

Asian Development Bank (ADB) (2014) *Gender Tool Kit: Micro, Small, and Medium-Sized Enterprise Finance and Development*: https://www.adb.org/sites/default/files/institutional-document/34125/gender-tool-kit-mse-finance-development.pdf

GSMA's *Bridging the Gender Gap: Mobile Access and Usage in Low- and Middle-Income Countries*: https://www.gsma.com/mobilefordevelopment/wp-content/uploads/2016/03/GSM0001_03232015_GSMAReport_Executive-Summary_NEWGRAYS-web.pdf

International Finance Corporation (IFC) and AXA's *She For Shield: Insure Women To Better Protect All*: http://documents.worldbank.org/curated/en/228381492593824450/pdf/114402-WP-SheforShield-Final-Web2015-PUBLIC.pdf

World Bank's Global Findex Database 2017: http://globalfindex.worldbank.org/

References

Ahmed-Karim, Z. and Alders-Sheya, J. (2017) *Empowering Women: Uncovering Financial Inclusion Barriers* [pdf], Ernst & Young <https://www.ey.com/Publication/vwLUAssets/EY-empowering-women-uncovering-financial-inclusion-barriers/$FILE/EY-empowering-women-uncovering-financial-inclusion-barriers.pdf> [accessed 28 March 2019].

AKI Press (2018) 'Women in Turkmenistan banned to drive car', [website], 6 January 2018, Bishkek, Kyrgyz Republic: AKI Press News Agency <https://akipress.com/news:600602/> [accessed 28 May 2018].

Ashraf, N., Karlan, D. and Yin, W. (2010) 'Female empowerment: impact of a commitment savings product in the Philippines', *World Development* 38(3): 333–44 <http://dx.doi.org/10.1016/j.worlddev.2009.05.010>.

Banithia, A., Johnson, S., McCord, M. and Matthews, B. (2009) *Microinsurance That Works for Women: Making Gender-Sensitive Microinsurance Programs* [pdf], Geneva: International Labour Organization <http://www.ilo.org/wcmsp5/groups/public/@ed_emp/documents/publication/wcms_124451.pdf> [accessed 28 May 2018].

Bin-Humam, Y. (2017) '5 challenges for women's financial inclusion' [blog], 13 February 2017, Washington, DC: Consultative Group to Assist the Poor (CGAP) <http://www.cgap.org/blog/5-challenges-women's-financial-inclusion> [accessed 28 May 2018].

Bin-Humam, Y. and Ayes, C. (2017) 'How social norms affect women's financial inclusion', [blog], 8 March 2017, Washington, DC: CGAP <https://www.cgap.org/blog/how-social-norms-affect-womens-financial-inclusion> [accessed 28 March 2019].

Blake, M. and Propson, D. (2018) *Advancing Financial Inclusion Metrics: Shifting from access to economic empowerment* [pdf], Geneva: World Economic Forum <http://www3.weforum.org/docs/WEF_White_Paper_Advancing_Financial_Inclusion_Metrics.pdf> [accessed 29 March 2019].

Burjorjee, D. and Bin-Humam, Y. (2018) *New Insights on Women's Mobile Phone Ownership* [pdf], Washington, DC: CGAP <https://www.cgap.org/sites/default/files/researches/documents/Working-Paper-New-Insights-on-Womens-Mobile-Phone-Ownership-Apr-2018.pdf> [accessed 31 March 2019].

Burjorjee, D., El-Zoghbi, B., Meyers, L. and Heilman, B. (2017) *Social Norms Change for Women's Financial Inclusion* [pdf], Washington, DC: CGAP <https://www.cgap.org/sites/default/files/researches/documents/Brief-Social-Norms-Change-for-Womens-Financial-Inclusion-Jul-2017_0.pdf> [accessed 28 March 2019].

Buvinic, M. and Jaluka, T. (2018) *Mindful Saving: Exploring the Power of Savings for Women* [pdf], Center for Global Development <https://www.cgdev.org/sites/default/files/mindful-saving-exploring-power-savings-women.pdf> [accessed 28 March 2019].

CGAP (no date) 'Frequently asked questions about financial inclusion' [online] <https://www.cgap.org/about/faq#who-funds-financially-inclusive-markets> [accessed 28 March 2019].

Convergences (2018) *Microfinance Barometer 2018* [pdf] <http://www.convergences.org/wp-content/uploads/2018/09/BMF_2018_EN_VFINALE.pdf> [accessed on 29 March 2019].

Demirguc-Kunt, A., Klapper, L. and Singer, D. (2013) *Financial Inclusion and Legal Discrimination Against Women: Evidence from Developing Countries* [pdf], Washington, DC: World Bank Group <http://documents.worldbank.org/curated/en/801311468330257772/pdf/wps6416.pdf> [accessed 28 May 2018].

Demirguc-Kunt, A., Klapper, L., Ansar, S. and Hess, J. (2017) *The Global Findex Database 2017: Measuring Financial Inclusion and the Fintech Revolution* [online], World Bank Group <http://globalfindex.worldbank.org/> [accessed 4 May 2018].

Ferracuti, A. (2018) 'Women's empowerment through digital finance: golden or rotten egg?', [online], 15 June 2018, UNCDF <https://www.uncdf.org/article/3754/womens-empowerment-through-digital-finance-golden-or-rotten-egg> [accessed 30 March 2019].

Global Banking Alliance for Women (2018) *The Women's Market for Insurance: An Emerging Business Opportunity* [online], MicroInsurance Centre <http://www.microinsurancecentre.org/resources/documents/the-women-s-market-for-insurance-an-emerging-business-opportunity.html> [accessed 28 May 2018].

GSM Association (GSMA) (2015) *State of the Industry 2014: Mobile Financial Services for the Unbanked* [pdf], London: GSMA <https://www.gsma.com/mobilefordevelopment/wp-content/uploads/2015/03/SOTIR_2014.pdf> [accessed 29 March 2019].

Hasler, A. and Lusardi, A. (2017) *The Gender Gap in Financial Literacy: A Global Perspective* [pdf], Global Financial Literacy Excellence Center <http://gflec.org/wp-content/uploads/2017/07/The-Gender-Gap-in-Financial-Literacy-A-Global-Perspective-Report.pdf?x87657> [accessed 28 May 2018].

Hewlett, S. and Turner Moffitt, A. (2014) 'The financial services industry's untapped market', [online], 8 December 2014, *Harvard Business Review* <https://hbr.org/2014/12/the-financial-services-industrys-untapped-market> [accessed 29 March 2019].

Holloway, K., Niazi, Z. and Rouse, R. (2017) *Women's Economic Empowerment Through Financial Inclusion: A Review of Existing Evidence and Remaining Knowledge Gaps* [pdf], Innovations for Poverty Action <https://www.poverty-action.org/sites/default/files/publications/Womens-Economic-Empowerment-Through-Financial-Inclusion.pdf> [accessed 28 March 2019].

International Finance Corporation (IFC) (2015) *She for Shield: Insure Women to Better Protect All* [pdf], Washington, DC: World Bank <http://documents.worldbank.org/curated/en/228381492593824450/pdf/114402-WP-SheforShield-Final-Web2015-PUBLIC.pdf> [accessed 28 May 2018].

IFC (2016) *SolTuna: Tuna Processing, Solomon Islands* [report], Washington, DC: IFC <https://www.ifc.org/wps/wcm/connect/d4561543-cc39-4a9d-9963-26eb5ab4169c/soltuna_updated_May2017.pdf?MOD=AJPERES> [accessed 28 May 2018].

Jones, L. and Grundling, I. (2016a) *Women and Financial Inclusion in Zambia*, FinScope Focus Paper 1, Financial Sector Deepening Zambia <https://www.fsdzambia.org/publication/finscope-focus-1-women-and-financial-inclusion-in-zambia/> [accessed 17 July 2019].

Jones, L. and Grundling, I. (2016b) *Women Farmers' Access to Finance*, FinScope Focus Paper 2, Financial Sector Deepening Zambia Lusaka: fsdZambia <https://www.fsdzambia.org/publication/finscope-focus-2-women-smallholder-farmers-managing-their-financial-lives/> [accessed 17 July 2019].

Kc, D. and Tiwari, M. (2015) *Innovative and Interactive Ways to Improve the Financial Capability and Savings of Women* [pdf], Institute for Money, Technology and Financial Inclusion <https://www.imtfi.uci.edu/files/

docs/2015/IMTFI%20Report-%20Women%20study_KC%20and%20 Tiwari_Final.pdf> [accessed 17 July 2019].

Klapper, L. (2019) 'Want to fix the financial inclusion gap? Ask better questions', [online], Accion <https://www.accion.org/want-to-fix-the-financial-inclusion-gender-gap-ask-better-questions> [accessed 31 March 2019].

Klapper, L., Lusardi, A. and van Oudheusden, P. (2015) *Financial Literacy Around the World: Insights From The Standard & Poor's Ratings Services Global Financial Literacy Survey* [pdf], Global Financial Literacy Excellence Center <http://gflec.org/wp-content/uploads/2015/11/3313-Finlit_Report_FINAL-5.11.16.pdf?x87657> [accessed 28 May 2018].

Lensink, R., Mersland, R., Hong Vu, N. and Zamore, S. (2017) 'Do microfinance institutions benefit from integrating financial and nonfinancial services?' *Applied Economics* 50(21): 2396–401 <https://dx.doi.org/10.1080/00036846 .2017.1397852>.

Microinsurance Network (2015) 'Key concepts' [online] <https:// microinsurancenetwork.org/microinsurance/key-concepts> [accessed 28 March 2019].

Miriri, D. (2018) 'Kenya's Safaricom takes M-Pesa global with Western Union', [online], 6 November 2018, Reuters <https://af.reuters.com/article/kenya News/idAFL8N1XH3KJ> [accessed 29 March 2019].

Napier, M., Melamed, C., Taylor, G. and Jaeggi, A. (2013) *Promoting Women's Financial Inclusion: A Toolkit* [pdf], DFID and GIZ <https://assets.publishing. service.gov.uk/government/uploads/system/uploads/attachment_data/ file/213907/promoting-womens-financial-inclusion-toolkit.pdf> [accessed 29 March 2019].

Nel de Koker, J. (2015) 'Why are women in developing economies excluded from banking?' [online], Geneva, Switzerland: World Economic Forum <https:// www.weforum.org/agenda/2015/09/why-are-women-in-developing-economies-excluded-from-banking> [accessed 28 May 2018].

Niner, S. (2018) 'Why microfinance as aid isn't enough to empower women', [online], 23 May 2018, The Conversation <https://theconversation. com/why-microfinance-as-aid-isnt-enough-to-empower-women-96632> [accessed 29 March 2019].

OECD (2013) *Women and Financial Literacy: OECD/INFE Evidence, Survey and Policy Responses* [pdf], Russia Financial Literacy and Education Trust Fund, OECD <http://www.oecd.org/daf/fin/financial-education/TrustFund2013_ OECD_INFE_Women_and_Fin_Lit.pdf> [accessed 29 May 2018].

Pomeranz, D. (2014) *The Promise of Microfinance and Women's Empowerment: What Does the Evidence Say?* [pdf], Ernst & Young <https://www.hbs.edu/faculty/ Publication%20Files/EY-The%20promise-of-microfinance-and-womens-empowerment_14123436-7f3a-4a87-a76f-94e931c9ed5e.pdf> [accessed 28 March 2019].

President's Advisory Council on Financial Literacy (2009) *2008 Annual Report to the President: Executive Summary 2009* [pdf], President's Advisory Council <https://www.treasury.gov/about/organizational-structure/offices/ Domestic-Finance/Documents/PACFL_Draft-AR-0109.pdf> [accessed 28 May 2018].

Robino, C., Trivelli, C., Villanueva, C., Caro Sachetti, F., Walbey, H., Martinez, L. and Marincioni, M. (2018) *Financial Inclusion for Women: A Way Forward* [online], G20 Insights <https://www.g20-insights.org/policy_briefs/financial-inclusion-for-women-a-way-forward/> [accessed 28 March 2019].

Robinson, A. (2019) 'Microfinance and women: assumptions and reality of empowerment impact', [online], 3 January 2019, Australian Institute of International Affairs <https://www.internationalaffairs.org.au/australian outlook/microfinance-women-assumptions-reality-empowerment-impact/> [accessed 29 March 2019].

Sahay, R., Cihak, M., N'Diaye, P., Barajas, A., Mitra, S., Kyobe, A., Nian Mooi, Y. and Reza Yousefi, S. (2015) *Financial Inclusion: Can It Meet Multiple Macroeconomic Goals?* [pdf], IMF <https://www.imf.org/external/pubs/ft/sdn/2015/sdn1517.pdf> [accessed 11 May 2018].

Siddik, N. (2017) 'Does financial inclusion promote women empowerment? Evidence from Bangladesh' *Applied Economics and Finance* 4(4) <10.11114/aef.v4i4.2514>.

Suri, T. and Jack, W. (2016) 'The long-run poverty and gender impacts of mobile money', *Development Economics* 354(6317): 1288–92 <https://www.findevgateway.org/sites/default/files/publication_files/new_jack_and_suri_paper_1.pdf> [accessed 29 March 2019].

Women's World Banking (2016) *Women's Financial Inclusion: A Driver for Global Growth* [pdf] <https://www.womensworldbanking.org/wp-content/uploads/2016/09/Womens-Financial-Inclusion-Driver-Global-Growth.pdf> [accessed 29 March 2019].

Women's World Banking (2017) 'Banking Rwanda's women: what she wants from her bank', [online], 9 January 2017 <https://www.womensworldbanking.org/insights-and-impact/banking-rwandas-women-wants-bank/> [accessed 31 March 2019].

Women's World Banking (2018) 'Ten years later: what has digital technology done for women's financial inclusion?' [online], 15 January 2018 <https://www.womensworldbanking.org/insights-and-impact/ten-years-later-digital-technology-done-womens-financial-inclusion/> [accessed 29 March 2019].

World Bank (2018) 'Financial inclusion on the rise, but gaps remain, Global Findex Database shows', [online], 19 April 2018 <https://www.worldbank.org/en/news/press-release/2018/04/19/financial-inclusion-on-the-rise-but-gaps-remain-global-findex-database-shows> [accessed 29 March 2019].

CHAPTER 6

Gender lens investing for business growth and impact

Carolyn Burns

Abstract

The chapter discusses the rise and importance of gender lens impact investing within the international development sector to increase gender equality and women's economic empowerment. It provides approaches, strategies, and tools for integrating gender into investment portfolios and environmental, social, and governance (ESG) standards.

Keywords: gender equality, women's economic empowerment, gender lens investing, gender-smart investing, impact investing, gender equality mainstreaming

Introduction

Zyanna grew up in Odisha, India and graduated from secondary school with English language and basic computer skills. She felt very fortunate that her parents were committed to her education as some of her friends had married and left school before graduation. Despite a good education, Zyanna still found it difficult to find a job – being a girl from a marginalized ethnic group, Zyanna was sure that the odds were stacked against her. Zyanna learned that some young people from her town were getting jobs as nursing assistants in Karnataka and Maharashtra, and so she decided to take a short government course to train as a nursing assistant and hoped this might improve her employment prospects. Zyanna completed the nursing course at the top of her class, after which she and two classmates were offered jobs with a healthcare company in Bangalore, Karnataka that provided home health-care services for the elderly and infirm. Although it was far from home, she would not be alone, and this was the kind of opportunity she had wished for. They began work immediately, and the company began to train and prepare them in their new roles. Zyanna was surprised to receive training not only on technical aspects of the job but on gender awareness, confidence, work-life balance, harassment, and company policies and procedures. Zyanna was so happy to be respected and supported in her work; she did not know that her

http://dx.doi.org/10.3362/9781780447506.006

employer had received investment from a fund manager who was concerned with gender inclusion and equality in business. Through this investment, her company had now embraced gender inclusion as a corporate strategy and was pursuing initiatives to achieve positive gender outcomes.

While women are involved in many aspects of a company's value chain – from being a supplier of raw inputs to a manufacturer and distributor of finished products or services to a customer purchasing the final product or service – their full participation in the business world is often limited by systemic barriers rooted in gender biases. An estimated 'USD $12 trillion could be added to global GDP by 2025 by advancing women's equality' (Woetzel et al., 2015), which shows the economic impact that gender inclusion can have on national economies. This chapter will demonstrate that gender lens investing (GLI) is an increasingly recognized and effective women's economic empowerment strategy that is poised for continued growth.

GLI tries to advance women's economic empowerment by incorporating a gender perspective into the financial analysis of a business prospect with the intention of deriving and measuring a better business outcome and addressing gender disparities at the company and ecosystem level (Anderson and Miles, 2015; Global Impact Investing Network, n.d.). When successfully embedded into investment negotiations, GLI can have positive effects on a company's:

- return on equity: 'companies with gender-diverse boards generate a higher return on equity than those without' (IFC, 2017);
- share price: 'companies with gender-diverse boards outperform those with no women in terms of share price performance during times of crisis or volatility' (IFC, 2017);
- performance: 'high-performing companies are almost 50% more likely than low-performing companies to report that men and women have equal influence on strategy development' (IFC, 2017);
- growth rate: 'investors in companies with strong gender diversity strategies receive excess returns running at a compound annual growth rate (CAGR) of 3–5%' (IFC, 2017).

A GLI strategy typically emphasizes a 'gendered lens' as opposed to a 'sex-based approach', because the term 'gender' recognizes that these prejudices stem from a malleable set of cultural patterns, rather than innate biological differences. The GLI movement, therefore, aims to bring both men and women into a conversation about how the financial system can better encompass notions of gender equality (Kaplan and VanderBrug, 2014). The Criterion Institute, a globally recognized GLI think tank, stresses that venture capital investors need to become more attuned to the merits of investing in women-led businesses that typically follow a normal growth curve that 'grow[s] one revenue line at a time' (Brush et al., 2014: 7). Women entrepreneurs' limited success in raising early-stage financing should not be attributed to a skills deficiency, but rather structural biases that favour 'high, swift growth companies' (Brush et al., 2014: 7). As such, the GLI community challenges financial markets to shift their appraisal metrics and rethink their definition of value to better accommodate women business leaders' differing capital needs (Anderson and Miles, 2015).

GLI experts argue that women are a globally underserved market that is 'ripe with opportunity' (Anderson and Miles, 2015: 11). Women's consolidated spending power is expected to rise to US$40 tn in 2018 (Statista, n.d.) and reach an estimated collective earning power that is twice as big as the economies of China and India combined (Anderson and Miles, 2015). Since women are often the primary buyer for others in their network, their purchasing patterns have a significant multiplier effect on companies' sales, brand loyalty, and market share (Brennan, 2015). Their influence will be further magnified by receiving 60 per cent of the intergenerational wealth transfer in the Global North over the next 20 years (Anderson and Miles, 2015).

At the company level, companies that embrace GLI values, such as the recruitment and advancement of women, reflect not just a socially progressive corporate culture, but an understanding that gender diversity is a significant value driver: 'companies that had strong female leadership generated a Return on Equity of 10.1% per year versus 7.4% for those without (on an equal-weighted basis).' (Lee et al., 2015: 4). The link between gender inclusivity and strong corporate performance holds true regardless of a business's geography. For instance, 'organizations ranked highly on Fortune's *World's Most Admired Companies* list have twice as many women in senior management than do companies with lower rankings' (Weber Shandwick, 2016). To stay economically competitive, companies need to better support women's leadership through gender-inclusive hiring and promotional policies and practices.

At the ecosystem level, industries that support women as employees, consumers, and suppliers can capitalize on strategic advantages, such as increases in productivity, revenue growth, and innovation. Since companies that enable women to work in non-traditional jobs are poised to increase their productivity by 13–25 per cent (IFC, 2013), the consolidated effects of these efficiency gains can lead to massive economic changes on a macroeconomic scale. Similarly, companies that have a strong understanding of women consumers can launch innovative products that can attract the attention of larger players whose support can help establish new product categories. For instance, the success of clothing retailers ASIYA, Capsters, and Artizara in creating an athletic hijab prompted sportswear giant Nike to create its own Pro Hijab in the hopes of also unlocking the strong sales potential of Muslim women customers (Nike, n.d.). Moreover, companies that work with women suppliers have an opportunity to source more exclusive products and services. For example, Ten Thousand Villages' first-mover advantage in sourcing uniquely created handicraft products from women suppliers insulated its value chain from competitive forces (Ten Thousand Villages, n.d.). However, the success of the Ten Thousand Villages business model has catalysed other retailers to also procure ethically and sustainably sourced products from women entrepreneurs.

Investors – both asset owners and asset managers – that implement GLI strategies tangibly demonstrate their financial support for women's growing economic influence, effectively 'putting their money where their mouth is'. GLI is not a substitute for traditional philanthropy, but rather a commitment to invest capital in a socially progressive manner. Its flexibility allows investors of every background to participate in its gender-inclusive movement. GLI can be applied as a stand-alone impact investment practice or integrated into a multi-pronged impact investing approach (e.g. it can be interlinked with climate-focused investing, or affordable housing-centred investment models). GLI can also be concentrated in one asset class (e.g. debt, equity, or mezzanine finance) or span a multi-asset class portfolio. Likewise, it can be used in single- or multi-country geographies. Finally, there are no restrictions on what types of industries are candidates for GLI. Ultimately, investors' variations in GLI investments stem from differences in their return expectations, risk tolerance, and time horizon profiles. Investors with varied commitments to GLI can be rewarded with strong risk diversification benefits and a larger breadth of gender equality impacts.

While investors who utilized GLI strategies in the past may have been mainly impact investors, 'the GLI ecosystem is growing in depth, breadth and complexity' (Veris Wealth Partners, 2018: 7). GLI investors now range from concessionary players (e.g. private foundations, government agencies, and NGOs) to commercially oriented institutional and individual investors. Several trends are responsible for this growth in the GLI investor base. Firstly, the larger volume of retail-focused products and services has increased investors' access to and knowledge of GLI strategies (Veris Wealth Partners, 2018: 3). Veris Wealth Partners (2018) comments that, 'the accessibility of these liquid, relatively low-fee, and low-minimum vehicles are on-ramps for millions of investors supportive of gender equality'. An illustration of the democratization of GLI product information is As You Sow, a US non-profit leader in shareholder advocacy founded in 1992, who launched a tool to score US mutual funds and exchange traded funds based on the gender balance of the underlying companies' leadership and workforce, as well as their policies that promote gender equality (As You Sow, 2019). Secondly, GLI investors have successfully used shareholder activism tactics to increase mainstream investors' knowledge of gender equality issues. The Pax Ellevate Global Leadership Fund's use of proxy voting (e.g. categorically voting against the approval of all-male boards) and shareholder resolution tactics (e.g. urging companies to implement greater gender diversity measures) showcases that gender-inclusive corporate structures and processes have become material issues that investors are willing to unite and exert their influence over (PAX World Funds, n.d.). Thirdly, GLI investors have pushed the market to evolve beyond offering independent products and services towards multidimensional GLI-themed portfolios (Veris Wealth Partners, 2018). The WomenInvest InFaith Portfolio's mandate to target the root causes of violence against women by deploying financial resources across a suite of deals linked to women's causes illustrates the maturation and variation of GLI deal flow (InFaith Community Foundation, 2018). Likewise,

Chordata Capital Partners' establishment of an advisory practice centred on structuring intersectional social justice portfolios (i.e. opportunities that advance racial, gender, and economic justice) exemplifies the increased depth and breadth of impact for GLI products (Chordata Capital, n.d.). Investors' push for more GLI opportunities has enabled the market to soar from $100 m in 2009 to an estimated size of $2.4 bn in 2018 with now more than 35 GLI strategies being operationalized (Veris Wealth Partners, 2018). Veris Wealth Partners (2018: 9) comments that, 'Given the rapid expansion of the GLI ecosystem, the future looks bright for those committed to bending the arc of finance for women and girls'.

Blended finance is one financing mechanism by which capital resources can be mobilized from a variety of investor types to increase the scale and impact of gender equality outcomes achieved. Convergence (2018: 4) defines 'blended finance' as the use of 'public, private, and philanthropic sources to scale up private sector investment in emerging markets to realize the [Sustainable Development Goals]'. It reports that '42% of blended companies have had a gender focus, with 10% of companies having had a principal focus on women and girls and 32% of companies having had a partial focus on women and girls' (Convergence, 2018: 2). Collectively, these deals have raised '$11 billion for gender-related projects in developing countries' (Convergence, 2018: 2). Investors in gender-related deals range from development finance institutions and multilateral development banks to private sector companies with an impact lens to private sector companies with a commercial lens to foundations/NGOs and development agencies. Respectively, these actors account for 26 per cent, 22 per cent, 20 per cent, 17 per cent, and 15 per cent of capital placed into gender-themed deals (Convergence, 2018). The four most common architectures of gender-related blended finance deals include design-stage grants, concessional capital, technical assistance funds, and guarantees/risk insurance (Convergence, 2018). De-risking tools, such as guarantees and risk insurance, provide private sector companies with a commercial lens with assurances that their funding of gender-themed deals can achieve both a financial and social purpose. In addition, the programmatic nature of design-stage grants gives foundations/NGOs a platform to apply their largely unencumbered capital towards creating innovative initiatives that can better meet the needs of their women customers. Likewise, technical assistance funds afford a wide circle of impact-oriented actors (e.g. development finance institutions and multilateral development banks, private sector companies with an impact lens, foundations/NGOs, and development agencies) an opportunity to pilot new gender equality business models and demonstrate a successful proof of concept. The concessional vs. commercial tiering of blended finance deals creates an environment whereby shared value among GLI investors can be created.

Investors can support the continued growth of the GLI industry by increasing their exposure via a progressive asset class strategy (e.g. a debt instrument that transitions into an equity investment once a certain threshold of deal maturity has been reached), co-investments with other gender-smart investors, and/or the recycling of returns into follow-on gendered investments. These tactics can assist gender-inclusive businesses in maintaining a positive track record and, subsequently, increase the size of the overall GLI pool. Investors can also strengthen the GLI cause by encouraging their investees to participate in gender-themed investment initiatives and holding their investees accountable to their gender-inclusive pledges. Investors can suggest that their investees join the 30% Club, a global campaign to drive positive gender equality outcomes by having companies earmark 30 per cent of their board of directors and senior leadership positions to be filled by women (30% Club, 2019). Investors can also ask their peers to join them in publicly announcing their support for GLI. By signing the six Principles for Responsible Investment, a global movement to have investors voluntarily incorporate environmental, social, and governance (ESG)-themed activities into the investment process (Principles for Responsible Investment, n.d.), investors can codify their support for GLI. Finally, investors can also release their GLI deal term sheets and track records to reduce informational asymmetries and encourage greater uptake in GLI.

GLI investment strategies

Experienced GLI investors tend to focus their efforts on pursuing three gender-inclusive strategies to influence company and ecosystem level changes: placing capital into women-led businesses, investing into companies that produce and market gender-smart products and services, and providing finance to companies that mainstream gender across their ESG policies. The first two approaches are described briefly in this chapter, while the third – gender equality mainstreaming – is reviewed in greater detail with an accompanying case study to illustrate its use. All GLI models are based on investors having a close relationship with their investees and all parties agreeing to a shared vision for gender equality outcomes.

Investing in women-led businesses

This section identifies the difficulties that women-led businesses often face in attracting external financing and outlines three examples of investors deploying their capital with the intention of reducing this gendered funding gap.

Women entrepreneurs face many challenges in accessing the capital required to launch and expand their businesses, whether this be as microentrepreneurs, small business operators, or the executive of a large corporate entity. While banking regulations tend to be universally applied to all borrowers, they often fail to recognize the business opportunity of supporting the unique circumstances of women-led ventures. Women entrepreneurs are often unable to collateralize a loan against the value of their property and/or equipment because cultural and legal norms often hold that they do not have ownership over such collateral. In many developing or emerging markets, women are also not able to provide the required personal identification and/or company registration paperwork to open a bank account (IFC, 2014). Finally, women frequently run smaller-sized firms, have limited formal business training, and have access to narrower professional networks (IFC, 2014). These circumstances can cause women to struggle with maintaining records, securing contracts, and managing short-term loan repayment conditions (IFC, 2014). Due to these issues, banks have become accustomed to perceiving women-operated enterprises as riskier, costlier to service, and more likely to generate a lower return regardless of the circumstances of a woman entrepreneurs' funding proposal (IFC, 2014). These challenges have culminated in a global gender-based credit gap of approximately $260–320 bn (Kipnis, 2017).

Investments into women-led businesses provide an opportunity to overcome the gendered credit gap by pairing investors' financial requirements with their social values. To be considered a women-led venture, a company must have been founded by a woman, over half of its ownership structure must be controlled by women, and/or over half of its executive team must be women. Investments into women-led business can vary in size; for the purposes of this chapter, the term will be seen to encompass deals that are upwards of $20,000 and below $2 m. Like other GLI strategies, investments into women-led businesses can take multiple forms depending on investors' return expectations, risk tolerance, and time horizon profiles. These deals are also not restrained by asset class, geography, or industry.

Investors can support women-led businesses by applying a positive investment screen towards businesses that meet the requisite ownership and/or leadership criteria. Their investment can be structured as: financial support for a GLI-focused product, non-financial support (i.e. technical assistance) for a GLI-focused project, and a comprehensive approach (i.e. support for a combined financial and non-financial investment facility). A closer examination of each investment sub-domain will help to further evidence the importance of placing capital into women-led businesses to drive more inclusive business growth.

Financial support approach: investment into a women-focused fund. Patamar Capital and the Australian-funded Investing in Women programme have created a fund to support six to eight early-stage women-led businesses in Southeast Asia (Patamar Capital, 2017). This fund will interweave women's economic empowerment themes throughout its due diligence and portfolio monitoring activities. Third-party investors can support the underlying women entrepreneurs by investing in this fund that will on-lend their finances to local funds that directly finance the women-led businesses. The impact of this fund's investments at the company level include the increased capacity of the investees to scale-up their existing operations and expand into new markets via product and/or service enhancements, greater geographic diversification, and/or the targeting of a wider range of consumers. At the ecosystem level, this fund hopes to demonstrate that an early-stage GLI strategy can successfully crowd-in commercial capital and return investors' capital at a competitive rate of return.

Non-financial support approach: investment into a women-focused technical assistance programme. The European Bank for Reconstruction and Development (EBRD) has utilized a non-financial support strategy through its Finance and Advice for Women in Business programme, an entity that seeks to increase Turkish banks' and women-led businesses' ability to partner with each other. This programme will allow women entrepreneurs to upgrade their skills (e.g. leadership, financial literacy, and marketing and communication support) and networks so that they become a more attractive client category to Turkish banks (EBRD, 2013). Third-party investors cannot support the underlying women entrepreneurs involved in this programme because this is a closed investment opportunity between the EBRD and the Turkish banks that offer the training. The effects of this programme at the company level include the greater capacity of Turkish banks to manage non-traditional clients and the enhanced capability of women entrepreneurs to present their business as a viable investment opportunity to commercial lenders. At the ecosystem level, this programme intends to illustrate that more gender-inclusive client management processes can lead companies towards servicing more clients and ultimately achieving higher revenue growth.

Comprehensive support approach: investment into a women-focused facility. Goldman Sachs and the International Finance Corporation (IFC) developed the Women Entrepreneurs Opportunity Facility to expand financial institutions' ability to service women-led businesses operating across emerging markets (Goldman Sachs, 2018). This facility allows banks to upgrade their service offerings to better support women-led businesses and enables women entrepreneurs to better access bank loans (Goldman Sachs, 2018). This facility represents a watershed moment in GLI, with a $600 m commitment size and ability to reach across 17 emerging markets to 30,000 women entrepreneurs. Third-party investors can support the underlying women entrepreneurs by investing in this facility which will on-lend their finances to local banks that directly finance the women entrepreneurs. The effects of this facility at the company level include the greater capacity of banks in emerging markets to manage non-traditional clients and the increased capability of women entrepreneurs to access growth capital. At the ecosystem level, this facility seeks to showcase that a women's entrepreneurship-focused GLI strategy can successfully crowd-in commercial capital and return investors' capital at a competitive rate of return. In addition, this facility evidences that gender-inclusive client management processes can lead companies to being able to service more clients.

Investing in companies that produce gender-smart products and services

This section discusses the struggles that women consumers face in relating to companies' products and services and highlights two cases where investors can use their financial resources to help influence companies' adoption of gender-smart design and marketing practices.

Until recently, companies often failed to consider women's unique consumer needs and values. Instead of recognizing women's wealth as an emerging source of consumer growth, many companies relied on outdated gender-based stereotypes effectively treating women as subpar customers. When companies with low gender intelligence engage in market research activities, this can result in reduced access to products and services for women. Women may also choose to avoid or disengage with companies whose products and services fail to satisfy their requirements. Whether women are left behind by companies' indifference to their needs or by their own choice, women consumers are still unable to equally participate in the economy and companies forgo earnings from a valuable market segment.

Investments into businesses that dedicate resources into developing and nurturing their relationships with women customers can achieve greater financial success and spur more equitable economic growth. 'Gender-smart' products and services are an effective medium to increase women's access to and uptake of economic goods. The term 'gender smart' is not meant to describe gender-neutral goods that have been 'women washed' through the addition of superficial feminine features, such as a pink-coloured product line and/or a charitable relationship with a women-friendly cause (e.g. a 'buy one, give one' corporate social responsibility campaign). Instead, gender-smart products and services are intentionally designed for women to meet their specific needs. Like other GLI strategies, investments into businesses that support smart products and services can take multiple forms depending on investors' return expectations, risk tolerance, and time horizon profiles. These deals are also not restrained by asset class, geography, or industry.

Investors can support gender-smart businesses by applying a positive investment screen towards companies that meet the requisite gender-inclusive criteria. Their investment can be structured as financial support for businesses that design gender-smart products and services and financial support for businesses that market gender-smart products and services. An investigation of these approaches will help to explain how investments into companies that promote gender-smart products and services acknowledge gender differences in a positive manner.

Financial support approach: investment into businesses that design gender-smart products. The Clean Cooking Alliance, a consortium of players interested in developing, selling, distributing, and using clean and efficient household cooking solutions (Clean Cooking Alliance, n.d.), showcases how the adoption of a gender lens in the design of cooking products can pair investors' support with the enhancement of women's livelihoods. Unlike traditional cookstove manufacturers that employ a gender-neutral, top-down design strategy, the Clean Cooking Alliance promotes the application of a women-centred, bottom-up design strategy to ensure that their products encompass the right mix of consumer preferences regarding performance, affordability, and usability characteristics (Clean Cooking Alliance, n.d.). The clean cookstove is a gender-smart product design because its impetus is to reduce the health and environmental impacts of burning traditional fuels (e.g. charcoal, kerosene, wood, and animal dung) in poorly ventilated cooking environments; an activity that disproportionately affects women who serve as their family's primary cook. By gaining reliable access to clean fuels, women can spend their time on more economically productive activities (e.g. upgrading their education or managing their businesses). At the company level, third-party investors can support the Clean Cooking Alliance's underlying member companies by investing in a single firm deal or constructing a portfolio by investing in several members. The influx of investors' funding will allow the Clean Cooking Alliance's members to scale-up their operations and continue designing products that meet low-income women consumer needs. At the ecosystem level, the Clean Cooking Alliance hopes to illustrate that investors can benefit from supporting businesses that co-design products and/or services alongside their target users.

Financial support approach: investment into businesses that use gender-smart marketing. The marketing of Sustainable Health Enterprises' menstrual hygiene products demonstrates how the execution of a gendered promotional strategy can align investors' capital with an increase in women's dignity. Traditional menstrual hygiene products are difficult for rural Rwandan girls and women to source because import costs necessitate that distribution companies must charge consumers a pricing premium to recover their costs (Sustainable Health Enterprises, n.d.). This means most products are sold at a price that most Rwandan girls and women can't afford (Sustainable Health Enterprises, n.d.). As a result, many girls and women forgo using safe menstrual hygiene products in lieu of freely available substitutes (e.g. old rags, leaves). By contrast, Sustainable Health Enterprises' Go! Pads manufactures and distributes its products locally. Go! Pads uses gender-smart marketing because it relies on women sales agents to act as knowledge ambassadors and product vendors (Sustainable Health Enterprises, n.d.). This peer-to-peer marketing channel has been successful in reducing social stigma around menstruation and has enabled low-income women to be a viable consumer category that other menstrual hygiene product distributors could target for business growth. At the company level, third-party investors can support Sustainable Health Enterprises by investing into the company through a single deal or a series of deals based on operational milestones achieved. The influx of investor funding will allow Sustainable Health Enterprises to scale-up its operations and continue targeting its marketing efforts to reach the low-income women consumer segment. At the ecosystem level, Sustainable Health Enterprises seeks to showcase what investors can gain from endorsing businesses that market their products and/ or services through mediums that resonate with their target users.

Investing in companies that mainstream gender

Despite women's increasingly prominent role in the corporate world, they continue to face challenges in overcoming hiring and promotional barriers. Women may face discriminatory recruitment practices, such as hiring managers scrutinizing their personal circumstances instead of their professional qualifications. In addition, job advertisements containing traits often considered masculine (e.g. leader, competitive, and dominant) to describe an ideal candidate can dissuade women from applying to the position (Gaucher et al., 2011). Women's inability to be hired into career advancing roles perpetuates a gendered division of labour and the prevalence of women's employment in 'pink collar' jobs (i.e. working in lower-paying, irregular work arrangements). Women who are on a gendered professional track may experience fewer opportunities for career progression. Without stretch assignments (i.e. a specific task that will help a worker expand their knowledge, network, and experience), mentors, and networks to support their candidacy for promotion, women who are competitive applicants may face opposition to their leadership from both internal (e.g. 'old boys' clubs') and external (e.g. social media) forces. Such negativity may deter women from applying for career advancement positions or cause them to decline promotional opportunities. Collectively, these barriers have resulted in only 23 women currently presiding as CEOs of Fortune 500 companies (Fortune, 2017).

Women's limited participation in corporate decision-making roles can obstruct their ability to influence a business's policies and practices. The failure of company policies and practices to represent women's perspectives often perpetuates gender inequalities. Through this cyclical pattern, structural gender biases can become established business norms. Corporate policies may overtly discriminate against women via their failure to guard against inappropriate workplace behaviours (e.g. no inclusion of an anti-sexual harassment clause in the employee handbook), unsafe working conditions (e.g. failure to reprimand staff who violate women's human rights), or unjust practices (e.g. no guarantee of equal wages for equal work). Corporate policies may also inadvertently victimize women by not taking their personal circumstances into account (e.g. the rejection of flexible working arrangements may punish women who disproportionately suffer from the double burden of being a worker and a primary caregiver for their families).

Similarly, a gender-biased corporate culture may prevent it from developing a meaningful relationship with women customers. Companies without an appreciation for women's purchasing power may not understand the value addition of developing and marketing women-centred products and/or services. Additionally, businesses may fail to reach women by treating them as one homogeneous consumer category. An internal study conducted by Unilever (2016) discovered that '40% of women say they do not identify at all with the women they see in adverts'. Stereotypical portrayals of gender roles in advertising can leave women consumers feeling offended, left out, or believing that they are not as important as male customers.

Moreover, a company with an ungendered outlook may struggle to create business partnerships with women suppliers. Since women-owned businesses are smaller in size and have narrower professional networks (IFC, 2014), women entrepreneurs have a difficult time competing for new business development opportunities. Without strong business partnerships, women suppliers are unable to grow their client base and compete with more established players. These structural barriers have resulted in 'women-owned businesses earn[ing] less than 1% of the money spent on vendors by large corporations' (WeConnect International, n.d.).

Businesses that support women by mainstreaming a gender lens across their policies and practices may find they are in a more competitive position via higher profitability levels, stronger employee relations, and improved gender equality outcomes. The National Women's Business Council found that 34 per cent of companies that have diversified their supplier base by working with women report a higher impact on their profitability (National Women's Business Council, 2009). Companies that install gender-balanced teams throughout their corporate structure yield higher rates of employee engagement (Landel, 2015). Additionally, companies that draw on a diverse supplier base experience many benefits and 'reducing costs, enhancing innovation, successfully integrating acquired businesses and reaching new markets ' (Whitfield and Farrell, 2010: 31). In addition, the establishment of a gender-diverse value chain can crowd-in additional business partnerships with firms that share similar gender-inclusive values and/or turn suppliers into new customers (Chin, 2017). These business benefits make women suppliers an attractive investment opportunity.

A gender equality mainstreaming framework

Women's challenges in achieving equal economic prosperity prompted Mennonite Economic Development Associates (MEDA) to develop an innovative approach for identifying, implementing, and measuring gender equality strategies across a company's existing ESG policies and practices (MEDA, 2018b). MEDA's Gender Equality Mainstreaming (GEM) Framework is a step-by-step manual that seeks to educate investors and capacity builders (i.e. technical assistance providers, consultants, incubators, accelerators, business development service providers, and NGOs) about 'the different ways in which women and men participate in, contribute to, and benefit from gender-inclusive business operations' (MEDA, 2018b: 3). Its integration of gender throughout ESG policies and its application in developing economies makes it a complementary tool to existing gender equality assessment approaches. In addition, it builds off stand-alone applications of ESG that pigeonhole gender into the social element, thereby limiting a company's ability to understand how gender can be a cross-cutting theme – the GEM Framework stresses that gender needs to be mainstreamed across a company's ESG strategy (MEDA, 2018b).

The GEM Framework is a flexible roadmap for driving positive gender norms across the investment cycle by 'support[ing] active management, value creation and effective risk monitoring' (MEDA, 2018a: 5). When completed in full, it can be compartmentalized into six steps: 1) identification; 2) scoping assessment; 3) full assessment; 4) strategy development; 5) implementation; and

6) monitoring and learning and impact measurement (MEDA, 2018b). Within each step, guidance tools, tip sheets, and communication aids are included to assist users in implementing the requisite activities. The GEM Framework also features several examples of key performance indicators to help measure and track GEM-related results, as well as two case studies to guide users' knowledge of practical GEM applications. All GEM activities can be modified by the user to better fit their specific needs and local context (MEDA, 2018b).

While 'capacity builders are typically the most appropriate to facilitate a gender equality mainstreaming process, offering both the requisite technical expertise as well as an unbiased perspective that is essential for gender-based analysis and decision making' (MEDA, 2018b: 4), soliciting the services of a capacity builder is not mandatory. Some investors may already have the capacity to implement elements of the GEM Framework themselves, while others may face resource constraints limiting their ability to engage a capacity builder (MEDA, 2018b). Investors that choose to not use a capacity builder are likely to find the GEM Framework's online self-assessment tool to be of great assistance. The self-assessment tool enables users to self-select whether they would like to complete some or all the questionnaire(s) on ESG topics. Upon close of the exercise(s), users receive rapid feedback on their result(s) and are ranked on a gender-integration scale on each specific ESG topic. Users are also provided with advice that is appropriate for their stage of GEM maturity.

This section identifies the different ways that investors can use their capital to influence the enhancement of gender equality outcomes by mainstreaming gender across the ESG spectrum. To achieve the desired results investors will need to work alongside their portfolio companies to ensure that a gender lens is applied to every ESG business decision.

Like other GLI models, investments into businesses that apply the GEM Framework can take multiple forms depending on investors' return expectations, risk tolerance, and time horizon profiles. These deals are also not restrained by asset class, geography, or industry. The time required for companies to participate in the GEM Framework assessment can also vary. MEDA suggests that the scoping and full assessment can take up to one month to complete. After completing this step, a company may want to spend a minimum of nine months working on its implementation strategy and an additional year measuring its impact. These varying timelines may affect investors' ability to source and deploy capital into companies applying the GEM Framework.

Investors can support the adoption of the GEM Framework by applying a positive investment screen towards companies that are interested in or have previously participated in the assessment. Likewise, investors can use structured investor–investee communication channels (e.g. references to a GEM Framework implementation in an investor side letter) to influence companies to participate in GEM-themed activities. In addition, investors can sponsor their investees to participate in GEM-themed technical assistance programmes. An investigation of these approaches will help to explain how investments into companies that support the GEM Framework enable companies to grow in a more gender equitable direction.

Gendered environmental strategy. A gendered environmental strategy means that a company has taken into consideration the different needs of women and men stakeholders in its environmental policies and practices. Successful applications of a gendered environmental strategy can entail providing both women and men employees with environmental training, encouraging both men and women employees to participate in a corporate 'green team', selling green products to both women and men customers, or sourcing products from companies implementing strong environmental practices (e.g. ISO 14001 certified). To prevent cultural norms from influencing the discounting of women's views, a company can encourage women from all organizational levels to participate. This helps to ensure that all implementation activities are undertaken with the intention of bringing about positive outcomes for both men and women stakeholders.

The GEM Framework recommends analysing a company's environmental impact from a gender perspective because an enhanced relationship with women stakeholders can help a business to mitigate any reputational damages associated with environmental missteps (MEDA, 2018b). For instance, a business may suffer from a gendered media backlash if its operations damage the quality of the local water supply (MEDA, 2018b). Cultural norms often regulate women to be the primary collectors and users of water for their households. A contaminated water supply will likely affect women's livelihoods to a greater degree than men's (MEDA, 2018b). A company with strong ties to women community members will likely have a deeper understanding of the gender impact(s) of an environmental issue and may be able to rectify the situation in a more efficient manner.

A gendered awareness of a company's environmental impact can also help it to uncover new business opportunities and strengthen its value chain. The ExxonMobil Foundation has been instrumental in helping its investees to scale-up their gender-smart environmental policies and practices to become more competitive. ExxonMobil Foundation's partner, Solar Sister, recruits, trains, and supports women entrepreneurs to run a localized clean energy business (Solar Sister, 2019). The use of solid fuel for energy can cause users to suffer from premature deaths, respiratory and vision problems, and lock communities into cycles of poverty (Solar Sister, n.d.). Solar Sister was created to enable African 'communities [to] benefit from the financial, education and health benefits of clean energy' (Solar Sister, n.d.). ExxonMobil Foundation's financing has helped Solar Sister to scale-up its presence beyond Uganda into Kenya, Tanzania, and Nigeria (Solar Sister, n.d.) and thereby encouraged more women to become sustainable energy advocates. Through this partnership with Solar Sister, ExxonMobil has 'provid[ed] women with [the] support to increase their productivity and financial resources, and realize their fullest potential' (Morningstar, 2019).

Gendered social strategy. A gendered social strategy means that a company encompasses the different perspectives of women and men stakeholders in its social policies and practices. Successful applications of a gendered social strategy can entail tracking and reviewing human resources statistics (e.g. number of full-time and part-time employees, employee turnover rates, number of employees at each hierarchical level and in each department, compensation metrics, number of occupational injuries and fatalities, number of employees involved in professional development opportunities) disaggregated by sex. The GEM Framework can help companies to understand the business value of examining and re-examining a company's customers and sales track record (e.g. total annual sales, average profit margin generated by specific product and service lines, percentage of repeat customers, average sales by employees, numbers of suppliers, business values of suppliers) from a gendered perspective. To prevent cultural norms from influencing the discounting of women's views, a company can encourage women from all organizational levels to participate. This helps to ensure that any implementation activities are undertaken with the intention of bringing about positive outcomes for both men and women stakeholders.

The GEM Framework stresses reviewing a company's social impact from a gender perspective because strong partnerships with women employees, customers, and suppliers can help a business to reduce any branding fallouts related to socially charged issues. For instance, a business may suffer from a gendered media backlash if its corporate policies do not feature mechanisms to mitigate inappropriate workplace behaviours (e.g. a confidential feedback system to encourage its employees to come forward with reports of sexual harassment). Gender-based workplace violence is often directed towards women. A company that fails to provide support for employees to disclose and discuss their feedback will likely affect women employees' perception of safety and engagement on a greater depth and scale. Likewise, a company that fails to consider how its products affect men and women customers differently could suffer from the boycott of its goods. Many companies reduce costs by field-testing their safety protocols with only men's physical dimensions in mind (e.g. the use of crash test dummies to test out a car's seat belt features; Ely, 2018). Should an accident occur, a company that does not have experience in understanding women's needs may face public unrest for its disregard of women's safety. Finally, a company that does not understand the importance of supplier diversity could find itself in trouble, should one of its core suppliers engage in unethical business dealings. Men's propensity to hold corporate leadership positions often affords them greater opportunities to become involved in unethical business dealings. A company that has unethical business partners may find itself in trouble by extension of its association with such firms. A company with strong ties to women community members can have a deeper understanding of the gendered impact of the social issues affecting their employees, customers, and suppliers and may be able to overcome their challenges in a more effective manner.

An investor's gendered awareness of a company's social impact can also help it to capture new business opportunities by unlocking the economic power of women as employees, customers, and suppliers (MEDA, 2018b). The IFC has made significant headway in helping its partners to adopt more gender-inclusive social policies and practices to become more competitive. IFC's partner, Meghmani Organic Limited, faced a staffing shortage at its newest chemical plant, the Meghmani FineChem Limited plant (IFC, 2017). The IFC supported Meghmani Organic Limited in designing a new recruitment strategy to be able to target Indian women engineers as new employees. Since the company had not hired any women at any of its other plants, the IFC's funds were essential in helping it to partner with educational institutes to source recently graduated female engineers and work with its community engagement officer to publicize its gendered recruitment efforts (IFC, 2017). With women representing 7 per cent of the workforce at its new plant (IFC, 2017), the company was able to capture some benefits of a more gender-diverse talent pool (i.e. increased creativity and innovation among its gender-diverse teams) (Karve et al., 2017).

Gendered governance strategy. A gendered governance strategy means that a company has reviewed the different values of women and men stakeholders in its governance policies and practices. Successful applications of a gendered governance strategy can consist of reviewing an organization's hierarchy and power structures (e.g. identification of owners or participation on internal committees) from a gendered perspective. To prevent cultural norms from influencing the discounting of women's views, a company can encourage women from all organizational levels to participate. This helps to ensure that any implementation activities are undertaken with the intention of bringing about positive outcomes for both men and women stakeholders.

The GEM Framework suggests examining a company's governance impact from a gender perspective because strong partnerships with women business leaders can help to curtail any scandals related to governance mishaps. For instance, a business may suffer from gendered media scrutiny if it does not practice gender equality in its board hiring decisions. A position on a company's board of directors allows women business leaders an opportunity to shape the direction of the company's governance outlook. A company that continuously fails to approve the appointment and/or reappointment of women to the board will affect women's interest in applying for vacant board seats. A company with strong ties to women business executives can have a deeper understanding of the gendered impact of their governance challenges and may be able to rely on these relationships to guide their problem-solving activities.

A gendered awareness of a company's governance impact can also help it to leverage the strength of its diverse leadership team and, subsequently, enhance its profitability. The CDC Investments Group, a British development finance institution founded in 1948, has made great strides in helping its investees to embrace more gender-inclusive governance policies and practices to become more competitive. CDC partner TheBoardroom Africa (TBR Africa) helps source and place experienced, peer-endorsed women African business leaders into firms looking to diversify their top management teams (CDC, 2019). TBR Africa was launched to increase the number of African women on boards from its current rate of 14 per cent (CDC, 2019). African boards of directors comprising at least 25 per cent women provides both positive gender equality outcomes and, on average, a 20 per cent higher earnings before interest and taxes (EBIT) margin than the industry average (Moodley et al., 2016). The CDC's funds were instrumental in helping TBR Africa to 'expand its membership and client base across key growth markets on the [African] continent and support the development of its accredited board training and mentorship programs tailored to women in the African business community' (CDC, 2019). Through this partnership with TBR Africa, CDC has increased the number of women on its investees' boards and investment committees.

Case study on gender lens investing via the application of the GEM Framework

The United States Agency for International Development's Asia and Middle East Economic Growth Best Practices (AMEG) project attempted to address gendered cultural and operational inequalities in small and medium enterprises (SMEs). AMEG partnered with local investment funds to access SMEs that were interested in enhancing their relationship with their women employees to prove the business case for enhancing gender equality (MEDA, 2018b). The AMEG project targeted SMEs because smaller firms have a stronger cultural influence over their employees' lives. The AMEG project sought to raise business leaders' awareness of the unique needs of women employees and encouraged firms to build a better relationship with their women employees.

One AMEG partner firm, Health Vista India Pvt. Ltd (Portea), is a leading Indian healthcare provider serving patients through a home-based service model (e.g. physiotherapy, nursing services, vaccination, and eldercare; Portea, n.d.). Through Portea's previous round of investment by VenturEast III, which then received investment by Sarona Frontier Markets Fund I, Portea became eligible to participate in the AMEG project.

Portea chose to focus its AMEG project on enhancing the personal and professional development of its nursing attendants and nursing staff. Many of Portea's employees are women who come from low socio-economic backgrounds and through their employment with Portea may be entering the formal sector for the first time (MEDA, 2018b). The growth of Portea's business is, therefore, linked to the reduction of cultural biases that suggest that women should be at home acting as the primary caregiver for their families (MEDA, 2018b). This case illustrates Portea's use of the GEM Framework to increase its women employees' engagement in their work and increase Portea's employee retention rate.

Portea received a $40,000 grant to deliver a series of trainings to 2,252 nursing attendants and nurses (MEDA, 2018b). The three learning modules included an in-classroom session on happiness (i.e. lessons on self-esteem, self-care, self-confidence, and professionalism), an interactive voice response training (IVR) on emotional intelligence and financial management, and an on-the-job training (OJT) on work-life balance and infection control (MEDA, 2018b).

After participating in the training sessions, Portea's female and male employees initially rated that their self-confidence scores had increased from 2.9 to 4.1 to 4.5 and from 2.7 to 4.1 to 4.4, respectively (all scores are based on a 1–5 ranking, with 5 being the top-rated score) (MEDA, 2018b). Many of Portea's nursing attendants reported that these learning modules helped them to become more aware about how to avoid uncomfortable working situations (MEDA, 2018b). In addition, the activities' focus on quality of care helped Portea's staff to realize the intrinsic value of the work that they offered their patients (MEDA, 2018b). This positive sentiment helped them to re-engage and recommit to their work with Portea.

Portea believes that the GEM Framework was catalytic in allowing it to understand how to listen to and satisfy its employees' needs. After participating in the AMEG programme, Portea has achieved higher employee engagement and retention rates among staff and boasts more satisfied customers and higher profitability levels (MEDA, 2018b). Portea intends to build on the positive momentum generated by the AMEG project by continuing to fund additional learning opportunities for its staff (MEDA, 2018b). Portea expects future learning modules to focus on progressing lower-ranking staff into managerial positions (MEDA, 2018b). The effects of Portea's professional development programme will likely enable many women employees to progress up the corporate ladder and escape the feminization of poverty. Achieving strong gender equality results would make Portea an attractive investment opportunity for other GLI players.

Useful resources

Criterion Institute's *The State of the Field of Gender Lens Investing*: http://criterion institute.org/wp-content/uploads/2012/06/State-of-the-Field-of-Gender-Lens-Investing-11-24-2015.pdf

Croatan Institute's *Investing for Positive Impact on Women: Integrating Gender into Total Portfolio Activation*: http://www.trilliuminvest.com/wp-content/uploads/2015/11/Investing-for-Positive-Impact-on-Women1.pdf

Hackett Group's *Beyond Compliance: Top Supplier Diversity Programs Aim to Broaden Value Proposition*: https://weconnectinternational.org/images/supplier-inclusion/HackettGroup_SupplierDiversity_2016.pdf

MEDA's *The GEM Framework: Gender Equality Mainstreaming for Business Growth and Impact*: https://www.meda.org/news/publications-main/technical/gem-framework/531-gem-framework-online-final2/file

Mercy Corps' *The Power of the Purse: A Market Systems Approach to Stimulating Private Sector Investment in Women as Consumers*: https://www.mercycorps. org/sites/default/files/Mercy%20Corps%20Power%20of%20the%20Purse. pdf

United States Agency for International Development's (USAID) *Gender Lens Investing in Asia*: https://www.usaid.gov/sites/default/files/documents/1861/ Advancing%20Gender%20Lens%20Investing%20in%20Asia%20(2015). pdf

UN Women's *The Power of Procurement: How to Source from Women-Owned Businesses*: http://www.unwomen.org/-/media/headquarters/attachments/ sections/library/publications/2017/the-power-of-procurement-how-to-source-from-women-owned-businesses-en.pdf?la=enandvs=237

Women Effect's 'Women Effect Landscape Map' (tracker of gender lens advisors, entrepreneurs, experts, investors, philanthropists, and vehicles): http://www.womeneffect.com/map/

References

30% Club (2019) 'Homepage' [online] <https://30percentclub.org/> [accessed 19 March 2019].

Anderson, J. and Miles, K. (2015) *The State of the Field of Gender Lens Investing*, 1 October 2015 [online], Criterion Institute <https://criterioninstitute.org/ gender-work/state-of-the-field/> [accessed 1 May 2018].

As You Sow (2019) 'Gender equality funds' [online] <https://genderequality funds.org/> [accessed 1 April 2019].

Brennan, B. (2015) 'Top 10 things everyone should know about women consumers', [online], 21 January 2015, *Forbes* <https://www.forbes.com/ sites/bridgetbrennan/2015/01/21/top-10-things-everyone-should-know-about-women-consumers/#656a50166a8b> [accessed 1 May 2018].

Brush, C.G., Greene, P., Balachandra, L. and Davis, A. (2014) *Women Entrepreneurs 2014: Bridging the Gender Gap in Venture Capital* [pdf], Arthur M. Blank Center for Entrepreneurship, Babson College <https://www. babson.edu/media/babson/site-assets/content-assets/about/academics/ centres-and-institutes/blank-institute/global-research/diana-project/diana-project-executive-summary-2014.pdf> [accessed 1 May 2018].

CDC Investment Works (2019) 'CDC backs TheBoardroom Africa with £1.6m funding to increase women's representation in African boardrooms', [online], 22 January 2019 <https://www.cdcgroup.com/en/news-insight/ news/cdc-backs-theboardroom-africa-with-1-6m-funding-to-increase-womens-representation-in-african-boardrooms/> [accessed 28 March 2019].

Chin, K. (2017) *The Power of Procurement: How to Source from Women-Owned Businesses* [pdf], UN Women <http://www.unwomen.org/-/media/head quarters/attachments/sections/library/publications/2017/the-power-of-procurement-how-to-source-from-women-owned-businesses-en. pdf?la=enandvs=237> [accessed 1 May 2018].

Chordata Capital (no date) 'Homepage' [online] <https://www.chordatacapital. com/> [accessed 27 March 2019].

Clean Cooking Alliance (no date) 'About' [online] <https://www.cleancookingalliance.org/about/index.html> [accessed 25 March 2019].

Convergence (2018) *Data Brief: Blended Finance and Gender Equality* [pdf] <https://assets.ctfassets.net/4cgqlwde6qy0/CeoeP3RBrt8yli PNKmDM3/97ea11b03c70fa31f65079b67cf07b90/Convergence_ _Gender_Data_Brief__2019.pdf> [accessed 16 April 2019].

Ely, K. (2018) 'The world is designed for men: how bias is built into our daily lives', [online], 8 September 2018, *Medium* <https://medium.com/hh-design/the-world-is-designed-for-men-d06640654491> [accessed 16 April 2019].

European Bank for Reconstruction and Development (EBRD) (2013) *Strategic Gender Initiative* [pdf] <http://www.ebrd.com/downloads/sector/gender/strategic-gender-initiative.pdf> [accessed 24 April 2018].

Fortune (2017) 'These are the women CEOs leading Fortune 500 companies', 7 June 2017 [online] <http://fortune.com/2017/06/07/fortune-500-women-ceos/> [accessed 27 April 2018].

Gaucher, D., Friesen, J. and Kay, A.C. (2011) 'Evidence that gendered wording in job advertisements exists and sustains gender inequality', *Journal of Personality and Social Psychology* 101(1): 109–28 <http://dx.doi.org/10.1037/a0022530>.

Global Impact Investing Network (GIIN) (no date) 'Gender lens investing initiative' [online] <https://thegiin.org/gender-lens-investing-initiative> [accessed 1 April 2019].

Goldman Sachs (2018) '10,000 women' [online] <http://www.goldmansachs.com/citizenship/10000women/#> [accessed 1 May 2018].

International Finance Corporation (IFC) (2013) *IFC Jobs Study: Assessing Private Sector Contributions to Job Creation and Poverty Reduction* [pdf], Washington, DC: IFC <https://www.ifc.org/wps/wcm/connect/0fe6e2804e2c0a8f8d-3bad7a9dd66321/IFC_FULL+JOB+STUDY+REPORT_JAN2013_FINAL.pdf?MOD=AJPERES> [accessed 16 April 2019].

IFC (2014) *Women-Owned SMEs: A Business Opportunity for Financial Institutions – A Market and Credit Gap Assessment and IFC's Portfolio Gender Baseline* [pdf], Washington, DC: IFC <https://www.ifc.org/wps/wcm/connect/b229bb004322efde9814fc384c61d9f7/WomenOwnedSMes Report-Final.pdf?MOD=AJPERES> [accessed 1 May 2018].

IFC (2017) *Investing in Women: New Evidence for the Business Case* [pdf], Washington, DC: IFC <https://www.ifc.org/wps/wcm/connect/ac8fca18-6586-48cc-bfba-832b41d6af68/IFC+Invest+in+Women+October+2017.pdf?MOD=AJPERES&CVID=lYLVAcA> [accessed 17 July 2019].

InFaith Community Foundation (2018) *Introducing WomenInvest inFaith Portfolio* [pdf] <https://www.infaithfound.org/sites/default/files/pdf/Introducing_WomenInvest_InFaith_Portfolio.pdf> [accessed 27 March 2019].

Kaplan, S. and VanderBrug, J. (2014) 'The rise of gender capitalism', [online], *Stanford Social Innovation Review* [pdf], Fall 2014 <http://www.ssireview.org/articles/entry/the_rise_of_gender_capitalism> [accessed 16 April 2019].

Karve, S., Moritz, B. and Flood, A. (2017) *Winning the Fight for Female Talent: How to Gain the Diversity Edge through Inclusive Recruitment* [pdf], PwC <https://www.pwc.com/gx/en/about/diversity/iwd/iwd-female-talent-report-web.pdf> [accessed 22 November 2017].

Kipnis, H. (2017) *Women Entrepreneurs Are Essential for Private Sector Development in Emerging Markets*, Washington, DC: IFC <https://www.ifc.org/wps/wcm/connect/179d5b804b3a16138f35ff4149c6fa94/Entrepreneurship+Offering+Brochure+Dec+2015wJKquote.pdf?MOD=AJPERES> [accessed 22 November 2017].

Landel, M. (2015) 'Gender balance and the link to performance', [online], February 2015, McKinsey & Company <https://www.mckinsey.com/global-themes/leadership/gender-balance-and-the-link-to-performance> [accessed 16 April 2019].

Lee, L., Marshall, R., Rallis, D. and Moscardi, M. (2015). *Women on Boards: Global Trends in Gender Diversity on Corporate Boards* [online], MSCI <https://www.msci.com/documents/10199/04b6f646-d638-4878-9c61-4eb91748a82b> [accessed 1 May 2018].

Mennonite Economic Development Associates (MEDA) (2018a) *The Case for Gender Lens Investing: Alitheia Fund*, Waterloo, Canada: MEDA <https://english.dggf.nl/publications/publications/2018/9/3/case-study-gender-lens-investing> [accessed 20 July 2019].

MEDA (2018b) *The GEM Framework: Gender Equality Mainstreaming for Business Growth and Impact* [online], MEDA <https://www.meda.org/resources/publications/technical/gem-framework/531-gem-framework-online-final2/file> [accessed 1 May 2018] <https://www.meda.org/news/publications-main/technical/gem-framework/531-gem-framework-online-final2/file> [accessed 20 July 2019].

Moodley, L., Holt, T., Leke, A. and Desvaux, G. (2016) *Women Matter Africa* [online], McKinsey & Company <https://www.mckinsey.com/~/media/McKinsey/Featured%20Insights/Women%20matter/Women%20matter%20Africa/Women%20Matter%20Africa%20August%202016.ashx> [accessed 17 July 2019]

Morningstar (2019) 'ExxonMobil grants to support women entrepreneurs and "She Counts" program', [online], 8 March 2019 <https://corporate.exxonmobil.com/news/newsroom/news-releases/2019/0308_exxonmobil-grants-to-support-women-entrepreneurs-and-she-counts-program> [accessed 17 July 2019]

National Women's Business Council (2009) *Research on Women's Participation in Corporate Supplier Diversity Programs, Part 1* [pdf] <https://www.nwbc.gov/2016/12/07/research-on-womens-participation-in-corporate-supplier-diversity-programs-part-1/> [accessed 1 May 2018].

Nike (no date) 'The Nike Pro Hijab' [online] <https://www.nike.com/ca/en_gb/c/women/nike-pro-hijab> [accessed 1 May 2018].

Patamar Capital (2017) 'Patamar Capital launches impact investment fund to drive growth of women's SMEs in Southeast Asia', [online], 29 May 2017 <http://patamar.com/patamar-capital-launches-impact-investment-fund-drive-growth-womens-smes-southeast-asia/> [accessed 26 April 2018].

PAX World Funds (no date) 'Pax Ellevate Global Women's Leadership Fund: investing in companies that invest in women' [online] <https://paxworld.com/funds/pax-ellevate-global-womens-leadership-fund/> [accessed 2 May 2018].

Portea (no date.) 'Homepage' [online] <https://www.portea.com/> [accessed 1 May 2018].

Portea Investment (no date) 'About the PRI' [online] <https://www.unpri.org/about-the-pri> [accessed 19 March 2019].

Solar Sister (no date) 'Homepage' [online] <https://solarsister.org/> [accessed 28 March 2019].

Statista (no date) 'Total consumer spending of women worldwide in 2013 and 2018' [online] <https://www.statista.com/statistics/578492/women-buying-power-worldwide/> [accessed 16 April 2019].

Sustainable Health Enterprises (no date) 'Homepage' [online] <http://sheinnovates.com/> [accessed 26 April 2018].

Ten Thousand Villages (no date) 'Homepage' [online] <https://www.tenthousandvillages.ca> [accessed 1 May 2018].

Unilever (2016) 'Unilever to unstereotype portrayals of gender in advertising', [online], 23 June 2016 <https://www.unilever.com.au/news/press-releases/2016/unstereotype-portrayals-of-gender-in-advertising.html> [accessed 1 May 2018].

Veris Wealth Partners (2018) *Gender Lens Investing: Building the Arc of Finance for Women and Girls* [online] <https://www.veriswp.com/research/gli-bending-arc-of-finance-women/> [accessed 27 March 2019].

Weber Shandwick (2016) *Gender Forward Pioneer (GFP) Index 2016* [pdf] <https://www.webershandwick.com/wp-content/uploads/2018/04/gender-forward-pioneer-index-infographic.pdf> [accessed 28 March 2019].

WEConnect International (no date) 'About us' [online] <https://weconnectinternational.org/en/about-us/who-we-are> [accessed 1 May 2018].

Whitfield, G. and Farrell, D. (2010) 'Diversity in supply chains: what really matters?' *Journal of Diversity Management* 5(4): 31–41 <10.19030/jdm.v5i4.341>.

Woetzel, J., Madgavkar, A., Ellingrud, K., Labaye, E., Devillard, S., Kutcher, E., Manyika, J., Dobbs, R. and Krishnan, M. (2015) 'How advancing women's equality can add \$12 trillion to global growth' [online], McKinsey & Company <https://www.mckinsey.com/featured-insights/employment-and-growth/how-advancing-womens-equality-can-add-12-trillion-to-global-growth> [accessed 28 March 2019].

CHAPTER 7

Enterprise development: starting and building businesses

Jennifer Denomy

Abstract

The chapter discusses the complex economic and sociocultural barriers inhibiting women entrepreneurs and women-owned small- and medium-sized businesses and outlines the enterprise development approach, strategies, and tools for reducing those barriers within a market system.

Keywords: women's economic empowerment, market systems development, enterprise development, small- and medium-sized enterprises, business training, financial inclusion

Introduction

Rania lives in Tripoli, Libya and recently graduated with a degree in mechanical engineering. Despite the ongoing civil and political unrest, she was determined to start her own business and was fortunate to have family support for the idea, which is unusual in Libya due to prevailing sociocultural norms. Lacking business experience, Rania began looking for training opportunities, and was excited to learn about the Libya Women's Economic Empowerment (LWEE) project that was facilitating skill building opportunities for women in Tripoli (MEDA, 2018). Through this service, Rania along with many other women learned how to conduct a feasibility study, assess market opportunities, and develop a business plan. The training provided her not only with needed skills, but also a network of like-minded contacts – and future colleagues. By the time Rania had completed training, she and a group of fellow trainees had already agreed to start an engineering company together. Launching a business in Libya's unstable economy presents significant challenges, particularly for young women, due to the lack of services and support in general and especially those appropriate for women. Despite these obstacles, Wadi al Namel, or 'Valley of Ants', is now a well-known engineering company that works on public sector and university-funded projects. Rania and her business partners demonstrate the role Libyan women can play in building the economy of

http://dx.doi.org/10.3362/9781780447506.007

their country – particularly when they have access to needed services, socio-cultural support, and networking with other women (MEDA, 2018).

From a market systems development (MSD) perspective, enterprise development is an approach that can upgrade enterprise ecosystems so that a range of appropriate and sustainable services and supports are available to enable businesses to flourish. These services allow enterprises to start, grow, become more viable, and, in many cases, create more and better-quality employment. In developing economies, however, the provision of business products and services is inconsistent and of variable quality, and business owners face numerous access challenges. Even if services are present, women face additional challenges accessing them due to mobility limitations, multiple demands on their time, and societal perceptions that women cannot run businesses effectively. Moreover, regulatory frameworks are often weak and, in some instances, discriminate against women.

Support to micro-, small-, and medium-sized enterprises (MSMEs) is vital for the overall success of business ecosystems and national economies. MSMEs are numerous, making up more than 90 per cent of the world's businesses, providing over half of global employment and more than a third of gross domestic product (Boyle et al., 2016). In developing economies, microenterprises make up the vast majority of MSMEs: over 900 million microenterprises, including approximately 500 million smallholder farmers, constitute 93 per cent of businesses in these countries (Boyle et al., 2016), while informal companies, the majority of which are run by women, constitute up to half of all economic activity (UN Foundation and ExxonMobil Foundation, 2016).

Enterprise development can be a strategic MSD women's economic empowerment (WEE) approach because of the potential for scale, given the significant number of women-run businesses, and the scope to shift enterprise ecosystems to improve access to vital resources, information, and markets for many women. The scale of women-run enterprises is significant, both in absolute numbers and in their proportional representation within the global economy. Globally, women own over a third of all formal businesses (ILO, 2016), and the World Bank estimates that women own 30 to 37 per cent of all small and medium enterprises (SMEs) in developing economies, which translates into 8 to 10 million actual women-owned businesses (Kumar, 2017). Entrepreneurship also constitutes a significant proportion of women's paid work in many countries and is therefore a critical avenue to promote WEE (Patel, 2014).

In order to thrive in market systems, enterprises require different levels of support and types of services at different points in their life cycle. An early stage microenterprise might require intensive capacity building to develop or refine products, set product pricing, and secure start-up funding. A more established enterprise may benefit from support to expand or diversify its clientele through new product development or linkages to new markets. Other important services include business management, mentoring and coaching, access to finance, linkages to markets and market information, and legal advice.

Significant donor money has been invested in MSME development – Donor Committee for Enterprise Development (DCED) estimates US$24.5 bn – despite an ongoing debate on whether targeting smaller businesses will benefit low-income workers (DCED, 2017). Proponents of this approach point to the large numbers of people, particularly low-income workers, who find jobs with smaller enterprises. Smaller firms often have lower skill and educational requirements, providing an important employment avenue for those having difficulty securing jobs in larger companies. As noted above, most women-run businesses are MSMEs, meaning that approaches targeting smaller businesses are more likely to include them. Most enterprise development programmes target businesses of a specific size or stage in an enterprise ecosystem, tailoring the upgrading of services to the context, the needs of the clients, and the market gaps. For example, the LWEE project (MEDA, 2018) focuses on women-run start-ups, all of which are currently microenterprises and face similar challenges, as described above.

Opponents argue that these jobs may be low quality, poorly paid, and insecure. In addition, as small enterprises fail in greater numbers than larger businesses, many of these jobs are lost through 'churning', as new businesses enter and leave the market. So-called 'graduate enterprises' that start small but grow to 10 or more staff members contribute disproportionately to job growth, accounting for only 1 per cent of MSMEs but creating a quarter of the new MSME jobs (DCED, 2017). Good jobs are created and sustained by initiatives – whether donor-funded or otherwise – that remove obstacles to business growth, rather than targeting services to firms of a specific size (Page and Söderbom, 2012).

Shifting the system for enterprise development is key for long-term and widespread change. DCED emphasizes that the success of individual enterprises – and resulting large-scale poverty reduction – requires that whole systems work effectively, not just individual enterprises (DCED, 2017). A systems approach to enterprise development is now the commonly accepted strategy among the majority of donors including the UK's Department for International Development (DFID), Australia's Department of Foreign Affairs and Trade (DFAT), the Swedish International Development Cooperation Agency (Sida), and the Swiss Agency for Development and Cooperation (SDC), among others. Nevertheless, the sustainability of local support services remains weak, and training services (a key 'push' component in developing the market system) are often provided by projects rather than by sustainable market actors.

Sustainable MSD involves the building of accessible and affordable services such as training for business management, provision of market information, access to needed resources such as finance and transportation, and improved linkages to markets. Whereas in the past an enterprise development approach prioritized firm-level changes, a market systems approach aims to address broad gaps in an enterprise ecosystem, with the assumption that individual firms within that system will access the services, change their behaviour, and adopt more productive practices. This, in turn, increases productivity and overall competitiveness in the market systems, with new entrants offering a more robust range of services (DCED, n.d.).

Enterprise development and women's economic empowerment

Many women choose to run an enterprise because they lack alternatives. Jobs are scarce and women are often at a disadvantage when applying for or seeking work. Young women face additional challenges in securing work and are unemployed at even higher rates than young men. For example, in the Middle East and North Africa, the female youth unemployment rate is over 44 per cent, almost double that of young men (ILO, 2016). In contexts where women face mobility restrictions, the labour market may be effectively closed to them and entrepreneurship is the only option (Kabeer, 2017).

However, when women do take up the challenge, they benefit not only themselves, but other women in business, their households, and communities as well as business sectors and national economies.

Women benefiting from enterprise development

Though starting and running an enterprise may be a decision driven by necessity, the experience of taking control over income and time can be very empowering for women.

Even 'necessity' entrepreneurs are making a choice, whether it is to avoid inconvenient, unsuitable, exploitative, or dangerous employment, or to create their own opportunities rather than relying on an uncertain market. The act of making this choice can be empowering in itself; and even more so, the subsequent choices opened by the act of running a business presents opportunities for women to develop their own skills, to hire other women or men, or to invest in their families and communities. A great example of this is CARE and H&M Foundation's Strengthening Women programme, which supports 100,000 women entrepreneurs in 11 countries, most of whom started their businesses out of necessity. With increased control over their time, income, and business operations, women in the project showed improved self-esteem, with many taking on leadership and mentorship roles for other women (CARE and H&M Foundation, 2017).

Enterprise development provides income generating opportunities that are flexible and can be combined with women's other obligations, such as domestic work or caregiving responsibilities. Women may run multiple enterprises, for example, shifting activities to benefit from seasonal work such as agriculture or tourism. In addition, non-seasonal activities such as catering, tailoring, or petty trade can provide income during other times of the year and be organized to fit into women's daily and weekly schedules.

Prior to the revolution in Libya, working women across the socio-economic spectrum were concentrated in public-sector positions. Ongoing instability has made these public-sector jobs unattractive because of late and irregular wages and high inflation. Enterprise development is increasingly seen as a viable option despite low levels of business ownership – 8 per cent compared with 25 per cent in other 'factor-driven economies' (those based mainly on low-skilled labour and natural resources); about 85 per cent of Libyans view owning a business as a good career choice with high status in society (OECD, 2016).

Women benefiting women

Women who run enterprises provide benefits to other women, both intentionally and by chance. Numerous examples exist of women who mentor and support other women in starting and growing businesses. The Goldman Sachs 10,000 Women initiative provides business and management education, mentorship, networking, and access to credit. Almost 90 per cent of the 10,000 women in the programme subsequently mentored other women entrepreneurs in their communities (Kelley et al., 2015).

When women's businesses grow, they provide employment opportunities that are likely to benefit other women, particularly when operating in female-dominated sectors. In gender-segregated contexts, women may structure their businesses to minimize interactions deemed inappropriate, resulting in women-only workplaces or value chains. This is often reinforced by the perception that women are better suited than men to particular tasks, such as those requiring detailed handiwork or strong interpersonal skills. As early as 2011, researchers were examining the role of women in the mobile communications value chain, and found that across multiple stakeholders, women were consistently identified as having better customer service skills than their male counterparts. Women are perceived as more trustworthy and patient with customers, and more willing to ensure complex products are understood (Cherie Blair Foundation for Women, 2011).

Women benefiting families and communities

Women entrepreneurs contribute to social development and economic prosperity by reinvesting in those around them. It is well documented that women invest in their families; one study quantified this investment, specifying that women directed 90 cents of every dollar they earned to their families' education, health, and nutrition, compared with 30 to 40 cents contributed by men (Kelley et al., 2015).

Many women-led enterprises contribute significantly to the social and economic performance of their communities, providing fair wages, healthcare, and educational support, as well as local environmental protection. These social enterprises tackle community-level problems, while simultaneously generating the income with which to address these issues – a sort of social and economic Yin and Yang where the profit motive is intertwined with solving a social crisis. After completing LWEE's training on management and entrepreneurship, several women in the project have chosen to start community organizations. Two examples include educator and family counsellor, Ghaida Albajghny, who now trains women in handicraft production and Huda Hrewit., who opened a kindergarten in 2009, which she has steadily expanded, offering new grades every year into which the students advance.

Barriers for women in enterprise development

There are several systemic barriers that result in significant differences in the opportunities, inputs, resources, and growth potential for women running businesses compared with those of their male counterparts. These include discriminatory legal and policy frameworks, such as inheritance and property laws, and social and community attitudes that dictate whether business is deemed acceptable for women, in addition to the choice of sector and their ability to expand operations and move into the formal sector. Restrictions on mobility and decision making have a negative impact on women's ability to start and grow businesses.

Women tend to start businesses in competitive, low-return, labour-intensive sectors with low capital requirements because of challenges in accessing external financing. These businesses are typically informal and survival-focused rather than growth-oriented. In Grimm's 'Constrained Gazelle' study conducted in seven West African capitals, 87 per cent of survival businesses surveyed were run by women (Grimm et al., 2012). Though sub-Saharan Africa has the highest percentage of women entrepreneurs in the world, most of these are self-employed rather than employers. In fact, globally, twice as many male business owners than women business owners are employers (Hallward-Driemeier, 2013).

Becoming an entrepreneur is a challenging choice for a woman since numerous barriers stand in the way of success. Supporting women's success in business requires understanding the various constraints across an ecosystem and responding with tailored interventions. Two cross-cutting, system-wide constraints are discussed in more detail here: socio-economic exclusion and regulatory frameworks. Such enabling environment challenges are dealt with more broadly in Chapter 3 and are referenced here as they specifically pertain to enterprise development.

Socio-economic exclusion

Social norms, or rules of behaviour that are considered acceptable in a given society, impact women in business in multiple ways. A country or community's attitudes contribute to the 'entrepreneurial culture' that the Global Entrepreneurship Development Institute (GEDI) describes as the way a population views entrepreneurship, risk assessment, and the degree to which business ownership is considered a viable career option (Terjesen and Lloyd, 2015). This, in turn, influences individuals' willingness to start and grow an enterprise.

Social norms also dictate the degree to which women are supported to start businesses. The Global Entrepreneurship Monitor (GEM, 2018) notes that these social constraints affect men and women differently, resulting in the most significant enterprise challenges that women face worldwide. For example, subtle social biases persist that perceive women to be less ambitious, or that business is not an appropriate pursuit (Kelley et al., 2015). These attitudes can limit women's access to vital resources such as networks, mentors, education, and financial services (Terjesen and Lloyd, 2015).

Social norms also contribute to women being concentrated in specific sectors and occupations. As noted earlier, women's enterprises are concentrated in labour-intensive sectors with low returns. Although non-traditional sectors can be much more profitable, women are often blocked from participation by higher capital requirements and educational barriers, both of which are driven, at least in part, by gendered social norms. This occupational segregation means that increasing women's empowerment requires work to be done to influence social norms.

When women earn an income, particularly in the public sphere, the gender dynamics at the household and community levels may be disrupted, and women may be at increased risk of violence (Gennari et al., 2015). Violence or fear of violence is fundamentally disempowering, and limits women's ability to participate fully in the economy, often resulting in lower earnings. A study in Tanzania found that women experiencing intimate partner violence earned 29 per cent less than women who did not; and earnings were up to 43 per cent less if the violence was severe (Gennari et al., 2015). The Violence Against Women and Girls Resource Guide recommends that economic empowerment programming, including support for enterprise and entrepreneurship development, include a component addressing social norms and behaviour change. Studies point to a reduction in violence against women in economic empowerment programmes that include activities on household communication strengthening, conflict resolution strategies, and training on violence against women. These could be stand-alone activities or incorporated into business services, such as business development training or financial education (Gennari et al., 2015).

Though enterprise ownership may bring women greater control over their lives through increased income and enhanced recognition among family and community members, running a business often decreases overall time women have available for leisure and other activities. Business activities add to women's already busy days. Women running enterprises usually continue to do most of the domestic chores and childcare or share it with other female members of the household, such as their daughters. Balancing business and family life may require women to devote fewer hours to their business: in a study of 303 entrepreneurs in Ghana, 39 per cent of men said they worked more than 12 hours per day in their business, compared with 25 per cent of women. Women were more likely to be willing to give up their business if their families needed more attention (Kabeer, 2017).

Women are disproportionately limited in their access to financial and business services, including business and management training, professional networks, and market information. These barriers are often structural, based on societal norms such as women's unequal access to land, which reduces their ability to provide loan collateral. Other barriers stem from biases, or 'capability perceptions' (Kelley et al., 2015), such as the misconception that women lack the ability to run a business. Household and community attitudes exclude women from business activities, but also from business culture. Women are not invited to join networks or associations, or if they do join may lack the confidence to speak out and benefit fully. Huda Al Shabaa, a client in MEDA's LWEE project, is an environmental scientist who runs a recycling organization mobilizing youth. She dreams of expanding into manufacturing paper, despite the scepticism of those around her: 'My mother tells me this business is for a man to run, but I tell her that I have to make this factory happen - I am going to be a businesswoman!' (MEDA, 2016)

Globally, women are excluded from financial services at higher rates than men, and women entrepreneurs face significant challenges in securing financing for business start-up or growth. The OECD (2013) conducted a study of banks in the Middle East and North Africa (MENA) region and found that while 90 per cent of the institutions stated that loans for women-led businesses were profitable for them, the volume of loans granted to women-led SMEs represented only a small fraction of their portfolios – less than 10 per cent in most cases. This funding gap increases for high-potential female entrepreneurs who require larger amounts of capital, typically provided by venture capital. Though gender-disaggregated data is not widely available, what is known is that men dominate top management positions in venture capital firms (Terjesen and Lloyd, 2015). Furthermore, many decisions about funding are made through networks, and women's more limited networks work against them.

Women are similarly underserved by business training and capacity building services. Where such training exists, women's access may be limited by low literacy, lack of time, cost, and mobility constraints. Fewer professional networks, an important source of information and resources, are available to women. Many business and contracting opportunities are made available through formal and informal networks, and women's exclusion places them at a significant disadvantage. This combined with the lack of suitable training and capacity building services forces women to rely on friends or family for business advice and guidance (ILO, 2016).

Disempowering regulatory frameworks

In general, countries with greater legal protection of women's economic rights have higher rates of female employers (Hallward-Driemeier, 2013). Several regulatory areas impact specifically on women and enterprise development, which will be discussed here.

Laws that disincentivize hiring or retaining female employees contribute to already high rates of self-employment among women. Paid maternity leave is common in most countries, though whether the costs are covered by the government, employers, or both varies greatly. When companies are responsible for covering the cost of paid maternity leave, the cost of hiring women becomes significantly higher than men. The World Bank's *Women, Business and the Law* notes that governments pay maternity leave benefits in just over half of countries with paid maternity leave as opposed to only 30 per cent where the employer pays and 19 per cent where the cost is shared between the two (World Bank, 2015).

Another example of a policy designed to support women resulting in unintended consequences is a Jordanian labour law requiring companies employing 20 or more married women to provide and pay for childcare (European Diversity Research and Consulting, 2012). While such laws are crafted to support working women, in reality they often lead employers to simply avoid hiring women of reproductive age.

The process of registering a business is onerous in many countries, requiring extensive paperwork, fees, and travel to multiple offices. For women not based in regional or national capitals, the travel may be prohibitive in terms of cost, time required, or mobility restrictions. Regulations and procedures are frequently unclear or lack transparency, which can compound the time required to successfully register a business. In addition, women in many countries cite fear of harassment by officials when attempting business registration (ILO, 2016).

Regulations that hinder women attempting to start, grow, or formalize businesses may contribute to the large numbers of women-led businesses that remain small and informal. Business registration is important for successful, scalable enterprises (Terjesen and Lloyd, 2015); formalization facilitates access to other services, including financing, and to contracting opportunities and national or export markets. Formal financing is especially important for female entrepreneurs, who tend to have less personal capital to invest in their businesses.

Women's access to and control over property and land increases their financial security and bargaining position within the family and is vital for the success and stability of both agricultural and non-agricultural enterprises. However, inheritance and marriage laws often restrict women's asset ownership, with consequences for women's ability to engage in the economy. Even in cases where women have the legal right to inherit, they may be pressured by relatives into giving up assets. In 2010, Jordan passed a law designed to counteract this social pressure by preventing women from waiving inheritances and requiring inherited property to be registered in their name upon execution of the will (World Bank, 2015).

Data from Tanzania found that women with strong land rights more than tripled their earnings and were three times more likely to participate in off-farm employment (USAID, 2016). For agricultural enterprises, women's reliable access to land boosts farm productivity: they are more likely to invest in inputs and activities that improve land quality, such as leaving plots fallow to allow soil to regenerate. Rwandan women with formal land rights were 19 per cent more likely to use soil conservation techniques, compared with 10 per cent of men (USAID, 2016).

Lack of access to land limits women's access to credit. Land and property are commonly used as loan collateral, and women who lack property – or proof of legal ownership – are less likely to have access to external sources of funding. Alternative forms of collateral are necessary to increase women's financial inclusion. A recent CGAP blog recommends creation of collateral registries for moveable assets such as household contents, jewellery, and livestock, which women are more likely to own (El-Zoghbi, 2015). Non-bank sources of credit such as microfinance institutions and retailers may be able to rely on alternative collateral, such as records of successful repayment or even mobile financial transaction records (World Bank, 2015). The 2019 *Women, Business and the Law* report examines 10 years of data around economic decisions women make in their working lives. Out of the eight indicators, 'Managing Assets' examines gender differences in property and inheritance law and had the fewest reforms of all eight indicators (four in total), revealing the pace of reform is very slow and there is significant room for progress (World Bank, 2019).

Designing and implementing an enterprise development initiative

Within MSD, several approaches and strategies can be used to maximize WEE. This section discusses the importance of beginning MSD with a gendered market assessment, to understand the profile of entrepreneurs to be reached, and the opportunities, bottlenecks and constraints that face them. MSD initiatives typically focus on supporting increased access to finance, improving market access, improving the enabling environment, strengthening business development services and enhancing agency and empowerment.

Understanding context faced by women entrepreneurs

Effective MSD programming begins with a gendered market assessment, providing critical information on opportunities, bottlenecks, and constraints. Women entrepreneurs are not homogeneous, and an assessment should consider critical differences that will impact success, including age, experience level, sector, and motivation. For example, enterprise growth is often assumed to be necessary for success, and those that are not growing are sometimes described as 'stagnating'. However, for many women, growth – or growth beyond a certain threshold – is contrary to their business objectives. A larger business may require more time, more resources, and more risk. In many cases, a more valuable and empowering MSD approach for women may be to improve enterprise efficiencies and facilitate a shift to higher value activities.

Anastasia de Santos's Women's Entrepreneurship Diagnostic tool presents a useful assessment framework, identifying and prioritizing the most binding constraints, or those that if overcome will have the greatest impact. Using a decision tree, the diagnostic focuses on identifying constraints to women's entrepreneurship in investment, enabling environment (corruption, registration, and contracts enforcement), property rights, market failures (which includes sectoral segmentation, information, and household demands), infrastructure, and human capital (De Santos, 2013).

Facilitating women's changing roles in enterprise development may result in increased risks to women. Assessments should include analysis of risk potential associated with women's participation in market activities, as well as strategies to mitigate potential harm (World Bank 2015). Assessing and mitigating risks for women in business is covered in more detail in Part 3.

The following sections describe a range of solutions that MSD projects can implement to overcome systemic barriers for women in enterprise ecosystems.

Single or multi-service provision to entrepreneurs or enterprises

Women's enterprise development typically focuses on access to finance, improving market access for women's businesses, improving the enabling environment, business development services, including training, technology transfer, incubation, and association strengthening, and enhancing agency and empowerment (Patel, 2014). Programmes may focus on a single type of intervention, such as facilitating increased access to finance or skills development, or may combine many interventions. A BRAC programme that combined asset transfer, training, and regular follow-up visits had significant impacts on vulnerable women in Bangladesh, increasing their incomes and transforming their occupational choice from casual day labourers to self-employment (Buvinic and Furst-Nichols, 2014). Evaluations of International Labour Organization (ILO) training and capital programmes in Uganda and Sri Lanka found more mixed results, with increased profits for men but not women. The differences were attributed to family pressure; women were expected to hand over earnings to relatives, while men employed their family members (Buvinic and Furst-Nichols, 2014).

Provision of multiple services can have a mutually reinforcing effect making the whole enterprise ecosystem more robust. For example, business training and informal mentorship have been found to increase repayment of microfinance loans (UN Foundation and ExxonMobil Foundation, 2016). Mobile financial services can strengthen other interventions such as facilitating improved privacy for women around finances, increasing the likelihood that they will be able to invest in their businesses rather than turning over profits to family members.

Financial inclusion and women's economic empowerment

According to the latest Findex report (World Bank, 2017), in the last three years the number of financially excluded adults – those without an account at a financial institution or through a mobile money provider – dropped from 2 billion to 1.7 billion. Despite an 18 per cent global decrease in unbanked adults from 2011 to 2017, the gender gap persists, with fewer women than men accessing savings and credit in every region of the world. Globally, 72 per cent of men and 65 per cent of women have an account, a 7 per cent gender gap that has not changed since 2011; in developing economies, the gender gap remains unchanged at 9 per cent (World Bank, 2017). Financial inclusion initiatives may focus on modifying products or delivery channels to improve suitability for women entrepreneurs. An ILO study found that women's business growth has been positively impacted by greater flexibility in loan repayment terms, larger financing amounts, and more consistent access to financing over the long term (Patel, 2014). The UN Foundation and ExxonMobil Foundation Roadmap report (2016) echoes this call for larger financing amounts for women's businesses, citing evaluations of 31 microcredit programmes that found small grants or loans failed to stimulate growth in women's microbusinesses. By contrast, larger amounts of capital, particularly when offered as in-kind productive assets (such as livestock or inventory), achieved greater impact, particularly when accompanied by training and follow-up visits (UN Foundation and ExxonMobil Foundation, 2016).

Business training

Business training is essential for entrepreneurs in starting or growing businesses, but evidence is mixed on the optimal content, duration, delivery method, and follow-up required. Training alone seems to have more of an impact on profit for business start-ups, while business growth requires other services in addition. Studies have linked business training with improved business practices among women entrepreneurs, but fewer effects were recorded on profits or business longevity (UN Foundation and ExxonMobil Foundation, 2016). When targeting women entrepreneurs, the duration and timing of training must accommodate their time constraints. While longer courses are likely to have more impact, women may be unable to attend multi-day or multi-week programmes.

Though business training is frequently unsustainable as it is heavily subsidized by donor or public-sector funding, some companies directly offer training to strengthen their supply chain. For example, The Coca-Cola Company has made WEE through entrepreneurship a signature corporate issue, pointing to the central role women play in their business and distribution system. In 2010, the company launched the 5by20 programme, which aims to reach 5 million women entrepreneurs in their global supply chain by 2020. To address the most common barriers faced by women producers, suppliers, distributors, and retailers, the initiative offers business skills training, financial services, and linkages to peers and mentors. By the end of 2016, 5by20 had reached more than 1.75 million women in 64 countries (Coca-Cola Company, 2017).

Building business and professional networks

Access to networks is a frequently cited gap for women in business. The UN Foundation and ExxonMobil Foundation (2016) identify professional networks as high-potential interventions, empowering women through access to contacts, advice, and mentorship, as well as a range of information and training opportunities. MEDA's LWEE project in Libya facilitated the launch of informal 'business tea parties', which were extremely popular; as intended, they have evolved into more formal business networking events run independently by participants. Some meetings feature local business people sharing expertise, others are designated discussions on specific topics, and still others offer opportunities for members to display products or services, such as catering. Since women are the primary customers for such services, the meetings are an important marketing channel. Meetings provide important information-sharing opportunities for women entrepreneurs, who lack the networks enjoyed by their male counterparts. For example, Sara, an LWEE client and graphic designer, decided to open an office to attract new clients. She had trouble finding affordable options, but after raising this problem at a project networking event, she was referred to an excellent location that she now rents.

Market access: mitigating risk through linkages

Commercial sales agent networks and micro-franchising offer market access for enterprising women. Distinct from simply reselling products, women participating in such networks benefit from identification with a recognized brand, and often receive support, including business and product training from the parent company. In return, sales agents frequently gain access to the base of the pyramid clientele, which may be inaccessible through traditional sales channels. The sales agent model has been successfully implemented in several sectors, with the distribution of dairy, cosmetics, health products, and mobile telecommunications.

Cosmetic giant Avon is the world's largest direct seller, operating in more than 75 countries through approximately 6 million agents; over half of their sales are in the developing world, with Brazil as the largest market (Avon, 2016).Living Goods, founded in Uganda in 2007, has replicated elements of the Avon model, with women selling health products to rural markets. Describing themselves as 'the Avon of health', Living Goods trains a network of women as Community Health Promoters who earn an income by providing vital health information and products to underserved rural markets. Agents also sell consumer goods such as soap, diapers, solar lamps, and clean cookstoves. The product mix is critical for meeting both social and commercial goals: promoters are often the main delivery channel for health products, and the consumer goods have a higher profit margin for the agent (Militzer, 2013). These micro-entrepreneurs earn a margin of approximately 20 per cent on their sales; top agents can make sales worth up to $500 per month (Kubzansky and Cooper, 2013). From an empowerment perspective, women benefit from income and the networks they develop, but also from the credibility they gain providing health information to their communities.

In the telecommunications sector, a strong cadre of female agents provides benefits to both mobile companies and female clients. In regions where interactions between men and women are limited, women customers may not be able to purchase products from men. GSM Association (GSMA) calculated that the gender gap in mobile money access was 14 per cent in low- and middle-income countries and 38 per cent in South Asia in 2015, with social norms a major contributing factor (Hendricks and Loupeda, 2017). Female agents may be able to build trust with female clients more easily and demystify a service that could otherwise prove intimidating. Women agents provide mobile network operators with access to new markets, or enhanced access to existing markets through their strong social connections within communities. As with Living Goods, women sales agents in the mobile value chain require training on products, marketing, financial management, and communication skills to boost confidence. However, the investment could pay dividends: the gender gap in mobile money alone is an estimated $170 bn (Hendricks and Loupeda, 2017).

Greater empowerment through social interventions

Some enterprise development programmes support empowerment outcomes for women through activities specifically designed to increase women's agency. These are typically project-based and are meant to be short-term subsidized initiatives that lead to long-term sustainable change for women's beneficial engagement in a market system. This strategy is most effective when constraints to women's business activities can be traced to gender-related barriers.

For example, the Unites States Agency for International Development (USAID)-funded Southern Africa Trade Hub project included the Persuasive Communications and Assertiveness training for Persuasive Communications and Assertiveness Workshop for Women in Business in Botswana, Zambia, and Namibia, created and delivered by Banyan Global (SATH, 2018). This interactive communications workshop increased women entrepreneurs' credibility and maximized impact through more effective communication. Sessions included presentation techniques, confidence and assertiveness, and negotiation, as well as discussions on how culture and gender influence communication. The workshop incorporated results from regional gender analyses and was tailored to address the specific needs, constraints, concerns, and opportunities experienced by women business owners and entrepreneurs in Southern Africa.

Case study: MEDA'S Libya Women's Economic Empowerment project

Since the 2011 revolution, Libya has struggled with the transition to a more inclusive economy that is less dependent on the oil industry. Entrepreneurship, the engine for growth and innovation in many economies, was not previously encouraged and remains underdeveloped. Challenges persist for entrepreneurs, including limited access to finance and ongoing security issues. In addition, Libyan women are hampered by the country's lack of entrepreneurial culture, compounded by scepticism of women's ability to do business. Despite almost universal literacy and high levels of educational attainment, less than one-third of women enter the formal workforce, compared with 78.7 per cent of men (UNDP, 2015). Women lack information on business and have few opportunities to learn entrepreneurial skills. Networks for women are scarce, and business associations or chambers of commerce that focus on or include women are non-existent. It is a tough environment for an MSD programme, and one where there is often more 'push' than 'pull' in activities that aim to overcome market failures.

Ongoing insecurity in Libya presents challenges for women entrepreneurs, but, paradoxically, it is also creating opportunities. As increasing numbers of men are pulled into the conflict, women are assuming some of the economic and social roles left vacant by husbands and sons. In her address to the Oslo Freedom Forum, Alaa Murabit (2015) describes how women are addressing community needs, including approaching ministries to ensure secure access to public spaces.

Launched in 2012, MEDA's LWEE project facilitates an integrated service model, with capacity building, networking, and financial services for women.

Business empowerment through networking

In the absence of female-friendly business associations or service providers, LWEE promoted monthly business networking events with opportunities for women to discuss business issues and source products and services from other women. In addition to linking women, these networks have allowed the project to expand across the country, as women initiate events in their hometowns.

Access to finance

Businesswomen received start-up and growth capital through business plan competitions, held in 2014 and 2016, where 21 women received matching investments of 5,000 to 30,000 Libyan dinars (approximately $3,700 to $22,000). Recipients stated that the award acted as a catalyst, providing 'seed' money that helped them to gather funds from other sources.

Capacity building

Leadership and negotiation training is offered through Springboard Corporation's network of licensed trainers. Business skills training was initially conducted by the project in-person, and the discussion-based format became cathartic for many participants, helping them cope with trauma from the conflict in addition to practising communication skills. However, ongoing instability led to the development of alternative delivery channels. Almost all participants own smartphones or laptops, so an approach was adopted that turned the business training into a self-guided online course, designed to be accessible with minimal bandwidth. The online platform aids businesswomen to overcome mobility limitations, but also offers flexibility, allowing them to balance the multiple demands on their time.

Together, these integrated services have enabled many businesswomen in Libya to successfully launch or grow enterprises. Almost all report having increased confidence – in their business skills and in their own abilities more broadly. This confidence has allowed them to take steps they could not have otherwise imagined, secure in their new networks of business peers.

Useful resources

Aspen Network of Development Entrepreneurs' (ANDE) *Entrepreneurial Ecosystem Diagnostic Toolkit*: https://assets.aspeninstitute. org/content/uploads/files/content/docs/pubs/FINAL%20Ecosystem%20 Toolkit%20Draft_print%20version.pdf

BEAM Exchange's *WEAMS Framework*: https://beamexchange.org/resources/794/

CARE's *Growing Together: Strengthening Micro-Enterprises in Value Chains*: https://insights.careinternational.org.uk/media/k2/attachments/Growing-together_CARE-SABM-BFP-HKS_09-2016.pdf

Donor Committee for Enterprise Development's (DCED) *Current Debates on Small Enterprise Development*: https://www.enterprise-development.org/ wp-content/uploads/DCED_SE_SynthesisNote.pdf

Food and Agriculture Organization of the United Nations' (FAO) *Developing Gender-Sensitive Value Chains: A Guiding Framework*: http://www.fao.org/3/a-i6462e.pdf

International Labour Office's (ILO) *Small and Medium-Sized Enterprises and Decent and Productive Employment Creation*: http://www.ilo.org/wcmsp5/ groups/public/---ed_norm/---relconf/documents/meetingdocument/ wcms_358294.pdf

UN Foundation and ExxonMobil Foundation's *A Roadmap for Promoting Women's Economic Empowerment*: http://www.womeneconroadmap.org/ sites/default/files/WEE_Roadmap_Report_Final.pdf

References

Avon (2016) *Avon Annual Report 2016* [pdf] <http://investor.avon company.com/Cache/1500098010.PDF?Y=andO=PDFandD= andfid=1500098010andT=andiid=3009091> [accessed 17 April 2019].

Boyle, G., Cornes, P. and Gilbert, R. (2016) *Growing Together: Strengthening Micro-Enterprises in Value Chains* [pdf], CARE International <https://insights. careinternational.org.uk/media/k2/attachments/Growing-together_CARE-SABM-BFP-HKS_09-2016.pdf> [accessed 15 May 2019].

Buvinic, M. and Furst-Nichols, R. (2014) *Promoting Women's Economic Empowerment: What Works?* Washington, DC: World Bank Group.

CARE and H&M Foundation (2017) *From Necessity to Opportunity: Women Entrepreneurs in the Global South* [pdf] <https://www.care-international. org/files/files/care-h-m/Global%20report%20CARE-HMFoundation.pdf> [accessed 15 May 2019].

Cherie Blair Foundation for Women (2011) *Women Entrepreneurs in Mobile Retail Channels: Empowering Women, Driving Growth* [pdf] <http:// www.cherieblairfoundation.org/wp-content/uploads/2012/07/

Women-Entrepreneurs-in-Mobile-Retail-Channels.pdf> [accessed 17 April 2019].

Coca-Cola Company (2017) *2016 Sustainability Report: Women's Economic Empowerment* [online] <https://www.coca-colacompany.com/stories/2016-womens-economic-empowerment> [accessed 2 May 2018].

De Santos, A. (2013) *The Women's Entrepreneurship Diagnostic* [pdf], USAID <https://pdf.usaid.gov/pdf_docs/pbaaa923.pdf> [accessed 15 May 2019].

Donor Committee for Enterprise Development (DCED) (2017) *Current Debates on Small Enterprise Development* [pdf] <https://www.enterprise-development.org/wp-content/uploads/DCED_SE_SynthesisNote.pdf> [accessed 17 April 2019].

DCED (no date) 'Why market development?' [online] <https://www.enterprise-development.org/what-works-and-why/evidence-framework/rationale-for-market-development/> [accessed 17 April 2019].

El-Zoghbi, M. (2015) 'False neutrality: ensuring policies and regulations benefit women', [blog], 15 September 2015, Washington, DC: CGAP <http://www.cgap.org/blog/false-neutrality-ensuring-policies-and-regulations-benefit-women> [accessed 17 April 2019].

European Diversity Research and Consulting (2012) 'Legal obligation to provide childcare in Jordan has not translated to reality, yet', [online], 2 April 2012 <http://en.diversitymine.eu/legal-obligation-to-provide-childcare-in-jordan-has-not-translated-to-reality-yet/> [accessed 17 April 2019].

Gennari, F., Arango, D. and Hidalgo, N. (2015) *Violence Against Women and Girls Resource Guide: Finance and Enterprise Development Brief*, Washington, DC: World Bank Group.

Global Entrepreneurship Monitor (GEM) (2018) 'How GEM defines entrepreneurship' [online] <http://www.gemconsortium.org/wiki/1149> [accessed 17 April 2019].

Grimm, M., Knorringa, P. and Lay, J. (2012) *Constrained Gazelles: High Potentials in West Africa's Informal Economy*, Washington, DC: World Bank.

Hallward-Driemeier, M. (2013) *Enterprising Women: Expanding Economic Opportunities in Africa*, Washington, DC: World Bank Publications.

Hendricks, L. and Loupeda, C. (2017) 'How women help women gain control of their financial lives', [blog], 19 July 2017, Center for Financial Inclusion <https://www.centerforfinancialinclusion.org/how-women-help-women-gain-control-of-their-financial-lives> [accessed 17 April 2019].

International Labour Organization (ILO) (2016) *Women at Work: Trends 2016*, Geneva: ILO.

Kabeer, N. (2017) *Women's Economic Empowerment and Inclusive Growth: Labour Markets and Enterprise Development* [pdf], McGill University and International Development Research Centre <https://www.idrc.ca/sites/default/files/sp/Documents%20EN/NK-WEE-Concept-Paper.pdf> [accessed 15 May 2019].

Kelley, D., Brush, C., Greene, P., Herrington, M., Ali, A. and Kew, P. (2015) *Global Entrepreneurship Monitor – Special Report: Women's Entrepreneurship* [online], GEM <https://gemconsortium.org/report/gem-2014-womens-report> [accessed 15 May 2019].

Kubzansky, M. and Cooper, A. (2013) *Direct Sales Agent Models in Health*, Bethesda, MD: SHOPS Project, Abt Associates.

Kumar, R. (2017) *Targeted SME Financing and Employment Effects: What Do We Know and What Can We Do Differently?* [pdf], Washington, DC: World Bank Group <http://documents.worldbank.org/curated/en/577091496733563036/pdf/115696-REVISED-PUBLIC-SMEs-and-Jobs-final.pdf> [accessed 17 April 2019].

Mennonite Economic Development Associates (MEDA) (2016) 'LWEE Client Stories, Waterloo, Canada: MEDA.

Mennonite Economic Development Associates (MEDA) (2018) 'Libya – women's economic empowerment' [online] <https://www.meda.org/gender-equality-and-social-inclusion-projects/582-libya-libya-economic-empowerment> [accessed 20 July 2019].

Militzer, J. (2013) 'Avon, Amway ... Africa?: Can the direct sales agent model work for health goods at the BoP? Part 2' [blog], NextBillion <https://nextbillion.net/avon-amway-africa/> [accessed 17 April 2019].

Murabit, A. (2015) 'Arming women for peace in Libya' [video], Oslo Freedom Forum <https://www.youtube.com/watch?v=hgaO6HBYA2w> [accessed 17 April 2019].

Organisation for Economic Co-operation and Development (OECD) (2013) *Exploring Bank Financing for Women Entrepreneurs in the MENA Region: Working Draft* [pdf] <http://www.eban.org/wp-content/uploads/2014/05/Bank-Finance.pdf> [accessed 17 April 2019].

OECD (2016) *SMEs in Libya's Reconstruction: Preparing for a Post-Conflict Economy*, Paris: OECD Publishing.

Page, J. and Söderbom, M. (2012) *Is Small Beautiful? Small Enterprise, Aid and Employment in Africa*, Helsinki, Finland: United Nations University – World Institute for Development Economics Research.

Patel, P. (2014) *Effectiveness of Entrepreneurship Development Interventions for Women Entrepreneurs*, Geneva: International Labour Organization.

Southern Africa Trade and Investment Hub (SATH) (2018) 'Empowering women with communications in Namibia' [online], Southern Africa Trade + Investment Hub <https://satradehub.org/component/content/article?id=507:empowering-women-with-communications-in-namibia> [accessed 17 April 2019].

Terjesen, S. and Lloyd, A. (2015) *The 2015 Female Entrepreneurship Index*, Washington, DC: Global Entrepreneurship and Development Institute.

United Nations Development Programme (UNDP) (2015) 'Human development reports, Libya country profile' [online] <http://hdr.undp.org/en/countries/profiles/LBY> [accessed 17 April 2019].

UN Foundation and ExxonMobil Foundation (2016) *A Roadmap for Promoting Women's Economic Empowerment* [pdf] <http://www.womeneconroadmap.org/sites/default/files/WEE_Roadmap_Report_Final.pdf> [accessed 17 April 2019].

United States Agency for International Development (USAID) (2016) Land Tenure and Women's Empowerment, Washington, DC: USAID.

World Bank (2015) *Women, Business and the Law 2016: Getting to Equal*, Washington, DC: World Bank.

World Bank (2017) 'The Global Findex database' [online] <https://globalfindex.worldbank.org/node> [accessed 22 March 2019].

World Bank (2019) *Women, Business and the Law 2019: A Decade of Reform* [pdf], <https://openknowledge.worldbank.org/bitstream/handle/10986/31327/WBL2019.pdf> [accessed 17 April 2019].

CHAPTER 8

Labour force participation: a pathway to greater equality

Sara Seavey

Abstract

This chapter discusses the sociocultural barriers and regulatory environment restrictions inhibiting women's formal and informal participation in the labour force and provides approaches, strategies, and tools for greater participation of women with decent work within a market system.

Keywords: gender equality, women's economic empowerment, labour force participation, unpaid care work, decent work, employment

Introduction

Yasmin was 23 years old when she was interviewed for a National Public Radio interactive story on the people who sewed and produced the Planet Money T-shirt in 2013 (Planet Money, 2013). She lives in a tiny one-room house with her brother, sister-in-law, and roommate in Dhaka, Bangladesh. There is no running water in the house, and the only appliance is a small gas stove. Yasmin leaves for work at 7 a.m., six days a week. She makes the equivalent of USD$80 a month in a garment factory job. Most of her pay cheque goes to her family. Yasmin keeps $10 for herself for food, or occasionally an impulse purchase. She began working in the garment industry when her family fell into debt after paying for her sister's dowry. Yasmin grew up in a small, rural village in Bangladesh where her family was worried about having enough food to go around. In villages like the one where Yasmin grew up, daughters are often seen as an economic burden, and this often results in early and forced child marriage. Bangladesh continues to have one of the highest child marriage rates worldwide as parents want their daughters married as soon as possible to reduce the financial strain felt by the family. In rural areas, child marriage is more prevalent, with 71 per cent of girls married before the age of 18, compared with 54 per cent in urban areas (Human Rights Watch, 2015). While the short-term solution to reducing the family burden is marriage, finding a good husband costs money.

http://dx.doi.org/10.3362/9781780447506.008

In Bangladesh as well as other countries, women's labour force participation is challenging social norms and expanding economic opportunities for women. For example, the UN Foundation notes that jobs for women such as those in the call centre industry in India and factory jobs in the garment industry in Bangladesh illustrate the positive impact on women themselves and how future generations of female children are affected. The potential for a wage-paying job raises the value of girls in disadvantaged communities, changing traditional gender norms and reshaping family spending on both female and male children (Jensen, 2010). Girls' school enrolment has risen faster in Bangladeshi villages that are within commuting distance of garment factories, where most workers are female. No such effect was observed among boys (Heath and Mobarak, 2011).

Yasmin is one out of 4 million people in Bangladesh working in the garment sector, which is double the amount in the previous decade. Garment production in Bangladesh is a $28 bn industry – 12 per cent of national GDP – and the country is the second-largest supplier of clothes behind China (Akhter, 2017). Despite working long hours at a monotonous low-wage job, Yasmin prefers working at her current factory because she feels safer and the working conditions are better than the other factories where she has worked in the past. The job also offers her more benefits than staying in her local village with her family and is an improvement over the impoverished conditions she experienced there.

Employment provides women with opportunities, not only for increased income, but also for the chance to break the intergenerational cycle of poverty. However, with new opportunities come systemic risks, such as issues with 'decent' and safe work environments. The 2013 Rana Plaza tragedy in Bangladesh – when an eight-storey factory building collapsed, killing more than 1,100 people and injuring 2,000 others – was one example of the horrific working conditions for factory employees and the need for improved transparency, work conditions, wages, and representation around the supply chain. Despite this tragedy, Yasmin and other women in Bangladesh and beyond fear a lack of jobs over poor working conditions. As Dr Frank Hoffer of Action, Collaboration, Transformation shared during a 2018 workshop after the tragic incident, 'For the past 150 years, from Manchester to Myanmar, the garment industry has been shaped by a search for desperate young women, who would rather work 14 hour days than be in poverty in the village' (Evans, 2018).

Labour force participation and women

If women played an identical role in labour markets to that of men, it has been estimated that as much as $28 tn could be added to the global annual GDP by 2025 – a 26 per cent increase from 2015 (McKinsey Global Institute, 2015). International Labour Organization (ILO) (2017) discloses that global tax revenue could increase by $1.5 tn, most of it in emerging ($990 bn) and developed ($530 bn) economies. The greatest benefits would be seen in northern Africa, the Arab States, and southern Asia, as the participation gaps between men and women in these regions exceed 50 percentage points (ILO, 2017). Despite efforts for gender parity by government, civil society, business, and international organizations, the change in terms of the structural and sociocultural barriers and behaviours have been slow to non-existent in developing economies. Women tend to be concentrated in low-earning sectors, and are paid on average 24 per cent less than men globally for the same work. Women also make up a significant percentage of the informal workforce and are responsible for two-and-a-half times more care and domestic work in their families and communities. The burden of care work is not only unpaid but severely restricts women's time, preventing them from finding better employment or acquiring skills that could lead to better employment. Regardless of the type of work performed, women everywhere encounter widespread violence and harassment at home and in the workplace (ILO, 2016).

According to the ILO, the term 'labour force' refers to a country's legal working-age population that is actively engaged in work or is seeking active engagement in work. This definition obfuscates women's participation in the labour forces, however, as many face economic, sociocultural, and regulatory barriers that prevent them from full labour force participation. *The Global Gender Gap Report* reveals that globally 54 per cent of working-age women take part in the formal economy, on average, compared with 81 per cent of men. Women make up a larger proportion of discouraged job seekers and of those outside the labour force. On average, women's unemployment rate is nearly 2 per cent higher globally (World Economic Forum, 2016). According to the ILO, labour underutilization is the combination of unemployed people; those in the formal labour force who are not employed but actively searching for available work; and the potential labour force, those that are not part of the labour force and are not seeking work or are not able to obtain work due to conditions limiting their active job search or availability (ILO, n.d.).

In developing and emerging markets, working-age women in the labour force are either formal sector employees (where they earn a salary and receive social security, regulated by labour law) or informal workers of enterprises that are not regulated who are not legally protected. For women working in the formal sector, finding 'decent' employment can be difficult as these jobs are often low paying and menial. 'Decent work', according to the ILO, is productive work for women and men in conditions of freedom, equity, security, and human dignity. Decent work guarantees equal opportunity and treatment for all, provides security in the workplace and protections for workers and their families, a fair income, and better prospects for personal development and social inclusion (ILO, n.d.). Women in developing economies may have few opportunities to take work that is considered decent as those types of jobs may be the only opportunities that are open to them, and not earning an income is simply not an option.

For women working in the informal sector, this work is often stigmatized, and even criminalized. Most women in emerging and developing economies are performing informal work, not by choice but by the lack of opportunities in the formal economy and an absence of other means of livelihood. Informal employment constitutes more than one half of non-agricultural employment in most regions of the developing world (ILO, 2016). Whether informal or formal, there are a myriad of economic, sociocultural, and regulatory conditions that prohibit a woman's ability to access decent work; participate in decisions that affect their lives by advancing into leadership positions; have the freedom to express their concerns, especially regarding discrimination, sexual harassment, or unsafe work conditions; and organize and have their voices heard.

Challenges facing women in labour force participation

Inclusive labour force participation involves four key dimensions to promote market system change: equal access to decent work opportunities; equal access to advancement; equal pay for equal work; and the prevention of sexual harassment. All four of these dimensions need to be addressed at the systems level to achieve inclusive and equitable gender participation in the work environment. However, not all market systems development (MSD) programmes that target labour force participation will need to address all four dimensions, and different contexts will require different combinations of these dimensions to be addressed.

The sociocultural context surrounding women's labour force participation is an important part of the enabling environment as it forms the basis for gender norms. Gender norms are the socially constructed ideas about how men and women should behave and are internalized early in life and socialized through institutions such as family, school, religion, and community. These gender norms are often the source for gender-based constraints, factors that inhibit men's or women's access to resources, behaviours, and participation, time use, mobility, rights, and the exercise of power based on gender identity. They impact women's economic participation (including time allocation and division of labour), as well as their physical safety, mobility, access to training, and other opportunities for advancement and employment. Before finding employment, women deal with sociocultural issues of perceptions of hiring personnel, family expectations, mobility constraints, and acceptability of jobs. These constraints impact a woman's preference and choice to participate in the labour force, her ability to access better pay and status, and her opportunity for decent work and advancement.

Below are the three main MSD challenges facing women in the labour force in developing economies:

- Heavy family and care responsibilities, and a lack of flexibility by private sector employers and businesses in either their hours or maternity/paternity leave policies.
- The need for societal acceptance for labour force participation by family, community, employers, and businesses.

- Discrimination and stereotypes with respect to gender roles and abilities, including the lack of legal rights, restrictive laws and policies to
work in certain sectors, and lack of enforcement of gender equality laws.

The following sections will dive further into these challenges.

Family/care responsibilities

Women's responsibility for unpaid care work is the key underlying barrier
to women's labour force participation in developing economies. ILO (2016)
shows that the burden of unpaid care work contributes to a wide array of
labour market inequalities. Women with jobs typically work a greater number
of hours in total than men because of the double burden of paid work and
unpaid domestic responsibilities. Women who are less able to undertake paid
economic activities are pushed further into poverty (USAID, 2015). According
to UN Women, women carry out at least two-and-a-half times more unpaid
household and care work than men in both developing and developed countries (UN Women, 2017a). Research also shows that this imbalance starts early,
with girls spending 30 per cent more of their time on unpaid care work than
boys (UNICEF, 2016).

This invisible unpaid care work is essential for any country's economy to
function. Summarizing findings in *Counting on Care Work: Human Infrastructure
in Massachusetts*, Ansel shares that:

> Many economists call care work the 'human infrastructure.' Just as we
> depend on the bridges, roads, and railways that make up our physical
> infrastructure for society to function, we rely on the support of those
> caring for the elderly and nurturing the young (Ansel, 2016).

Care work impacts women's ability to be involved in paid employment,
unless support systems within their family, community, or employer exist.
Policies such as flexible working arrangements, affordable care for children
and the elderly, and affordable healthcare can support both men and women
and strengthen society and the economy.

A 2016 study in Kenya by the Growth and Economic Opportunities
for Women (GrOW) programme, a research initiative involving Canada's
International Development Research Centre (IDRC), the United Kingdom's
Department for International Development (DFID), and The William and
Flora Hewlett Foundation, found that subsidized access to childcare increased
women's economic participation. It stated that the percentage of working
mothers increased from 48.9 per cent among those without free childcare to
57.4 per cent among mothers with subsidized childcare (IDRC, 2017). The
8.5 per cent increase brings mothers closer to the levels of male participation
in the labour force in an environment where jobs and income-generating
activities are hard to come by. When the care burden is reduced, women are
more mobile and feel less tied down by the stresses and conflict over what is
happening at home. Women are then able to work and/or access and develop

their skills – both technical and soft – through training. These opportunities improve a woman's chances for career advancement and her ability to increase and control her income, which ultimately impacts her agency (intra-household decision making and negotiation), self-confidence, leadership, and status within her family and society.

Societal acceptance

In many countries, women attempting to enter the labour market must have approval from their husbands, from their family, or from their community, especially if there is a culture of shame that exists around certain industries and sectors. Societal acceptance is predicated on gender norms that view women as vulnerable and in need of protection to preserve their sexual and reproductive health, as it is their responsibility to care for children and their household. ILO findings show that having a spouse or partner reduces the probability of women participating in labour markets in Arab States and Northern Africa (ASNA) countries and other developing contexts (ILO, 2017).

Societal acceptance is also a factor in a woman's ability to choose a sector and field to work in. According to UN Women, sectoral and occupational segregation is a consequence of structural barriers and gender-based discrimination, such as poverty, inflexible working hours, limited or no access to affordable quality childcare, poor parental leave policies, and social attitudes, among many other factors (UN Women, 2017a). Here the sectoral and occupational segregation varies greatly by region and income level. In high-income countries, women are concentrated in health, education, wholesale, and retail trade sectors, whereas in low-income and lower-middle-income countries women are concentrated in agricultural labour (ILO, 2016). Women tend to go into sectors that are often considered 'women's work' or where the workforce is predominantly women because those sectors have already received societal acceptance. These sectors, however, tend to have lower paying job opportunities. Another barrier for women in the labour force is the lack of role models across all industries, which is due to women's historically low participation in the labour market. Families and communities fear women in majority-male workplaces, such as construction, mining, and engineering occupations, as they fear women will be exposed to higher rates of sexual harassment, discrimination, or even violence.

Societal acceptance can also be seen in the structures and practices of the private sector employers. Again, this is due to gender norms. The gender norms at play are the dual burden of caregiving and breadwinning, unconscious bias, and traditional organizational practices in the workplace. In the workplace, women earn as little as 20 per cent – but never higher than 80 per cent – of what men earn on average, depending on the country (World Bank, 2012). In sub-Saharan Africa and South Asia, the gender pay gap is 31 per cent and 35 per cent, respectively, for women with children, compared with 4 per cent and 14 per cent for women without children. UN Women calls this the motherhood penalty (UN Women, 2017a).

Women's mobility is a gender-based constraint and barrier to her labour participation. The ILO states that women's limited access to safe transportation is the greatest challenge to participation that women face in developing economies, reducing their participation probability by almost 16 per cent (Tobin, 2017). However, strategies can be developed to mitigate these gender-based constraints. One strategy is for a business to pay the first month's wage upfront or in weekly instalments rather than at the end of the month to ensure employees have access to cash for transport. While this is not a women-specific issue, one could argue that poor women face greater challenges to appropriate transportation than men as their lower income compounds their geographic exclusion from jobs and good public services. To encourage women's participation, businesses could also consider subsidizing transportation costs or assisting women employees by arranging transport if female employees are working late or night shifts, as transport at those times can be expensive, difficult to arrange, and potentially unsafe.

Women face insensitivity with respect to gender concerns (such as female-friendly facilities), perception of co-workers and managers over hours available for work outside the home, and sexual harassment. When women get jobs in fields with men, they are often paid less due to misconceptions about their abilities. These private sector employers lack formalized workplace policies and procedures preventing sexual discrimination and ensuring gender equity. Therefore, their conscious or unconscious bias put women in lower positions with lower pay than their male counterparts. When women lack opportunity for advancement within positions and lack access to equal pay for equal work, it is a signal to other women within the company that women are inferior to men.

Structural barriers of laws, policies, and rules

The ILO reports that the current global labour force participation rate for women is close to 49 per cent. For men, it's 75 per cent. That's a difference of 26 percentage points, with some regions facing a gap of more than 50 percentage points (ILO, n.d.). It is no surprise that women's labour force participation is lower than men when you look at the regulatory barriers to women's labour participation. The World Bank (Iqbal, 2018) reports that 104 countries have laws preventing women from working in specific jobs, such as mining (65), manufacturing (47), construction (37), energy (29), agriculture (27), water (26), and transportation (21). In Pakistan, a general misconception is that women are not capable of operating machinery. In Pakistan, a general misconception is that women are not capable of operating machinery; for example, The World Bank highlights Pakistan's regulations that prohibit women from working on, or even in the same room as machinery with moving part. Eighteen countries have regulations that allow husbands to legally prevent women from working. Other legal barriers include restricting the number of hours, especially at night, and lowering overtime limits for women workers as in Taiwan's 1984 Labour Standards Law. The lack of formal legal protections can similarly prevent women from accessing opportunities for decent work; 123 countries have no laws prohibiting sexual harassment in education and 59 countries have no law pertaining to sexual harassment in the workplace (World Bank Group, 2016). All these regulatory and structural barriers compound patriarchal norms for men, and limit women's access to opportunity for decent work.

It is also important to consider formal laws, policies, rules, legal systems, and national bureaucracies as these formal structures reflect countries' national values, norms, and commitments towards gender equality. If there are no national bureaucracies around gender equality, then there are no commitments to changing public structures around gender equality. The strength of a country's legal system is especially important; if a country has a pluralistic legal system considering both laws and customs, often laws can be negated by deeply entrenched sociocultural customs. This can be seen in Nigeria, where the tripartite legal system, which includes three bodies of law (statutory, customary, and sharia), has led to non-enforcement of international and federal commitments to eliminate all forms of discrimination against women. Even though Nigeria signed the Convention on the Elimination of All Forms of Discrimination against Women (CEDAW) in 1985, the discrimination of women based on customary and sharia law is still widespread in many parts of the country.

UN Women contends that the lack of law enforcement remains a major challenge, even in countries where women have legal protection and rights. Weak implementation by the authorities, low awareness among rights-holders and those responsible for implementing the law, and constraints on women's access to legal resources all limit enforcement of existing laws and undermine effective legal protection (UN Women, 2017a). As shown in the Nigeria example, if enforcement is weak, often restrictive sociocultural norms prevail. This limits women's economic empowerment and the desire by both the public and private sectors to adopt new and inclusive practices and behaviours towards women. Regulatory barriers impact and interfere with women and girl's access and ability to learn, study, and work in labour force development and their overall sense of agency and autonomy.

Mainstreaming women in labour force participation initiatives

To illustrate different ways to mainstream women into the labour force, this section will be divided into three parts. The first section focuses on how actors on the supply side can help upgrade women's skills and abilities in workforce and labour force initiatives. The second section highlights issues of the demand side, and how private sector employers can integrate gender considerations, host ongoing dialogue and awareness-raising, and target women in their workforce development initiatives. To address the scale and complexity of labour force participation, gendered research and analysis is necessary. Therefore, the last section focuses on the importance of data-specific information and analysis using systems tools and resources. Sex-disaggregated data, especially around participation and retention, is essential to understanding what is working and how to track progress.

Supply programming

In many developing economies, the supply side of the labour market (education and training) is carried out by the public sector. Many in the private sector fear that this education is not preparing youth, specifically women, with the required skills needed for gainful employment. Airing and Goldmark argue that economic development strategies, education systems, and employers need to provide greater input into workforce development systems, especially to meet the needs of target groups such as women (Airing and Goldmark, 2013). This trend has been the focus of the 2017 World Economic Forum's (WEF) Global Gender Gap Index, as there is an ever-increasing number of educated women who are not participating in the labour force. An additional explanatory factor – as well as unpaid reproductive work, discrimination, and bad enabling environments – is the skills differentials in the types of educational degrees that women and men seek. WEF asks: do these choices prepare women adequately for prospering in the labour market to the same extent as their male counterparts? How do you orient the human side of supply to be more market-focused? How can you integrate, target, and bring gender awareness to school-to-work programmes and vocational training to encourage women's participation in the labour force? (World Economic Forum, 2017).

The public sector must link with the private sector to incorporate demand needs and principles into education and vocational training. Educational institutions should communicate with employers about skills that are in demand, solicit feedback on their graduates, and act on this information to inform educational practice (Workforce Connections, 2014). This feedback can help address what employers call the 'skills mismatch'. The public sector can also assist in improving women's access to necessary skills, aptitudes, and experiences to close the gender gap.

United States Agency for International Development's (USAID) EQUIP3 project, a nine-year programme designed to improve earning, learning, and skill development opportunities for out-of-school youth in developing economies, showed that fewer female youth completed training programmes. Their review of 26 projects showed that 59 per cent of males completed work readiness training versus 40 per cent of females; 64.7 per cent of males completed vocational training versus 35.3 per cent of females; and 56 per cent of males completed entrepreneurship training versus 44 per cent of females (USAID EQUIP3, 2012). Participation (access to training and its quality) and retention is a large issue for women entering the labour force. To encourage women's labour participation, work readiness training should integrate gender-sensitive content, target women in growing sectors, and build awareness and dialogue on rights – especially sexual harassment and local labour laws – with students and partners in the private sector.

Universities and vocational technical training schools track and collect gendered data about students and graduates so that they can understand trends in the labour market and design strategies to better target, reach, and prepare women for the skills and challenges they may face in the workplace. Training should continue to include technical competencies, a set of job-related skills, knowledge, and abilities that are necessary for successfully performing in a specific job function, and behavioural competencies (sometimes also referred to as 'soft skills'), a set of behaviours based on individual values, personal attributes, attitudes, habits, and experiences that are necessary for success more generally in the workplace. These behavioural competencies include dependability, flexibility/adaptability, higher order cognitive skills (such as problem solving, critical thinking, and decision making), and inter- and intra-personal skills. Training should also provide students with opportunities to learn by doing. This can be accomplished through occupational skills training and summer employment opportunities linked to academic and occupational learning such as internships, apprenticeships, and job shadowing. Below are some strategies to improve women's access to such training and to improve the quality of that training to meet women's needs and ensure their participation.

Universities and vocational technical institutes should adopt a career centre model as a place to advise women and men on career readiness, job searching, access to training, potential career paths, and opportunities to network with role models, mentors, and other professionals, particularly alumni. Information for the career centres should be based on reliable market information on relevant economic trends, job opportunities, and entry-level skills requirements. Centres can provide skill seekers with positive role models, build awareness that women are in these fields, reinforce confidence, and help students adopt positive behaviours.

Information on career paths should be provided to students and their parents, who often try to influence their children into safe positions in the government (which may not exist). This information will guide young women on the courses of study and their associated career pathways, resulting in improved decision making and more realistic aspirations. For vocational technical training schools, similar coordination is necessary. Centres of excellence are public–private partnerships that feature stakeholders from government, education, and the private sector. These stakeholders work towards a common vision to provide the best technical skills for the workforce. Training in centres of excellence should be open and accessible for all.

Due to restrictive social norms, university and vocational technical institutes should consider providing female-only training to increase women's access to training and knowledge. USAID highlights the necessity for universities and vocational technical training institutions to be safe places for students to participate comfortably. Therefore, it may be necessary to separate female and male students in conservative contexts. Additionally, an appropriate balance of male and female trainers is necessary to ensure that women and men are comfortable and participating actively. Familial approval, the presence of same-sex trainers and mentors, and distance from home should all be considered when selecting locations for programme activities (USAID EQUIP3, 2012). Awareness-raising and dialogue with families and students can take place during training on labour force development.

Demand programming

When gender is mainstreamed into private sector operations it helps produce new social norms and creates a new inclusive enabling environment that is gender equitable for women in the labour force. The private sector can take the following steps, outlined in the UN Secretary-General's High-Level Panel on Women's Economic Empowerment report, *Leave No One Behind: Taking Action for Transformational Change on Women's Economic Empowerment* (UN Women, 2017b), to improve business operations for women employees and make meaningful progress towards closing the gender gap:

- Adopt policies/procedures/processes that protect employees from discrimination and improve the enabling environment for women.
- Develop internal mechanisms to track employment and social practices that are flexible and recognize women's care work.
- Hold discussions with staff on adverse gender norms to change the business culture and practice.
- Strengthen visibility, collective voice, and representation with positive role models.

Policies, practices, regulations, and procedures should be founded on gender-based analysis to ensure equal outcomes for women. To gather gender-based data, a business can use tools such as a gender audit to advise the organization on its gender policy and subsequent policies and procedures that form part of an overall gender strategy. Audits allow an organization to gauge how gender is mainstreamed across organizational processes, procedures, and perceptions. It is key for businesses to ensure that these surveys are anonymous, and that staff interviewed are representative of the organization. It can also include a gender pay gap analysis to identify and explicate the causes of other types of organizational gender pay gaps. If such gaps exist, action plans should be developed to ensure that issues are properly resourced.

A gender equality policy should highlight the company's commitments to supporting gender equality in its operations, organizational resources, and monitoring and evaluation mechanisms. It should also highlight the company's policies related to discrimination and sexual harassment in the workplace. In many countries, discrimination and sexual harassment in the workplace deter women from entering or staying in the formal economy. Gender equality policies and procedures can provide flexible work schedules or on-site childcare for women to increase their participation.

Policies and procedures alone do not create a gender-sensitive enabling environment for female employees. Businesses should also build systems to increase transparency and accountability, as well as increase investment in tracking employment and the collection of data related to hiring female employees. Data points to focus on in this data collection include: the types of roles women are recruited for (e.g. entry-level, mid-manager, or executive leadership team), the length of the employment contract (e.g. part-time, full-time, or contract), and features that are most attractive to female employees (e.g. daytime working hours or flexible working hours).

By mapping and monitoring management, businesses can begin to measure their performance in mainstreaming gender into their operations. They can also measure retention and capacity building within their business to ensure that they are not losing talent. Businesses should also increase their measurement and monitoring of gender equity in the rollout or implementation of human resource policies, including compensation policies, distribution of incentives, and training opportunities. If a business does not have a human resources department, a focal person within the organization can work with management to mainstream gender equity strategies into the business operations. This performance measure can also be used in tracking suppliers and helping the organization share success stories to inspire others.

In the recruitment and promotion process, businesses should consider at least one woman and one under-represented minority in the slate of candidates, especially for manager-level positions. Businesses can also implement blind screenings by removing names (or other gender identifiers) from résumés when selecting candidates for interviews to eliminate any chance of implicit gender bias.

Along with performance management systems, businesses should develop a human capital manual that standardizes job descriptions, pay scales, and annual job performance evaluations. Gender equality should be included in job description and performance criteria, as it is an organizational commitment for all staff. This helps ensure that performance measurement is based on merit. Included in the human capital manual are career pathways that outline the criteria required for promotion and advancement opportunities with the organization, including the required training, education, and experience.

Related to career pathways, businesses should aim to increase women's access to training through mentorship and sponsorship opportunities. It is important to provide women within a business with role models and mentors who can serve as coaches and sounding boards that provide advice, guidance, and support. Sponsors go further by requiring that the organization advocates to create opportunities for advancement for high-potential women and publicly declare their commitment within a company and outside in the community. Specialized training programmes, such as the ones mentioned above, have a high rate of return according to Dr Rohini Anand of Sodexo. In a Sodexo study, training programmes, workshops, and intentional hiring practices enhanced organizational engagement, productivity, and retention. Businesses should also link female employees with women's associations and networks to build their capacities and professional contacts (Durkee, 2017).

The private sector can invest in initiatives to reduce and redistribute unpaid care and work, such as family-friendly policies around maternity/paternity leave and free or subsidized childcare. Employers often believe a lack of work-life balance is a key deterrent to women's participation at work. This factor appears to influence all industries (World Economic Forum, 2017). Companies that invest in family-friendly, gender-responsive policies have found high returns on their investments, including reduced absenteeism and increased productivity. By providing healthcare for women and their children at the workplace, studies in Bangladesh and Egypt point to a $3 to $1 and $4 to $1, respectively, return on investment (Iversen, 2017). Employers should provide both maternal and parental leave in their policies and outline these policies in their human resource materials. Paternity leave also encourages men to be more involved at home and redistributes the care burden to allow women to be involved at work. As noted above, childcare programmes increase women's access to employment, with the emphasis on the need for affordable, cost-effective, and high-quality care. Therefore, organizations and businesses should also consider providing subsidized or free childcare. Investing in such policies and social protection systems develops an enabling environment for women to enter and thrive in labour markets. Additionally, flexible schedules are a consideration for employers, as women joining the workforce will often choose one sector over another based on their flexible schedules, especially if there are no support systems for childcare.

To encourage inclusive business culture and practice, dialogue with staff on adverse gender norms is necessary. Regular gender sensitization for all staff, particularly managers and decision makers, on issues related to gender equality concerns, especially women's participation and advancement in the labour force, is important. Sensitization should highlight implicit bias and major labour regulation, as well as ensure that staff are aware of the organizational gender equality policy and commitments.

Businesses can challenge stereotypes through their advertising and media communications by using gender-neutral terms, ensuring that gender balance is maintained in communication material, and by portraying the diverse roles of both women and men in the labour force. Businesses can also highlight and promote positive role modelling of economically empowered women and leaders. One of the gender-based constraints is the lack of successful role models to serve as an example for other women. These topics can also be discussed during gender sensitization.

Tools and resources for labour force participation

To understand the impact of the enabling environment – formal and informal – and the state of the market system, it is important to use tools that capture the interrelations, multiple perspectives, and boundaries of a workforce development system. The tools below show how stakeholders and institutions interact and engage, are affected by policy, and show areas for alignment, especially in the supply and demand of skills and demand of the labour market. A gender lens should be applied to examine the gender roles, norms, constraints, and barriers to women entering the labour force; to observe the underlying social structures, policies, and norms that perpetuate gender inequalities; and to identify opportunities to promote equality.

In *Women's Empowerment and Market Systems: Concepts, Practical Guidance and Tools* (WEAMS Framework), Jones (2016) describes gender mainstreaming as a three-pronged approach. This approach entails integrating gender in all planning phases and processes by incorporating gender-aware research, analysis, planning, implementation, monitoring, and evaluation; using targeted strategies to enhance integration efforts over the longer term; and internalizing dialogue by implementing organizations, partners, and other stakeholders.

Understanding women's labour force participation requires practitioners to shift their mindsets and build awareness of the labour force system. The structure and conditions of this system are based on relationships and networks, interdependencies that show demand and supply are interconnected. Therefore, labour market assessments should include gendered lenses from gender analysis to systems tools such as institutional systems maps and causal loop analysis, highlighted below.

Labour market assessments should outline stakeholders – including policy makers, private sector employers, education and training providers, students, parents, and others – that make up the ecosystem of labour force participation. Institutional systems maps show the key public and private actors, highlighting their interactions, where power is located, who can influence decisions, and, ultimately, who makes decisions. The purpose of this exercise is to identify opportunities to improve a system's overall performance by strengthening weak connections or filling gaps in the system. Some actors may not appear to be a stakeholder but may wield influence over the initiative and ultimate outcome.

Causal loop analysis is a tool that can provide practitioners, funders, and researchers with a comprehensive picture of the complexity and non-linear relationship of labour force participation and workforce development. It forces the individual to be problem-oriented, to think about the variables of the system, and to understand how the variables link to each other and affect each other. Causal loop analysis can show if gender-based constraints are reinforcing or changing the conditions and structures (i.e. enabling environment) for women's participation and the behaviour of the market towards gender norms. Awareness of the full system, gained by using systems tools in labour market assessments, informs actors in the better design of international development projects or decisions in labour force and workforce investments. Awareness of the system also allows stakeholders in the system to make informed choices, such as deciding which field to study for their personal careers; or for the public and private sectors to know in which areas to invest, which will ultimately allow the actors to influence and change the labour force system around them.

USAID's TOPS Program, funded by the Office of Food for Peace and implemented by Food for the Hungry, Food Security and Nutrition Network, and the Core Group, highlights the need to conduct a barrier analysis for food security and behaviour change programmes to identify why a promoted behaviour has low coverage or has not been adopted at all. A similar rapid barrier analysis could be applied to employers and employees in the labour force to understand the necessary positive actions required to change behaviours and reduce barriers to women's participation.

Case study: Macrosentra and gendered labour force development

Under the USAID Asia and Middle East Economic Growth Best Practices (AMEG) project, Mennonite Economic Development Associates (MEDA) partnered with local investment funds and small and medium enterprises (SMEs) to evaluate and upgrade gender practices within business operations. As part of AMEG, MEDA awarded $40,000 to Macrosentra Niagaboga (MN), which is part of the Cimory Group, a family business in Indonesia focused on consumer goods, such as processed meats, eggs, dairy, and soy products. MN received technical assistance support to mainstream improved practices around hiring, upgrading, and promoting women. Under the pilot, MN invested in developing a performance management system, establishing a mentorship programme for career development for female employees, and conducting gender sensitization for their staff. MEDA's investment pilot provided MN with an effective means to meet their demands for skills and improving business performance, while also enabling women to acquire knowledge, skills, and attitudes for gainful employment and advancement.

As noted in the programming section above, it is important for private sector companies like MN to track their employment and collect sex-disaggregated data to analyse promotions, retention, absenteeism, and resignations by women and men. Through technical support from local consultants and MEDA staff, MN was able to develop an employee diversity performance management system. This database tracks sex-disaggregated human resources data to allow managers to identify gender imbalances within various departments and levels of the company. As a result of this initiative, MN learned that women outperform men, especially in lower-level positions. MN's senior management have since established an action plan to conduct quarterly reviews of sex-disaggregated data to make more informed hiring and promotion decisions that improve gender equality. It also enables MN to better understand its baseline, as it set targets to increase its total workforce from 22 per cent women staff to 35 per cent, over the period 2017–19.

The performance management system has increased transparency around career development, providing clear guidance on the requisite experience and competence for both women and men employees for future promotion. The establishment of the career development programme provides specialized training to women within MN to understand the knowledge, skills, and attitudes required for advancement through a mentorship programme. This specialized training for interested employees involves biweekly mentorship sessions with their line managers that will expand their knowledge and skills while also expanding their growth within the company.

The last workforce investment conducted by MN, under the $40,000 investment, was to launch its first-ever training programme for staff in gender sensitization. MN trained 398 employees in gender awareness, 402 employees in induction and career development, and 241 employees on gendered division-specific topics, such as human capital, sales, finance, and procurement.

Useful resources

Gereffi, G., Fernandez-Stark, K., Psilos, P. and RTI International, *Skills for Upgrading: Workforce Development and Global Value Chains in Developing Countries*: https://d3n8a8pro7vhmx.cloudfront.net/fhi360/pages/213/attachments/original/1409156819/Skills-for-Upgrading-Workforce-Development-and-GVC-in-Developing-Countries_FullBook.compressed.pdf?1409156819

International Labour Organization's (ILO) InfoStories, 'The gender gap in employment: what's holding women back?' http://ilo.org/infostories/en-GB/Stories/Employment/barriers-women#intro

Rockefeller Foundation and Making Cents International, Demand-Driven Training for Youth Employment Toolkit: https://youtheconomicopportunities.org/DDTtoolkit

The United Nations Foundation and the ExxonMobil Foundation: *A Roadmap for Promoting Women's Economic Empowerment* http://www.womeneconroadmap.org/sites/default/files/WEE_Roadmap_Report_Final.pdf

UN Secretary-General's High-Level Panel on Women's Economic Empowerment, Reports and Toolkits: http://hlp-wee.unwomen.org/en/reports-toolkits#toolkits

Workplace Gender Equality Agency, Australian Government, Gender Strategy Toolkit https://www.wgea.gov.au/sites/default/files/Gender_Strategy_Toolkit.pdf

World Bank Group, *Women, Business and the Law 2019*: http://wbl.worldbank.org/

References

Airing, M. and Goldmark, L. (2013) *Skills for Jobs for Growth: Effective Human Capital Development in a Changing World of Work*, FIELD Report No. 17, Washington, DC: FIELD-Support LWA.

Akhter, A. (2017) 'An overview of Bangladesh RMG 2016', [online], Textile Today <https://www.textiletoday.com.bd/overview-bangladesh-rmg-2016/> [accessed 18 April 2019].

Ansel, B. (2016) 'This is the extent of the gender gap in unpaid work', [blog], 20 September 2016, World Economic Forum <https://www.weforum.org/agenda/2016/09/this-is-the-extent-of-the-gender-gap-in-unpaid-work> [accessed 18 April 2018].

Durkee, R. (2017) 'Four benefits gained from women's equality in the workplace: introducing The Modern Guide to Equality', [blog], 17 January 2017, Medium <https://medium.com/digital-trends-index/four-benefits-gained-from-womens-equality-in-the-workplace-5f13e320ff7c> [accessed 20 July 2019].

Evans, Alice (@_alice_evans). "For the past 150 years, from Manchester to Myanmar, the garment industry has been shaped by a search for desperate young women, who would rather work 14hr days than be in poverty in the village" - Dr Frank Hoffer (ACT)." 27 Apr 2018, 5:46 AM.

Heath, R. and Mobarak, M. (2011) 'Supply and demand constraints on educational investment: evidence from garment sector jobs and the female stipend program in Bangladesh', unpublished manuscript.

Human Rights Watch (2015) '"Marry before your house is swept away": child marriage in Bangladesh' [online] <https://www.hrw.org/world-report/2016/photo-essay-child-marriage-bangladesh> [accessed 20 July 2019].

International Development Research Centre (IDRC) (2017) 'Could affordable daycare be the key to unlocking women's earning power in Africa', [blog], 17 October 2017 <https://www.idrc.ca/en/stories/could-affordable-day-care-be-key-unlocking-womens-earning-power-africa?platform=hootsuite> [accessed 20 July 2019].

International Labour Organization (ILO) (2016) Women at Work: Trends 2016 [pdf] <http://www.ilo.org/wcmsp5/groups/public/---dgreports/---dcomm/---publ/documents/publication/wcms_457317.pdf> [accessed 20 July 2019].

ILO (2017) 'The gender gap in employment: what's holding women back?' [online], Infostories <http://ilo.org/infostories/Stories/Employment/barriers-women?utm_content=buffercb5b5andutm_medium=socialand utm_source=twitter.comandutm_campaign=buffer#header> [accessed 18 April 2018].

ILO (no date) 'Decent work' [online] <http://www.ilo.org/global/topics/decent-work/lang--en/index.htm> [accessed 20 July 2019].

Iqbal, S. (2018) Women, Business, and the Law 2018 [online], Washington, DC: World Bank <http://documents.worldbank.org/curated/en/926401524803880673/pdf/125804-PUB-REPLACEMENT-PUBLIC.pdf> [accessed 20 July 2019].

Iversen, K. (2017) '7 myth-busting reasons we should be investing in women', [blog], 1 February 2017, World Economic Forum <https://www.weforum.org/agenda/2017/02/7-myth-busting-reasons-we-should-be-investing-in-women/> [accessed 20 July 2019].

Jensen, R. (2010) 'The (perceived) returns to education and the demand for schooling', Quarterly Journal of Economics 125(2): 515–48 <https://doi.org/10.1162/qjec.2010.125.2.515>.

Jones, L. (2016) The WEAMS Framework – Women's Empowerment and Markets Systems: Concepts, Practical Guidance and Tools [pdf], London: The BEAM Exchange <https://beamexchange.org/uploads/

filer_public/0d/50/0d5009be-faea-4b8c-b191-c40c6bde5394/weams_frame-work.pdf> [accessed 19 June 2017].

McKinsey Global Institute (2015) 'The power of parity: how advancing women's equality can add $12 trillion to global growth' [online] <https://www.mckinsey.com/global-themes/employment-and-growth/how-advancing-womens-equality-can-add-12-trillion-to-global-growth> [accessed 18 April 2019].

Planet Money (2013) *People: The Lives of the Workers Who Made Our Shirts* [online], National Public Radio <http://apps.npr.org/tshirt/#/people> [accessed 20 July 2019].

Tobin, S. (2017) 'What causes gender gaps in the labour market?', [blog], 1 August 2017, ILO <http://www.ilo.org/global/about-the-ilo/newsroom/news/WCMS_566891/lang--en/index.htm> [accessed 18 April 2018].

UNICEF (2016) *Harnessing the Power of Data for Girls: Taking Stock and Looking Ahead to 2030* [pdf] <https://www.unicef.org/gender/files/Harnessing-the-Power-of-Data-for-Girls-Brochure-2016-1-1.pdf> [accessed 20 July 2019].

UN Women (2017a) 'Women in the changing world of work: facts you should know' [online] <http://interactive.unwomen.org/multimedia/infographic/changingworldofwork/en/index.html> [accessed 20 July 2019].

UN Women (2017b) *Leave No One Behind: Taking Action for Transformational Change on Women's Economic Empowerment* [pdf], Report of the UN Secretary-General's High-Level Panel on Women's Economic Empowerment <http://www2.unwomen.org/-/media/hlp%20wee/attachments/reports-toolkits/hlp-wee-report-2017-03-taking-action-en.pdf?la=enandvs=5226> [accessed 20 July 2019].

USAID (2015) *Gender and Extreme Poverty: Getting to Zero: A USAID Discussion Series* [pdf] <https://2012-2017.usaid.gov/sites/default/files/documents/1870/Gender_Extreme_Poverty_Discussion_Paper.pdf> [accessed 18 April 2018].

USAID EQUIP3 (2012) *Gender in Youth Livelihoods and Workforce Development Programs* [pdf], Program Note <http://idd.edc.org/sites/idd.edc.org/files/Gender%20in%20Youth%20Livelihoods%20-%20Report.pdf> [accessed 20 July 2019].

Workforce Connections (2014) 'What is workforce development?' [blog], May 2014 <https://www.wfconnections.org/what_is_workforce_development> [accessed 18 April 2018, no longer available].

World Bank (2012) *Gender at Work: A Companion to the World Development Report on Jobs* [pdf] <http://www.worldbank.org/content/dam/Worldbank/Event/Gender/GenderAtWork_web2.pdf> [accessed 20 July 2019].

World Bank Group (2016) *Women, Business and the Law 2016* [pdf], Washington, DC: World Bank <http://pubdocs.worldbank.org/en/810421519921949813/Women-Business-and-the-Law-2016.pdf> [accessed 20 June 2019].

World Economic Forum (2016) *The Future of Jobs* [pdf] <http://www3.weforum.org/docs/WEF_Future_of_Jobs.pdf> [accessed 20 June 2019].

World Economic Forum (2017) *The Global Gender Gap Report 2017* [pdf] <http://www3.weforum.org/docs/WEF_GGGR_2017.pdf> [accessed 20 July 2019].

CHAPTER 9

Information and communications technology for WEE

Adam Bramm

Abstract

The chapter discusses the increased use of information and communications technology (ICT) for international development and the complex political, economic, and sociocultural barriers that prevent women from benefiting from these transformative technologies. It provides approaches, strategies, and tools for increasing the use of ICT to benefit women and close the global digital divide.

Keywords: information and communications technology, digital gender gap, digital development, big data, blockchain, ICT4D

Introduction

Putri Hamzah is a single mother living in Kuala Lumpur, Malaysia. She is the owner of a flourishing tailoring business called This and That Enterprise and has launched her own design label, Hatasia Curvy, for women. She is also a mentee of the Cherie Blair Foundation's Mentoring Women in Business Programme, one of a community of nearly 4,000 mentors and mentees from 90 countries that support women-owned small and medium enterprises (SMEs) in underdeveloped countries who are all connected virtually.

In Malaysia, 32 per cent of GDP is attributed to SMEs, which comprise approximately 99 per cent of the economy (APEC Policy Partnership on Women and the Economy, 2013). Women-owned SMEs are estimated to grow by 10 per cent per year (APEC Policy Partnership on Women and the Economy, 2013) and Malaysia has a mobile phone penetration rate of 141 per cent (ITU, 2017b). This makes Malaysia a prime environment to deploy the virtual Mentoring Women in Business platform, which connects women entrepreneurs in underdeveloped countries with more experienced entrepreneurs and business advisers elsewhere in the world. In addition, the online platform provides training and webinars, hosts discussion forums, and provides business resources and templates. To make the programme work, the Cherie Blair Foundation partnered with Qualcomm, a leader in global wireless

http://dx.doi.org/10.3362/9781780447506.009

telecommunications products and services, to provide tablets to 200 women entrepreneurs. The partnership then negotiated with Maxis, Malaysia's communications service provider, to connect the tablets to the internet through Maxis' Tune Talk mobile data plan. The Foundation for Women's Education and Vocational Training, a Malaysian NGO, hosted a series of in-person trainings on computer literacy to ensure the women were ready and able to get the most from their experience (Cherie Blair Foundation for Women, n.d.; Qualcomm, n.d.).

Through the platform's unique matching algorithm, Putri was paired with mentor Philippe, an assistant professor at the Lebanese American University in Beirut. Together, Philippe and Putri discussed the details of her business plan and worked on better financial management. They also discussed how Putri would be able to increase her customer base through better marketing efforts. To raise the visibility of her products and reach more clients, Putri and Philippe use Instagram and Facebook, which are low-cost, user-friendly social media platforms that are widely used in Malaysia. Today, she has 994 followers on Instagram and has grown her business from less than 5 clients to more than 30, many of whom have become regular customers. As a result, revenue has increased by 86 per cent and has become a regular income stream for her. As Putri explains, 'When I was young, I never believed that one day I would be in business, nor did I believe that I could do anything but work for others' (Hamzah, 2015). Now she aspires to diversify her designs into women's lingerie and men's fashion, and to become a manufacturer as well as a clothing designer. Her mentor, Philippe, reflects on his experience as mentor, 'Putri deserves every success. She is determined and passionate against all odds' (Haddock-Millar and Clutterbuck, 2016; see also Cherie Blair Foundation for Women, n.d.; Qualcomm, n.d.). An in-depth case study of the Cherie Blair Foundation's Mentoring Women in Business Programme is provided at the end of this chapter.

What is ICT4WEE?

The above case study is a notable example of how technology, specifically information and communications technology (ICT), can overcome barriers for women in developing economies to realize greater economic empowerment and integration into market systems. Success stories such as the one above attract a lot of attention within the market systems development (MSD) field, particularly for their innovative use of ICTs. But the MSD industry, like society more broadly, has a mixed reaction to ICT use; some are quick to recognize the positive transformational effect of ICT solutions and incorporate them into MSD programmes, while others question whether ICTs should be considered at all given the often-underdeveloped conditions in which many of us work. But ICTs have revolutionized society today, fundamentally altering economic, political, and social systems in ways we have yet to understand. Discussions involving ICTs for development should be as ubiquitous as discussions of agriculture within the development discourse.

> Information and communication technologies (ICTs) are accelerators, amplifiers, and augmenters of change. They make it feasible to more flexibly and dynamically reconfigure, and hence transform all aspects of how resources are produced and used, fundamentally restructuring economies and redefining how we interact with each other and the world around us (Dr William Lehr, Massachusetts Institute of Technology (MIT)).

The field of ICT is an interdisciplinary area that combines the tangible innovations in technology with the less-tangible study of how humans process and communicate information. The rise and integration of ICTs into economic, social, and political systems has led to a gradual shift from the Industrial Age, marked by traditional forms of industry, to the Information Age, characterized by the central role of information, new pathways for communicating that information, and the rise of the knowledge economy. Since 2000, innovations in ICTs and their use have changed rapidly. Therefore, any definition of ICT is subject to change just as rapidly. For the purposes of this book, we will use an extremely broad definition of ICT, one that encompasses any electrical device or platform with the ability to store and transmit information (Zuppo, 2012). But that definition focuses on the technology itself and does not adequately capture the social dimensions. As ICTs increasingly integrate into every aspect of our society, profoundly altering traditional economic, political, and social systems and behaviours, some posit that information communication will become the driving force behind social evolution (Wu, 2014). Cutting edge trends in ICT, such as artificial intelligence (AI), big data, blockchain, virtual reality (VR)/augmented reality (AR), and the internet of things (IoT), will evolve the way we discuss and define ICTs from just the hardware and software components to also include the social dimensions.

The international development industry is just beginning to develop frameworks and strategies around ICT use, generically referred to as ICT for development and sometimes abbreviated ICT4D. The utilization of technology within a development context is not new, however. Older analogue forms of ICTs, such as television and radio, have been used extensively in international development interventions to disseminate information to target populations. Newer, digital forms of ICTs, such as the internet and smartphones, are gaining attention in MSD discourse as tools used by both practitioners and by low-income individuals for greater economic development and poverty reduction. ICT4D, like ICT, is a multidisciplinary area that draws on several fields and frameworks, but differs in its primary objective, which is to facilitate international development. It has often become synonymous with technology for development, though technology encompasses a much broader definition; the distinguishing factor is that ICT technologies seek to create market efficiencies by providing information and connecting people.

ICT4D practitioners are increasingly exploring the transformative effects of ICTs on women's economic empowerment (WEE), which I will refer to as ICT4WEE. Globally, women face many more barriers to the access to and use of ICTs than men, which means that they also miss out on the benefits that ICTs could have on their economic well-being. As ICTs play an increasingly vital part of the global economy, women, who are already economically vulnerable, could be further marginalized. The disparity between men and women's access to and use of ICTs has become known as the global digital gender divide (Broadband Commission Working Group on the Digital Gender Divide, 2017), and has gained increasing attention within the international development industry in recent years. The global digital gender divide recognizes women both as a significant market segment, under-represented in ICT-related jobs, and an under-served market for ICT goods and services, but also as a substantial portion of the population that is not actualizing the economic benefits of ICT access and use. As a recent report from the Broadband Commission's Working Group on the Digital Gender Divide plainly states:

> It is widely acknowledged that ICTs, including the Internet and broadband, have the potential to contribute positively to protecting women's human rights, and to their economic, social and political empowerment and development by, among other things, lowering information costs, creating information goods and expanding information bases, and boosting financial independence and productivity (Broadband Commission Working Group on the Digital Gender Divide, 2017: 13).

This chapter will explore ICT4WEE, explicating why ICTs are important for WEE in MSD programming, reviewing strategies and frameworks for integrating ICTs into MSD interventions, and providing case studies.

Why are ICTs important for women?

With the advent of the Information Age, starting roughly in the 1950s, the global economy has been transitioning from an industrial to a knowledge-based economy. ICTs are increasingly integrating into all aspects of our lives and are becoming an important economic sector within many national economies. In 2017, it was estimated that the global spending on ICTs, including software, hardware, and services, reached US$3.5 tn (Peterson, 2017). The IoT, referring to the number of devices, excluding personal devices, connected to and transmitting information via the internet, is growing exponentially; it was estimated that in 2017, there were over 20 billion devices connected to the internet, and that figure is projected to exceed 75 billion by 2025 (Statista, 2018). Remote sensing and GPS-enabled devices are among the many IoT devices being deployed to constantly collect and remit data that can be used to improve human decision making. For example, cities are using IoT devices to provide the public with better and more timely information on public transportation; to collect data and traffic patterns to better relieve congestion;

and to monitor public utilities to mitigate service interruptions. IoT devices are also being used in the agriculture sector to better monitor weather and soil conditions so farmers can make more informed decisions about agricultural activities. McKinsey Global Institute projects that IoT could contribute between $3.9 tn and $11 tn to global GDP by 2025 (Manyika et al., 2015).

ICT is proving to be a significant economic market system in and of itself; however, ICTs are having an even more profound impact on other sectors. It has been estimated that 90 per cent of all formal sector jobs globally will require an ICT skill, including sectors not traditionally thought of as ICT-specialized such as agriculture and manufacturing (Mlambo-Ngcuka, 2018). Moreover, it has been estimated that by 2020, 7.1 million jobs will have been displaced by technological advancements (Mlambo-Ngcuka, 2018). As these technologies become more pervasive throughout society, they are altering traditional business processes and fundamentally altering global economic systems in what has become known as disruptive innovation – technology that changes or replaces existing markets. In fact, new market segments are being created at alarming speed because of ICTs – including application development, gaming, and microwork (a series of small tasks that together comprise a large unified project, and are completed by many people over the internet) – that didn't even exist a few years ago. A Strategy& report projects that digital technologies, and the concomitant innovations in business processes, products, and services that result in emerging markets alone, could contribute $6.3 tn in additional GDP, 77 million new jobs, and more than half a billion people lifted out of poverty over the next 10 years (Bahjat El-Darwiche, 2015).

It is no surprise, then, that countries that have invested more heavily in ICTs and ICT infrastructure will benefit the most economically. This seems somewhat obvious but coupled with the fact that the digital economy is growing faster than the regular economy means that for countries that do not have decent ICT infrastructure the negative impact to their economies could be exponentially greater. A disproportionate amount of the economic benefits mentioned above are flowing to developed countries where most of the technology and the connectivity resides. This difference between a country's level of ICT use and investment is known as the global digital divide; not surprisingly the divide is most apparent between developed and developing economies. For example, in 2017, almost 85 per cent of households in developed countries had internet access, compared with less than 15 per cent in the world's least developed countries (ITU, 2017a).

The global digital divide has gained increasing attention in recent years from international organizations for its impact on the global economy and economic development. The International Telecommunications Union (ITU), the UN's special agency for ICTs, has focused on the growing global digital divide to measure and mitigate growing disparities in international development and poverty reduction. The ICT Development Index (IDI) is a tool developed by ITU to measure the digital divide and compare ICT use across countries. The IDI shows that there is a strong correlation between economic development and ICT development, with the top-ranking countries for ICT access, skills, and use also ranking towards the top of other economic prosperity indicators. According to the IDI, 37 of the 44 least connected countries are also the world's least developed countries (ITU, 2017a).

Just as the global digital divide can exacerbate economic disparities, there is a parallel digital gender divide that threatens to further marginalize women in developing economies in terms of ICT access, skills, and use. The digital gender gap represents both a significant loss to the global economy in terms of underserving women, but also identifies a substantial portion of the population that is not partaking in the economic growth generated by ICTs. ITU estimates that the digital gender gap in developed countries is around 3 per cent, while it is 33 per cent in the world's least developed countries, of which Africa alone accounts for 25 per cent, and appears to be growing (ITU, 2017a). ITU's research shows that closing the gender gap in mobile phone access and usage in low- and middle-income countries could unlock an estimated cumulative revenue opportunity of $170 bn for the mobile industry from 2015 to 2020 (ITU, 2016). The GSM Association (GSMA), the trade body that represents the interests of mobile network operators worldwide, estimates that digital finance, a new and growing area of ICT that includes mobile money services, could add around $3.7 tn in additional annual economic activity by 2025 by better serving women clients (GSMA mWomen, 2013). Intel has estimated that bringing 600 million additional women and girls online could contribute an estimated $13 to $18 bn to annual GDP across 144 developing economies (Intel Corporation et al., 2012). According to Nancy Hafkin, PhD Senior Associate, Women in Global Science and Technology:

> Women without access to the Internet risk getting left further behind. As more of the world's communications and business migrate online, women who cannot or do not use the Internet risk deeper isolation, including missed opportunities for education, jobs and career advancement (Intel Corporation et al., 2012: 33).

Mobile phones are the fastest growing and most ubiquitous ICT to date. The Measuring the Information Society Report noted that the total number of mobile-cellular subscriptions grew rapidly from 34 per cent in 2005 to 104 per cent in 2017, outpacing the growth of fixed telephone connections globally (ITU, 2017a). Similarly, the number of mobile-broadband subscriptions increased from 12 per cent to 56 per cent globally, and ITU estimates that between mobile and fixed connections, at least 53 per cent of households have access to the internet, with an estimated 3.5 billion individuals actively using the internet in 2017 (ITU, 2017a). The amount spent on mobile phones, laptops, and tablets alone was estimated as a $654 bn market in 2017 (Peterson, 2017), but a recent GSMA report on the mobile economy noted that the mobile industry alone generated 4.5 per cent of global GDP in 2017 and estimated that it would rise to 5 per cent by 2022 (GSMA, 2018c). That contribution includes not only device and service sales, but the subsequent increase in productivity and market efficiency supported by mobile technologies. As mentioned above, the greatest economic benefits of the mobile industry have been felt in developed countries; however, as these markets become saturated, 9 out of 10 new mobile subscribers will be in the developing world between 2017 and 2020 (Blockchain for Development, GSMA 2018a).

Mobile phones have gained attention in ICT4D initiatives because of their accessibility and reach in developing economies – mobile infrastructure has leapfrogged over fixed telephone infrastructure and declining prices in handsets and services has increased mobile penetration far beyond traditional infrastructure. But more importantly, mobile phones represent an incredible potential for delivering economic benefits to access and use, not least of which is the ability to connect to the internet. Perhaps not surprisingly, there is a gap in mobile phone access and use by women. Globally, women are 10 per cent less likely to own a mobile phone and 23 per cent less likely to use mobile internet (GSMA, 2018d). This mobile phone gap is greatest in Southeast Asia at 28 per cent and in sub-Saharan Africa at 15 per cent, and 70 per cent and 34 per cent, respectively, for mobile internet usage (GSMA, 2018d). This means that women are missing out on a hugely productive asset. The cost of mobile phone ownership and use remains a significant barrier for women. However, GSMA found that digital literacy and safety and security concerns are also significant educational and psychological barriers for women. Similarly, women experienced psychological barriers to mobile internet usage due to a perceived lack of (or in many cases actual lack of) internet content relevant to their circumstances (GSMA, 2018d).

How can ICTs economically empower women? Barriers and constraints

As can be seen from the above discussion, ICTs represent a significant economic sector where women are under-represented, but also underserved. ICTs have the potential to create greater WEE, but greater digital inclusion for women can have a far-reaching ripple effect on gender equality (GE) more generally. A 2016 Accenture study that combined UN data sets and survey results found that nations with higher rates of ICT access and use among women also had higher rates of workplace equality. According to the study's projections, 'At the current rate of digital adoption, developed nations likely won't achieve workplace gender equality until 2065, and developing nations until 2100' (Accenture, 2016: 2). This rate of gender parity is discouraging; however, this rate could be increased with the use of ICTs. As the report findings assert, 'if governments and businesses can double the pace at which women become frequent users of technology, we could reach gender equality in the workplace by 2040 in developed nations and by 2060 in developing nations' (Accenture, 2016: 2). This research points to the positive transformational effect that ICTs can have on women's economic empowerment. However, it does not elucidate the causal pathway between ICT use and greater economic empowerment for women. As Clare Twelvetrees from the Cherie Blair Foundation for Women explains:

> The gender digital divide is not just about ownership or access to technology. It's not enough to give a woman a mobile phone or connect her to the internet. She also needs the skills and confidence to use those tools to her benefit (ITU and UN University Computing and Society, 2016: 4).

Indeed, simply providing women access to ICTs will not ensure their use. Similarly, using ICTs does not automatically result in the full benefits for women. It should not be surprising that the digital gender divide very closely resembles the gender divide in terms of the structural inequalities between men and women. The digital divide, however, has also shown a gap in ICT access and use among women in urban and rural areas and among women of different economic classes. A more nuanced understanding of the digital gender divide would therefore move away from looking at simply providing the ICT hardware and software to how women are using ICTs to overcome the social, economic, and political barriers to greater economic empowerment.

Structural barriers to ICT use by women

Simply providing the technology will not ensure that women will use or even benefit from it; this is particularly true for women who face many more obstacles than men when it comes to ICT access and use. Practitioners of WEE and MSD will be familiar with the general dimensions of access and agency. These concepts must also be addressed in developing ICT4WEE interventions and cover social, cultural, economic, and political factors. Other chapters of this book explicate the social norms prohibiting WEE in more detail and Chapter 3 on enabling environments more thoroughly discusses the implications for women's entrepreneurship; however, we will provide a brief overview here as these factors relate specifically to ICTs. In their literature review on digital ICTs and women's empowerment, Cumming and O'Neil (2015) deal with access and agency through four structural barriers to ICT use by women: material, cultural, psychological, and political.

Material barriers to ICT use by women refer to the physical inability of women to access or use ICTs. Even with the falling prices of ICT devices (such as mobile phones) and services (such as the internet), women in developing economies may not have the ability to purchase these assets or services. Some women may simply not be able to use ICTs due to their physical locations, which might be out of range of a wireless or cellular connection or have infrequent or no electricity. Access to mobile phones on a fee-basis – for example, where one woman owns a mobile phone and rents out the use of the phone to other women for a fee – is one way of providing women with access and use, while at the same time providing a source of income for the woman-owner.

Cultural barriers affecting women's access to and use of ICTs are complex. Social norms pertaining to women and technology may directly prohibit them from using ICTs. In many conservative communities, for example, there is a cultural prohibition on women using the internet or owning a mobile phone, most stemming from misperceptions or fears on the part of men. Indirectly, social norms may prohibit women from using ICTs; for example, girls' education is not valued in many societies, which indirectly prevents them from using any form of written information. Similarly, many women shoulder the burden of unpaid care work within their families and communities; these responsibilities can take up most of a woman's time, leaving very little time to learn, access, or use ICTs.

Psychological barriers to women's access to and use of ICTs are closely linked with cultural norms. The world over, women and girls are under-represented in what are considered technology-heavy fields, or the STEM (science, technology, engineering, maths) fields. Several studies have shown the inherent bias in collegiate and corporate recruiting of women and girls into these career paths, yet many women feel a psychological barrier towards these areas. In developing economies, women may feel that ICT devices and services are not appropriate for them to use, in addition to or despite a cultural prohibition. More importantly, women may not have confidence because of a lack of education or experience in using ICTs, viewing these devices and services as too complex for them to use. In other cases, women perceive little value for them in ICTs; for example, many women in developing communities feel that internet content has little to no relevance for them or their lives.

Political barriers to women's access to and use of ICTs represent formal barriers. Government or institutional policies prohibiting women from accessing and using ICTs is common, such as school policies prohibiting girls' computer education. In some cases, it may also be illegal for women to personally own a cellular phone. Government-owned ICT systems may also actively discourage women's use through the types of platforms used or the content generated.

These barriers to WEE should not be surprising, especially for WEE practitioners. However, these barriers are important within an ICT4WEE context as any disruptive technology targeting women must not only disrupt the technological and market system, but also disrupt the power dynamics between men and women in one or more of the areas above.

ICT4WEE overcomes constraints

Despite these structural barriers, ICTs promise several benefits for GE/WEE. Interestingly, the United Nations Conference on Trade and Development (UNCTAD) recognized the importance of ICTs for women's economic development early on. Developed in coordination with the International Labour

Organization's (ILO) Women's Entrepreneurship Development (WED) Framework, UNCTAD produced *Empowering Women Entrepreneurs Through Information and Communications Technologies: A Practical Guide* (UNCTAD, 2014), which identifies four major areas where ICTs can contribute the most to WEE: access to finance, mobility constraints, time constraints, and education.

Access to finance. An International Finance Corporation (IFC) report found that globally there is an unmet financial gap in women-owned businesses of up to $320 bn, and the Global Findex found that women are still 15 per cent less likely to have a bank account than men globally (Murray, 2016). This is particularly true for women in underdeveloped communities who are more likely to be operating informal businesses. On the one hand, ICTs can improve women's access to information pertaining to financial options and financial rights. On the other hand, ICTs such as mobile money can greatly improve a woman's ability to conduct financial transactions via a mobile connection.

Mobility constraints. In many places in the world, women face mobility issues, both in terms of physical distance or barriers and sociocultural restrictions on mobility. ICTs can circumvent those restrictions by providing a remote link to these women regardless of their location. The changing nature of business and business-to-business (B2B) connections are making remote work not only more possible, but more acceptable. ICTs can connect home bound women with employment opportunities, or a home-based business with markets, vendors, and clients virtually.

Time constraints. Women everywhere in the world shoulder a disproportionate amount of household responsibilities. These responsibilities, known as unpaid care work, put demands on a woman's time that may impede her ability to partake in other activities, such as running a business. ICTs are changing the landscape of business so that women can work from anywhere, at any time, thereby increasing their employment opportunities and/or making business ownership possible.

Education. e-Education initiatives are overcoming barriers to providing much needed education and skills to women. This is particularly relevant for women's entrepreneurship, where ICTs can fill a gap in business development skills for women, not to mention providing vital market information to support women-owned businesses. It can also provide access to other types of vital information for women that may not be otherwise readily available, such as legal and human rights and information regarding women's health, particularly sexual and reproductive health.

In addition to the areas above, ICT use by women can also generate more self-confidence, self-reliance, and a greater sense of security. One report found that more than 70 per cent of women internet users considered the internet 'liberating' and 85 per cent said it 'provides more freedom' (Intel Corporation et al., 2012). In addition, a GSMA study on women's use of ICT found a positive correlation between mobile phone ownership and general feelings of well-being, which increased even more if the mobile phone had internet connectivity (GSMA, 2018b).

Approaches for ICT4WEE

As mentioned above, ICT4D initiatives have historically focused only on access to ICT hardware and software, seeing these technologies as solutions that can be delivered to developing communities. In these scenarios, low-income individuals become active users and beneficiaries of ICTs, but they are not in control of the technology itself. ICT4D discourse is now beginning to look at ways that low-income communities are actively using and innovating ICTs for their benefit. With the explosion of enormous amounts of data being produced as a result of increasing ICT usage globally, international development practitioners are also starting to look at ways that ICTs can be used to benefit development efforts more broadly. In examining ICT4D there are three areas that emerge with respect to use, ownership, and benefit:

- *ICTs for development practitioners*. These ICTs are used by development practitioners to better design and implement development initiatives. The substantial amounts of data that are being generated with ICTs can be utilized to gain deeper insights into human use patterns, especially for women, which can help development efforts, especially as more and more data can be disaggregated by sex. Low-income individuals, however, are not actively producing or consuming any of the ICTs and are only indirectly benefiting from them.
- *ICTs for developing countries*. This is the bulk of ICT4D initiatives where ICT strategies or components are integrated into development initiatives. Often these initiatives do not differentiate between men and women users or consider the unique barriers that women face in accessing and using the ICT solutions. The technologies are created and owned by the development practitioners, or non-local institutions, and provided to low-income communities to use. Low-income individuals are therefore actively consuming the technologies, but they are not the producers.
- *ICTs by inclusive innovation*. Regardless of where the base technology was developed, inclusive innovation allows developing economies to create new ICT devices or systems, or, through the process of convergence, adapt existing technologies for new uses, that directly meet their needs. This is where women can be particularly innovative in adapting technology to their specific use and why STEM education is vitally important to girls so that they feel empowered to innovate.

Let's look at these three areas more closely as they relate to GE/WEE.

ICTs for development practitioners: big data informing development efforts

Using data to inform development efforts in contraception and family planning. The United Nations Population Fund (UNFPA) supports the reproductive rights of women and girls by providing family planning services, contraceptives, reproductive care, and counselling services. The delivery of these much-needed services, however, is often made difficult by varying local attitudes and misconceptions about pregnancy and maternal health. Uganda is no exception, with a rapidly growing number of reproductive-aged women and teenage pregnancy estimated at 24 per cent, the challenges to family planning and health are complicated by attitudes towards pregnancy and understandings of contraception.

Working toward the alleviation of this situation, the UNFPA partnered with Pulse Lab Kampala, which uses a series of labs established by Global Pulse, a UN agency for big data. The pilot project mined publicly available digital data via Facebook and UNICEF's U-report platform, an SMS-based polling system, to gain insights into young Ugandans' perceptions towards pregnancy and contraception. The results were compiled in a real-time dashboard that supplies development organizations and national and municipal governments with information that can better target and support UNFPA programmes and other sexual and reproductive health services for women and girls (UN Global Pulse, 2014).

This is a notable example of how international development organizations are utilizing ICTs and the copious amounts of data they produce to assist with efforts to shift market systems. In this case, UNFPA and Pulse Lab Kampala created a platform for data extraction and added to it data already available via Facebook. In fact, there is already a large amount of data being created globally by ICTs that could be utilized by the development community. This has coined the term 'data-intensive development', or development that relies heavily on available or created data sets that provide feedback to the success of the development effort. In 2015, then UN Secretary-General Ban Ki-moon called for a Data Revolution to monitor and hold countries accountable for the Sustainable Development Goals (SDGs). Yet, as Mark Suzman explains, despite the large amount of data available:

> Up-to-date data exist for only a small fraction of the indicators that were developed to assess progress on the 17 SDGs – including the more than 40 that directly relate to gender equality. Of the 14 indicators of progress associated with the primary gender equity goal, SDG 5, most countries are measuring just three (Suzman, 2017).

To this end, the Bill & Melinda Gates Foundation has pledged $80 m for initiatives aimed at generating data on gender and development that can keep countries accountable to the SDGs and provide development organizations with reliable data to improve development programmes.

One programme that receives partial funding from the Gates Foundation is Data2X. Data2X is a collaborative technical and advocacy platform dedicated to improving the quality, availability, and use of gender data to make a practical difference in the lives of women and girls worldwide. In collaboration with other organizations, Data2X extracts data from four main sources:

- *Mobile phones*. Data2X calls this source 'Data Exhaust' as it includes data gathered from mobile phones, including call detail records, as well as any data generated via mobile applications like mobile money or mobile health platforms.
- *Online activity*. This includes social media platforms, blogs, and internet browser histories.
- *Sensing*. This has to do with any remote sensing (e.g. environmental monitoring sensors) or personal sensing (e.g. Fitbit) devices that transmit information, including any device that makes up the IoT.
- *Crowdsourcing*. This is information that is voluntarily provided from a crowd of people. A good example of this was provided above with UNICEF's U-report platform; it has also been used in humanitarian crisis situations, where information provided by many people can help form a more complete understanding of a crisis where real-time information is critical to response efforts.

Large-scale data collection for the UN's SDGs is a step in the right direction. However, we should be aware of what the data is not telling us. If women are under-serviced by ICTs, and a large amount of the data collected is being generated by ICT sources such as those above, then women are equally under-represented in the data. Moreover, data is often designed to capture formal economic transactions; transactions that are dominated by men. However, women often occupy informal economic niches. For example, UN Statistics Division reports that 80 per cent of the 126 countries surveyed regularly produce sex-disaggregated statistics on education and 65–70 per cent produce statistics on sexual and reproductive health and fertility, but only 30–40 per cent regularly produce statistics on informal employment, unpaid work, and violence against women (Levine and Buvinic, 2016). This is a critical gap not only in the data available on women, but also on our ability to collect data on the unique economic activities performed by women.

ICTs for developing communities: who is designing ICT systems and why?

A comprehensive system for healthcare delivery in Tanzania. In Tanzania, a country of 45 million, where many suffer from tropical and infectious diseases including HIV/AIDS, health data can be a critical missing link in delivering effective healthcare services. As Devex's Catherine Cheney explains

It is a common problem across countries that, because routine health data is generally low quality, health decisions are based on best guesses rather than reliable information. The insufficient use of data to inform planning decisions, manage programmes and deliver services can lead to life-threatening consequences, such as stock outs of medicines, delayed responses to outbreaks or wasteful health care spending (Cheney, 2017).

This is what the Data Use Partnership Project, implemented by PATH and funded by the Bill & Melinda Gates Foundation, is trying to address. By linking a disparate array of health systems and databases, the project hopes to be able to provide comprehensive, real-time data to patients, health workers, and government officials all with the aim of improving the overall health system within the country. The benefit to women is potentially greater as the prevalence of HIV/AIDS is slightly higher among women; women are often the primary caregivers within a family, which includes immunizing children; and women require additional care before, during, and after pregnancy (Stiffler, 2017).

What makes the Data Use Partnership Project most successful is that it is building on previously built and tested data platforms. The Better Immunization Data Initiative, also implemented by PATH and funded by Gates, created digital immunization records for children that allowed healthcare workers to track immunizations and to distribute needed vaccines across the country. In addition to these immunization records, the Data Use Partnership Project is linking together other databases that are already in use rather than creating an entirely new system. This not only retains old information but cuts down on the need to retrain health workers on an entirely new technology.

The other successful aspect of this project is that PATH has put the Tanzanian government as the lead design agent. It would be difficult in and of itself for one international NGO to coordinate a system like this, and dictating the system requirements would probably gain little traction with individual agencies. Instead, the project puts the Tanzanian government at the centre of the design coordination and allows for local input and feedback on system use and requirements, resulting in a system that local healthcare workers and government policy makers will find useful, and ultimately a better healthcare system for the people of Tanzania.

This is a classic example of an ICT4D initiative where the ICT system and skills are brought in by an international organization for local benefit. What is most notable about this example is the significant role that the Tanzanian government plays in designing the system based on their needs. It is also remarkable in its ability to reach scale – a country-wide system that knits together several other systems and builds upon previous ICT efforts. In fact, UNICEF played a pivotal role in the creation of the Principles for Digital Development, a set of nine guiding principles for organizations in designing and implementing ICT strategies for development. These Principles for Digital Development are:

1. design with the user;
2. understand the existing ecosystem;
3. design for scale;
4. build for sustainability;

5. be data driven;
6. use open standards, open data, open source, and open innovation;
7. reuse and improve;
8. address privacy and security;
9. be collaborative.

These guiding principles were based on the experience of numerous organizations implementing ICT4D programmes. As the Principles state clearly:

> While the potential is clear, the success of the thousands of projects that have sprung up using technology to close access gaps is less so. Pilots have failed to move into scalable and sustainable programmes. Solutions too often reinvent the wheel rather than build on robust platforms, infrastructure, and shared services. Applications and services designed thousands of miles from their use environment fail to meet user needs. The creation of duplicative tools and systems has made data difficult to access and use for decision-making. This is an inefficient use of scarce resources. We must do better, both to fulfill our own mandates and, critically, to deliver to the best of our ability for the people we serve (Luege, 2016).

And yet, the Principles for Digital Development were designed for use by international organizations implementing development programmes in developing economies. While the Principles may necessitate that local organizations play a role within the development process, the inherent assumption in the Principles is that ICT systems are something to be given to developing economies. That means that while the poor may benefit from a properly designed ICT system, they are still largely passive consumers. This is particularly true in the case of women, who are often left out of the design process for ICT4D initiatives. The Principles, while providing a general guideline for ICT4D initiatives, do not specifically address women, and therefore do not specifically address the digital gender divide. In addition, the Principles were not designed from a market systems perspective and because they are weighted more heavily toward the end user (i.e. individuals in developing economies), they disincentivize market actors. For example, the Principle of open source data is great from an international development perspective, but it reduces the incentive for market actors to provide quality data and/or to improve data quality methodologies, particularly those pertaining to women.

ICTs for inclusive innovation: producers and consumers of ICTs

Indian women use mobile phones for justice. It is estimated that nearly half of New Delhi's 18 million people reside in the city's outlying slums. In addition to living in below-standard conditions, slum dwellers, especially women, are routinely taken advantage of and denied services they are entitled to such as government rations and maternal health benefits. Aiswal lives in the New

Delhi slum of Bhim Nagar, and routinely educates other women on services entitled to them. She is one of six women paralegals trained under the SMS for Justice programme, implemented by the Indian NGO Nazdeek. In addition to the community paralegals, Nazdeek has developed an SMS-based system for reporting infractions. Just last year, Aiswal accompanied a woman from Bhim Nagar to a vendor who was denying the woman her government rations that helped feed her family of four. Following the refusal to serve the woman, Aiswal reported the infraction via SMS message to Nazdeek. Nazdeek followed up on the case and made an official report to the municipal authorities who issued a warning to the vendor. The vendor now supplies good quality rations to the woman.

Bhim Nagar was one of several New Delhi slums where women had to walk great distances for access to safe water. Several of the slum's women made reports via the SMS-based messaging system to Nazdeek, which was able to take the multitude of complaints to city officials. Today, Bhim Nagar has safe water taps installed outside every house. As Jayshree Satpute, Nazdeek's co-founder, explains, 'Most slum dwellers are unaware of various government schemes available to them. They are routinely denied basic entitlements such as maternal benefits because they simply don't know how to attain them' (Sahariah, 2017). Where women would otherwise not have the time or ability to travel to municipal centres to lodge complaints, the Nazdeek programme has adapted simple, mobile technology to empower women by providing direct recourse and civic participation (Sahariah, 2017).

Nazdeek is a fitting example of how low-income communities can directly adapt ICTs for their own benefit and is a great instance of convergence. Convergence is the adaption of an ICT device, service, or system to meet a need that may be different from that intended. In the Nazdeek example, SMS messaging was the primary tool used by the foundation to bring about social justice within a community. In the Mentoring Women in Business Programme in Malaysia example at the beginning of this chapter, Facebook was adapted from a social networking platform to a virtual marketplace for Putri's goods and services. In both examples, however, local people and communities have full control over the process of innovation from which they can benefit directly. Inclusive innovation is a key point to make in ICT4D discourse; all too often international development organizations fall into an ethnocentric mindset that developing economies do not have technology and so it must be delivered to them. This is not only false, but it is also not empowering to local communities. What some international development organizations also fail to realize is that when ICT systems are deployed to developing contexts, many of these technologies are owned by private companies in developed countries. Not only does that make it impossible for the host country to innovate on the technology, but many of the technologies come with licensing or use restrictions that make continued or expanded use of the technology difficult. One of the Principles of Digital Development attempts to address this issue by requiring open source technology, which would allow for full ownership and inclusive innovation by the host communities.

Challenges to ICT4WEE

In the previous section, we looked at the unique barriers that women face in accessing and using ICTs. ICT4WEE practitioners must directly address these barriers for their intervention to be successful. Addressing these barriers can be challenging enough; however, there are additional challenges of *doing* ICT4WEE that practitioners must be aware of. As should be evident from the above discussion, the international development industry is still struggling with how to fully utilize ICTs and, as such, the challenges are many and still evolving. The points below provide only a few challenges to be aware of when designing ICT4WEE initiatives.

Practitioners of women's economic empowerment must actively mitigate any unintended negative consequences of our development efforts and ICT4WEE initiatives are no exception. Just as ICTs open new opportunities for women, they also open new forms of discrimination and violence towards women. Discriminatory practices, such as online job applications or electronic voter registration, actively exclude women from economic and political activities without being overt in their discrimination. Even gender bias in machine learning programmes has been reported, purportedly learning from inherent gender bias in digital content (Report of the Inter-agency Task Force on Financing for Development, 2018). Women can also experience backlash from ICT use if that use challenges sociocultural norms, resulting in greater discrimination or even gender-based violence. Online communications, especially social media platforms, expose women to new forms of sexual violence and abuse, which can sometimes lead to physical assault. Any development intervention that seeks to utilize ICTs for greater women's economic empowerment needs to be aware of the potential negative consequences of women's ICT access and use.

ICT4WEE interventions must address the multiple dimensions of the digital gender gap (age, education, urban/rural, etc.). Women are not a homogeneous group, so a single ICT solution will not empower women uniformly. As mentioned above, ICT4D initiatives have historically focused on access to ICT devices and services, but a more nuanced approach would recognize the ways that different demographic groups of women access and use those products and services. Doing so can better target women and make sure that no woman is further marginalized by the divide. In addition, efforts to reduce the digital gender divide will require considerable cooperation at multiple levels from multiple stakeholders. This includes consolidating our understanding of ICT4WEE strategies and tools. Some have called for a 'Technology Roadmap' that would highlight the significant components of an ICT intervention, including the key policy, regulatory, technical, and capacity issues that need to be addressed for success (Global Pulse and GSMA, 2017). As Luna Doha of Bangladesh Women in Technology explains, 'It is critical to develop efforts at a global scale. There are many best practices that can be transferred and replicated. To do this, partnerships are essential' (ITU and UN University Computing and Society, 2016: 10).

While ICTs certainly pose many benefits to women's economic empower-ment, the technology should not serve as the initiative itself, but only a tool to support the initiative. As Kentaro Toyama explains:

> The focus when reporting ICT4D projects quickly slips into extolling the virtues of the technology itself, not the human component. This says much about the seductive quality of technology. Myths about its poten-tial persist because we have a strong desire to see the triumph of clever ideas and ingenuity, and to believe that one-time catalytic investments can have such an impact. The reality is always more complex (Toyama, 2010).

What practitioners of ICT4WEE must realize is that ultimately what we are trying to do is resolve a fundamentally human problem, not a technological one. As such, we need to be reconciled with the limitations of that technology to address the issue. A Data2X report specifically addresses this limitation with regards to big data. The report explicitly states that:

> Big data is not a panacea for all the challenges of development planning and research. The invisibility of women and girls in international and national data discourse is a political, not solely a technical, problem. New methods can indeed illuminate previously ignored aspects of the lives of women and girls, but it can also create a sense that technical advancements alone will compel investments in gender-sensitive data systems by national statistical agencies, civil society organizations, and international donors. They will not. In the worst-case scenario, they will have the opposite effect: the data deluge may shift policy focus towards the groups and regions for which the most information is available, not the people and places in greatest need. Even big data illuminates only small parts of the entire field of human experience (Data2X, 2017: 29).

Case study: virtual support to women entrepreneurs in Malaysia

The global entrepreneurial gender gap is not shrinking. Not only are women less likely to start their own businesses – according to the Global Entrepreneurship Monitor project, only 11 per cent of women start new businesses as opposed to 30 per cent of men – but women have a 10 per cent lower rate for sustaining those businesses (Blomqvist et al., 2014). The factors that contribute to that success or failure are varied; however, business associations and other types of networks, both formal and informal, have been identified as critical in provid-ing the knowledge and information that supports small- and medium-sized business owners the world over. Yet, in underdeveloped countries, women are often excluded from these networks, and thus are deprived of the kind of support that could facilitate the success of their businesses.

A study by the Boston Consulting Group highlights the role participation in these networks can have on women creating sustainable businesses, correctly identifying higher levels of social capital with increases in higher aspirations and better long-term planning; new or improved business skills and better business ideas; collaboration and credibility; greater access to funding; and emotional support for women. Using affiliation in business associations as a proxy for social capital, the study found that a 10 per cent increase in women's entrepreneurial affiliation reduced the sustainability gap between genders by as much as 25 per cent in Latin America and Caribbean countries (Blomqvist et al., 2014). Similarly, the Asia Foundation found that women who participated in business associations were 24 per cent more likely to report plans to increase their firm's size over the next three years (Blomqvist et al., 2014).

Recognizing this critical factor in women's successful business ownership, the Cherie Blair Foundation for Women launched its Mentoring Women in Business Programme in 2012. Since inception, the programme has connected over 4,000 mentors and mentees in 90 countries. The Foundation is capitalizing on modern technologies that facilitate these types of peer-to-peer relationships and can connect women who would otherwise not have opportunities to associate. A perfect example of this is in Malaysia, where the Cherie Blair Foundation partnered with Qualcomm, Maxis, and the Foundation for Women's Education and Vocational Training to connect women via the internet with business development services to grow their businesses. Malaysia was a great country in which to deploy the programme; Malaysia is a trendsetter among developing nations within the region, with higher-than-average internet coverage and internet usage (ITU, 2017a). The government continues to invest heavily in ICT infrastructure, not least of which is the National Broadband Initiative, which has a target of 95 per cent broadband coverage for urban areas by 2020 (ITU, 2017a).

A critical success factor of the platform is that it addresses several unique issues faced by women entrepreneurs, namely mobility, time, and information. Mobility is often a constraining factor for women, either directly, in places where women are not permitted to travel, or indirectly in places where the distance, time, or infrastructure to travel to a training or business incubation centre is prohibitive for women. Time is often a constraining factor for women who shoulder a disproportionate amount of unpaid care work; having access to information as needed works around these issues and reduces the demands on women's time. Lastly, information gaps are perhaps the most critical for women entrepreneurs; not only does this platform provide information on business development, but it provides it directly from a global community of peers. As Allison Kahn, Cherie Blair's Mentoring Programme Director, explains of the women participating in the programme, 'They can benefit from each other's knowledge and learn from those who have tried, failed, and succeeded in the real world' (Kahn, 2013). She comments on one online interaction she witnessed directly in a group discussion forum where a woman entrepreneur asked about how to handle losing a major client. Within days, information from all over the globe had poured into the discussion, providing insight and encouragement 'that would rival what one might find in a textbook, with the distinct advantage that it came with a personal touch and direct interaction' (Kahn, 2013).

The achievements of the Malaysian programme are inspiring and include the following:

- 98 per cent improved their English skills;
- 98 per cent improved their communication skills;
- 95 per cent gained strategy and planning skills;
- 86 per cent gained marketing skills;
- 90 per cent found ways to access new markets;
- 75 per cent increased their financial knowledge and knowledge on funding options;
- 95 per cent built networks and gained new business contacts;
- 97 per cent gained confidence;
- 68 per cent expanded their online presence (e.g. built a new website, launched a new Facebook page).

These results have a sustainable, lasting impact on the communities, economy, and women's economic empowerment, with 80 per cent of mentees reporting having passed along what they learned to others in their communities and half actively mentoring others. Furthermore, 47 per cent were still using the programme's online platform and more than half are still communicating with their mentor.

The Mentoring Women in Business Programme was the catalyst that facilitated greater market change in Malaysia. First, the successful partnerships with private sector telecommunications companies resulted in those companies recognizing the value in women as an important market segment, supplying data on women's internet and cellular use to better target products and services for women. Second, the programme increased women's knowledge of and comfort in utilizing digital tools and services, even adapting platforms such as Instagram, Facebook, and WhatsApp for business purposes. Coupled with business development knowledge and skills, women can now realize the full potential of the internet and other digital resources to achieve greater economic empowerment. Lastly, the peer-to-peer networks established by the programme will continue to grow and yield benefits to women entrepreneurs beyond the programme.

The key to the success of the Mentoring Women in Business Programme is that the Cherie Blair Foundation didn't let the technology act as the solution itself; instead, it accurately identified the unique barriers to women's economic empowerment and employed a digital solution to overcome those barriers that facilitated a greater market linkage for women. As Cherie Blair aptly says:

> The internet is more than just gadgets. We can use it to stretch out a hand across the virtual world to help some really great women improve their lives and the lives of those around them. It is a crucial life line which can mean the difference between success and failure (Cherie Blair Foundation for Women, 2014).

Information for this case study was sourced from the Cherie Blair Foundation for Women (http://www.cherieblairfoundation.org) and Qualcomm (https://www.qualcomm.com).

Useful resources

Broadband Commission for Sustainable Development's Working Group on the Digital Gender Divide: www.broadbandcommission.org/workinggroups/Pages/digital-gender-divide.aspx

GSM Association (GSMA) Mobile Connectivity Index: https://www.mobile-connectivityindex.com/

International Telecommunications Union's (ITU) ICT Development Index (IDI): https://www.itu.int/net4/ITU-D/idi/2017/index.html

ITU's *Measuring the Information Society Report 2017* Vol. 1 and Vol. 2: https://www.itu.int/en/ITU-D/Statistics/Pages/publications/mis2017.aspx

United Nations Digital Impact Alliance (DAIL): https://digitalimpactalliance.org/

United States Agency for International Development's (USAID) *Gender and Information Communication Technology (ICT) Survey Toolkit*: https://www.usaid.gov/sites/default/files/documents/15396/Gender_and_ICT_Toolkit.pdf

USAID's Gender Digital Divide Online Course: https://www.panoplydigital.com/gender-and-ict-online-course/

References

Accenture (2016) *Getting To Equal: How Digital is Helping Close the Gender Gap at Work* [pdf] <https://www.accenture.com/_acnmedia/PDF-9/Accenture-Getting-To-Equal.pdf> [accessed 15 May 2019].

APEC Policy Partnership on Women and the Economy (2013) *Access to Trade and Growth of Women's SMEs in APEC Developing Countries*, Singapore: APEC Secretariat.

Bahjat El-Darwiche, A.S. (2015) *Digitization in Emerging Economies: Unleashing Opportunities at the Bottom of the Pyramid* [pdf], PWC <https://www.strategyand.pwc.com/media/file/Strategyand_Digitization-in-Emerging-Economies.pdf> [accessed 15 May 2019].

Blomqvist, M., Chastain, E., Thickett, B., Unnikrishnan, S. and Woods, W. (2014) 'Bridging the entrepreneurship gender gap: the power of networks', [online], 21 October 2014, Boston, MA: Boston Consulting Group <https://www.bcg.com/publications/2014/bridging-entrepreneurship-gender-gap.aspx> [accessed 1 February 2018].

Broadband Commission Working Group on the Digital Gender Divide (2017) *Recommendations for Action: Bridging the Gender Gap in Internet and Broadband Access and Use* [pdf], Broadband Commission for Sustainable Development <https://broadbandcommission.org/Documents/publications/WorkingGroupDigitalGenderDivide-report2017.pdf> [accessed 15 May 2019]

Cheney, C. (2017) 'Can data drive better health outcomes in Tanzania?' [online], 5 September 2017, Devex <https://www.devex.com/news/

can-data-drive-better-health-outcomes-in-tanzania-90867> [accessed 20 September 2017].

Cheri Blaire Foundation for Women (2014) 'How the internet has become a lifeline for women around the world', [online], 18 February 2014 <http://www.cherieblairfoundation.org/how-the-internet-has-become-a-lifeline-for-women-around-the-world/> [accessed 20 July 2019].

Cherie Blair Foundation for Women (no date) 'Homepage', [online] <http://www.cherieblairfoundation.org> [accessed 18 April 2019].

Cumming, C. and O'Neil, T. (2015) *Do Digital Information and Communications Technologies Increase the Voice and Influence of Women and Girls?* London: Overseas Development Institute.

Data2X (2017) *Big Data and the Well-being of Women and Girls* [pdf] <https://eprints.soton.ac.uk/407908/1/Big_Data_and_the_Well_Being_of_Women_and_Girls.pdf> [accessed 20 July 2019].

Global Pulse and GSM Association (GSM) (2017) *The State of Mobile Data for Social Good Report* [pdf] <http://unglobalpulse.org/sites/default/files/MobileDataforSocialGoodReport_29June.pdf> [accessed 15 May 2019].

GSMA (2018a) *Blockchain for Development: Emerging Opportunities for Mobile, Identity and Aid* [pdf], London: GSMA <https://www.gsma.com/mobilefor-development/wp-content/uploads/2017/12/Blockchain-for-Development.pdf> [accessed 15 May 2019].

GSMA (2018b) *The Impact of Mobile on People's Happiness and Well-Being* [pdf], London: GSMA <https://www.gsma.com/mobilefordevelopment/wp-content/uploads/2018/01/The-Impact-of-Mobile-on-People%E2%80%99s-Happiness-and-Well-Being_report.pdf> [accessed 15 May 2019].

GSMA (2018c) *The Mobile Economy 2018* [pdf], London: GSMA <https://www.gsma.com/mobileeconomy/wp-content/uploads/2018/05/The-Mobile-Economy-2018.pdf> [accessed 15 May 2019].

GSMA (2018d) *The Mobile Gender Gap Report 2018* [pdf], London: GSMA <https://www.gsma.com/mobilefordevelopment/wp-content/uploads/2018/04/GSMA_The_Mobile_Gender_Gap_Report_2018_32pp_WEBv7.pdf> [accessed 15 May 2019].

GSMA mWomen (2013) *Unlocking the Potential: Women and Mobile Financial Services in Emerging Markets* [pdf], London: GSMA <https://www.gsma.com/mobilefordevelopment/wp-content/uploads/2013/02/GSMA-mWomen-Visa_Unlocking-the-Potential_Feb-2013.pdf> [accessed 15 May 2019].

Hamzah, P. (2015) 'Turning Dreams Into Reality Through The Power Of Mentoring', June 30, 2015 <http://www.cherieblairfoundation.org/turning-dreams-into-reality-through-the-power-of-mentoring/> [online] [accessed 20 July 2019]

Haddock-Millar, D.J. and Clutterbuck, P.D. (2016) 'Putri's story', [online], 21 July 2016, Cherie Blair Foundation for Women <http://www.cherieblairfoundation.org/putris-story/> [accessed 20 July 2019].

Intel Corporation, Dalberg Global, and GlobalScan (2012) *Women and the Web: Bridging the Internet Gap and Creating New Global Opportunities in Low and Middle-income Countries* [pdf], Intel Corporation <https://www.intel.com/content/dam/www/public/us/en/documents/pdf/women-and-the-web.pdf> [accessed 15 May 2019].

International Telecommunications Union (ITU) (2016) *How Can We Close the Digital Gender Gap?* Geneva: ITU.

ITU (2017a) *Measuring the Information Society Report*, Geneva: ITU.

ITU (2017b) *Measuring the Information Society Report 2017: Vol. 2 ICT Country Profiles*, Geneva: ITU.

ITU and UN University Computing and Society (2016) *Mapping Gender Digital InclusiveInitiatives* [pdf], ITU <https://www.itu.int/en/action/gender-equality/Documents/GDD%20Mapping%20-%20Presentation%20%281%29.pdf> [accessed 20 July 2019]

Kahn, A. (2013) *A Platform for Change: Using Technology to Support Women Entrepreneurs* [online] <http://www.cherieblairfoundation.org/a-platform-for-change-using-technology-to-support-women-entrepreneurs/> [accessed 20 July 2019].

Lehr, W. (2018) 'Why ICTs are critical for sustainable development', May 3, 2018   https://news.itu.int/icts-are-critical-for-sustainable-development/ [online] [accessed 20 July 2019]

Levine, M. and Buvinic, R. (2016) *Closing the Gender Gap* [pdf], Data2X <https://data2x.org/wp-content/uploads/2019/05/Closing-the-Gender-Data-Gap-Mayra-Buvinic-and-Ruth-Levine.pdf> [accessed 20 July 2019].

Luege, T (2016) '9 development principles to stop waste of time and money', [blog], 8 March 2016, Social Media for Good <http://sm4good.com/2016/03/08/principles-digital-development/> [accessed 20 July 2019].

Manyika, J., Chui, M., Bisson, P., Woetzel, J., Dobbs, R., Bughin, J. and Aharon, D. (2015) *The Internet of Things: Mapping the Value Beyond the Hype*, McKinsey & Company [PDF] <https://www.mckinsey.com/~/media/McKinsey/Business%20Functions/McKinsey%20Digital/Our%20Insights/The%20Internet%20of%20Things%20The%20value%20of%20digitizing%20the%20physical%20world/The-Internet-of-things-Mapping-the-value-beyond-the-hype.ashx> [accessed 15 May 2019].

Mlambo-Ngcuka, P. (2018) 'Reshaping the future: women, girls and tech for development', [online], 9 February 2018, IUT News <http://news.itu.int/reshaping-future-women-girls-icts/> [accessed 20 July 2018].

Murray, I. (2016) 'Catalyzing women's financial inclusion: the role of data', [blog], 17 February 2016 CGAP <https://www.cgap.org/blog/catalyzing-womens-financial-inclusion-role-data> [accessed 15 May 2019].

Peterson, B. (2017) 'Companies will spend $3.5 trillion on tech this year – the price it would cost to buy Apple 4.5 times', [online], 13 July 2017 *Business Insider*   <http://www.businessinsider.com/worldwide-it-spending-2017-7> [accessed 7 February 2018].

Qualcomm (no date) 'Homepage', [online] <https://www.qualcomm.com> [accessed 5 August 2017].

Report of the Inter-agency Task Force on Financing for Development (2018) *Financing for Development: Progress and Prospects 2018*, New York: United Nations.

Sahariah, S. (2017) 'Women in India's slums use mobile phones to fight injustice', [online], 11 September 2017, News Deeply <https://www.newsdeeply.com/womenandgirls/articles/2017/09/11/women-in-indias-slums-use-mobile-phones-to-fight-injustice> [accessed 12 September 2017].

Statista (2018) 'Internet of Things (IoT) connected devices installed base worldwide from 2015 to 2025 (in billions)' [online], Statista: The Statistics Portal <https://www.statista.com/statistics/471264/iot-number-of-connected-devices-worldwide/> [accessed 20 July 2019].

Stiffler, L. (2017) 'Gates Foundation and PATH wire up health data in Africa using a novel approach', [online], 3 September 2017, GeekWire <https://www.geekwire.com/2017/gates-foundation-path-wire-health-data-africa-using-novel-approach/> [accessed 19 April 2019].

Suzman, M. (2017) 'Data-driven gender equality' [online], New York: Project Syndicate <https://www.project-syndicate.org/commentary/better-data-for-gender-equality-by-mark-suzman-2017-09?barrier=accessreg> [accessed 19 April 2019].

Toyama, K. (2010) 'Kentaro Toyama: ten myths about technology and development', [online], 25 February 2010, Stanford Center on Democracy, Development and the Rule of Law <https://cddrl.fsi.stanford.edu/news/kentaro_toyama_ten_myths_about_technology_and_development_20100225> [accessed 5 February 2018].

UN Global Pulse (2014) *Analyzing Attitudes Towards Contraception and Teenage Pregnancy Using Social Data* [pdf], Global Pulse Project Series, No. 8 <http://www.unglobalpulse.org/sites/default/files/UNGP_ProjectSeries_Family_Planning_2014_0.pdf> [accessed 15 May 2019].

United Nations Conference on Trade and Development (UNCTAD) (2014) *Empowering Women Entrepreneurs Through Information and Communications Technologies: A Practical Guide*, UNCTAD Current Studies on Science, Technology Innovation No. 9, Geneva: UNCTAD.

Wu, T. (2014) 'As technology gets better, will society get worse?' *The New Yorker*, 6 February 2014.

Zuppo, C.M. (2012) 'Defining ICT in a boundaryless world: the development of a working hierarchy', *International Journal of Managing Information Technology (IJMIT)* 4(3):13-22 <http://dx.doi.org/10.5121/ijmit.2012.4302,pages 13-22>.

PART 3
Managing risk and assessing outcomes

Part 3 examines the potential risks to women when facilitating change to economic empowerment within a market system and provides strategies, frameworks, and tools to identify and mitigate against these risks. Chapter 11 looks at the importance of measuring women's economic empowerment and discusses approaches, frameworks, and tools for assessing impact within the market system. While we offer various ways for measuring and understanding change in gender equality, we do not advocate for any one single approach. Rather, we provide the means to assess the approach or framework and evaluate its appropriateness for the context.

Managing risk and assessing outcomes

CHAPTER 10

Managing risks for women's participation

Calais Caswell and Linda Jones

Abstract

This chapter outlines the various risks to women inherent in achieving greater economic empowerment and discusses the importance of assessing, managing, and mitigating gender-based risk. It provides approaches, strategies, and tools for assessing and reducing the level of risk for women within a market system development initiative.

Keywords: gender equality, women's economic empowerment, risk mitigation, gender-based violence, time poverty, gender wage gap

Introduction

Interventions that are aimed at creating the enabling conditions for the empowerment of women and advancing gender equality (GE) have inherent risks. As market inclusion often requires shifting normative behaviours in households, communities, and sectors, there can be negative spin-off effects that can manifest as risks to women's livelihoods and their ability to engage effectively in the targeted market system. These risks can not only cause harm to women personally but can also compromise programme and sectoral success.

When women's economic empowerment (WEE) initiatives target advancements in women's economic empowerment at the household and community levels of market systems, some of these risks include an increase in instances of gender-based violence, a deepening of patriarchal social norms and negative perceptions of women's economic participation, male capture, and an increase in women's time poverty. At the institutional or enabling environment level of market systems, there are risks that target sectors, market actors, supporting functions, and regulatory frameworks may be too gender-biased to meaningfully integrate women into business activities. This institutionalized and structural gender bias can be a risk to WEE programming and successful and sustainable outcomes for women. Nevertheless, even if market actors and functions in target sectors can adapt to be gender inclusive, women's participation may still be hampered by oppressive household and community gender norms, women may not ultimately benefit from increased incomes, or there may be serious side effects.

http://dx.doi.org/10.3362/9781780447506.010

Household and community level risks

As mentioned, it is essential to consider potential repercussions and retaliatory behaviours that could result from an increase in women's economic empowerment to effectively manage risk in a WEE intervention. Poverty is sexist and, throughout many societies, patriarchal power structures uphold discriminatory sociocultural norms that result in the oppression of women, gender and sexual minorities (GSMs), and other marginalized groups. At the household or community level, these risks are largely the result of the perpetuation of inequitable social norms within households and communities that inhibit women's voice, choice, and control. Risks also come from power imbalances in transactions where not only gender but also other intersectional identities, such as age, ability, race, class, and ethnicity, among other factors, can limit women's bargaining position. Interventions may unwittingly perpetuate or worsen these risks if women are treated as a homogeneous group without accounting for their differences and unique experiences within societies and market systems. As such, WEE programming must take an intersectional approach for it to be impactful and appropriately targeted (Gender and Development Network, 2015). A selection of notable risks that may result or worsen from WEE interventions are outlined below.

Gender-based violence and harassment

It has long been recognized, but is still relatively unaddressed within WEE programming, that gender-based violence presents a serious risk to women's meaningful and equal participation in market systems. Greater instances of harassment and violence towards women can result from women's increased access to economic resources and formal engagement in the economy as power relations between men and women shift (Hughes et al., 2015). The risk of harassment can also inhibit women from accessing financial services in formal banking institutions, as well as disincentivize women from entering into workplaces where they are potentially at risk, particularly if there are few safeguards or legal protections in place (V4W, 2013; Grantham et al., 2019). This is especially problematic for women working in low-skilled jobs in more informal sectors.

Patriarchal social norms

Further, other forms of risk including negative backlash can reverberate within communities where women become more visible within formal economic spaces resulting from market interventions that explicitly target women's increased participation. This can include the reification of discriminatory social norms towards women as market actors, and negative perceptions by men in the community where they may feel threatened due to shifting power dynamics. Consequently, men may resent women's growing economic independence and may impede women's engagement in market interventions if they believe that women are neglecting their domestic responsibilities (Eves and Crawford, 2014).

Male capture

A potential risk that can result from women's increased economic participation and independence within market systems is the risk of male capture of women's land or productive assets. Mennonite Economic Development Associates (MEDA) (2019) found through their GROW project in northern Ghana that women were often given less fertile lands and had to invest significant time and energy to make the land productive. Once the land started to generate yields men would take it back and would provide women with more unproductive land as the cycle continued (MEDA, 2019). This is an ever-present risk in agricultural development initiatives focused on women's economic livelihoods where men may usurp women's assets, including technological inputs provided through interventions, or even take control over women's businesses once they begin to generate a profit (World Bank Independent Evaluation Group, 2010; Oehmke and Post, 2015).

Women's time poverty

As has been highlighted in earlier chapters, women experience significant time poverty and shoulder a disproportionate amount of the productive and reproductive labour burden worldwide. Notably, women's contributions to the care economy are vastly under-recognized and unremunerated. WEE interventions can exacerbate women's workload and can increase time poverty when the outcome results in increased women's economic engagement in paid work. Without the corresponding 'recognition, reduction, redistribution and sharing of care responsibilities', the gender care gap will continue to widen, incurring negative impacts on women's well-being and ability to succeed economically (Grantham et al., 2019: 12). Furthermore, this challenge to balance competing priorities and greater demands on women's time with increased workloads can manifest in risks to women's stress levels and mental and physical health (V4W, 2013).

Enabling environment risks

Macroeconomic, political, and environmental shifts and trends throughout history, such as colonization, structural adjustment, globalization, financial crises, and climate change, among other events, have exacerbated existing inequalities. Market systems are flawed and are often gender blind or are modelled according to men's experiences as market actors. The results of which have worsened the effects of environmental and economic risks to women and other marginalized individuals. This gender blindness within markets can be perpetuated by practitioners within market systems development (MSD) interventions if gendered risks to women's participation and potential for socio-economic empowerment are not sufficiently accounted for and managed. Recognizing that markets are not ahistorical nor gender-neutral spaces is a crucial first step in designing interventions that address risks to women resulting from discriminatory sociocultural norms and inequitable institutional and systemic constraints. Furthermore, WEE interventions should address women's whole lives with targeted activities to promote individual transformation as well as systems change by addressing both social norms and regulatory and legal barriers.

Within the enabling environment of a market systems intervention, there are typical and oft-repeated categories of risks that stand in the way of advancing gender equality and women's economic empowerment as overarching goals of market systems development. These may include:

- Regulations that are either gender blind or actively discriminate against women.
- Business environments that relegate women to low-paying, risky, and vulnerable employment or enterprise development.
- Services and resources that are not readily accessible by women including financial services and other business supports, or other gender-specific resources such as childcare.
- Other market actors (e.g. government agencies, business owners, civil society stakeholders) that unconsciously or consciously behave in gender-biased ways.

Research has shown that to advance gender equality through market systems development and effect sustainable change and inclusive growth, WEE interventions should pay commensurate attention to structural inequalities and how they are reproduced in markets, and how these constrain women's choices and ability to succeed (Kabeer, 2012). In effect, a recent study demonstrated that 'where programs or policies did deliver resources to women they were targeting, the persistent structures of constraint may have prevented those resources from translating into enhanced capabilities for women and girls' (Kabeer, 2018: ii). Insufficient attention to these structural issues can also result in risks to attaining programming objectives. A selection of these structural gaps and barriers include:

Legal and regulatory barriers

Risks to implementing successful WEE interventions that can meaningfully advance gender equality include the prevalence of discriminatory legal and regulatory environments that circumscribe women's opportunities within market systems. According to UN Women (2012), women own just 20 per cent of global landholdings, and many countries lack legal frameworks to secure women's property rights, protect them from disinheritance, or insulate them from economic exploitation. Furthermore, approximately 104 economies have laws preventing women from working in specific jobs (Wood, 2018). Women entrepreneurs experience a multitude of challenges to starting and growing businesses, including institutionalized barriers to registering their businesses and to accessing financing and investment (Cornish, 2017). Moreover, studies have shown that 'legal gender disparities have been shown to have a strong link with female labor force participation' (World Bank Group, 2017: 3). For example, a study in Ethiopia found that after a reform in family law that established more equitable marital property rights, there was a consequent increase in women entering the labour market and other productive sectors (World Bank Group, 2017).

The gender wage gap and occupational segregation

Women remain at a disadvantage in their economic lives compared with their male counterparts, resulting in a persistent gender wage gap. The 'race to the bottom' on taxation, wages, and labour standards has resulted in the concentration of women and other minorities in informal sectors, gender-stereotypical employment, and the lowest rungs of economies with little protection or opportunity for advancement (Grantham et al., 2019). Where in the Global North women encounter obstacles to climbing the corporate ladder, aptly described as 'the glass ceiling', in developing economies structural gendered inequities have created a 'sticky floor' resulting in gender and occupational segregation with women concentrated at the bottom of the wage earning scale where they are often relegated to risky, informal, low-income work that serves to further circumscribe their rights, and which perpetuates gender inequality in the labour market (Puri, 2016). These gendered and occupational inequalities mean that women earn on average 24 per cent less than men, and not a single country has gender parity in pay (UN Women, 2015; World Economic Forum, 2015). Additionally, 61 per cent of all workers worldwide are in the informal economy, and women respectively make up 92 per cent (in low-income countries) and 84.5 per cent (in lower-middle-income countries) of all informal workers (ILO, 2018).

Consequently, some of the risks explored here can directly or indirectly result from WEE interventions or can have a knock-on effect on WEE intervention programming at multiple levels. These risks can negatively impact women's ability to take full advantage of market systems development as well as hinder programme success. The following section will examine a selection of available risk mitigation tools.

Gendered risk assessment

Throughout this volume, cases and examples illustrate the risks for women around the world and their participation in market systems. From Nepal, Ghana, Libya, Guatemala, and more, we have documented examples of women's exclusion due to gender discrimination, structural barriers to women's advancement, and possible solutions to overcome the constraints that women face. While it is helpful to our analysis to understand the general types of risks that exist across functions and actors in market systems, understanding context is key to performing a gendered risk assessment. This means that risk assessments must be carried out from the early stages of research and analysis of a market system to capture a nuanced perspective of women's lived experience. This attention to risk must be carried through the design of programme interventions and activities, during implementation, and throughout monitoring and impact measurement.

Programme design: conducting a gendered risk analysis

During the research or design phase of an intervention, risks to women's livelihoods and their ability to benefit from and contribute to market systems are assessed using gendered risk analysis methodologies. These analyses can accompany broader market assessment studies and can employ both secondary and primary research to assess the current context of gender relations and the presence of gender-related risks to enable the development of a risk mitigation strategy. This is also to ensure that the intervention is developed in a gender-aware manner so that it is not gender-blind or exploitative, as illustrated in Figure 10.1.

With experience, practitioners can develop the capacity to ask the appropriate questions to determine the specific risks that might be encountered. For example, the following series of questions were prepared by Australian Aid as guidance for practitioners on women's economic empowerment initiatives in agriculture sub-sectors (DFAT, 2015). Some sample research questions for a WEE risk analysis include:

- Are we entrenching gender roles through our interventions? Are we setting women up for poorly paid work that is not valued?
- Is there a risk that our work is deepening knowledge, skill, and asset inequalities?
- Are we inadvertently undermining financial and productive decision making in our interventions? What about women's leadership?
- Have we considered the impacts of the interventions on women's workload and therefore trade-offs, such as nutrition of feeding and care of infants and young children?
- Is there a risk that gender-based violence may increase as a result of our interventions? If so, what have we done to mitigate this? (DFAT, 2015 p 9)

For risk assessment to be inclusive, a key consideration is the application of participatory rural appraisal (PRA) techniques to ensure that the voices of those impacted by identifiable risks are heard and considered. For example, Oxfam has developed a Vulnerability and Risk Assessment (VRA) methodology to assess vulnerabilities experienced by women and other marginalized groups and susceptibility to environmental and economic shocks (Morchain

Gender blind	Gender exploitative	Gender accommodating	Gender responsive	Gender transformative
No analysis conducted in project as gender issues are not recognized	Basic analysis conducted for funder compliance. Project reinforces and takes advantage of gender inequalities and stereotypes	Analysis conducted that is context-specific. Strategy developed that is loosely tied to analysis but does not challenge gender norms	Comprehensive strategy based on gender analysis and implemented through a work plan. Strategy included some activities that challenge gender norms to influence behaviour change	Gender equality is internalized in systems. Project directly targets behaviour change and addresses power relations and structures of inequality

Gender Aware Programming Continuum

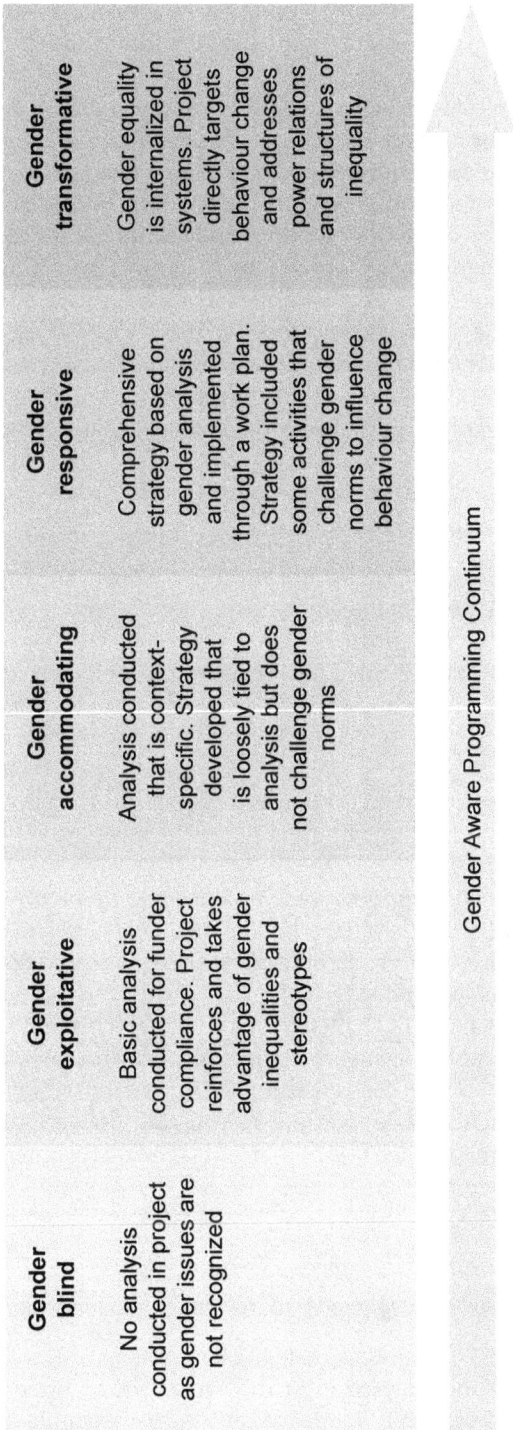

Figure 10.1 MEDA's gender equality project continuum

and Kelsey, 2016). The methodology emphasizes employing PRA approaches while scoping women's vulnerability to risk. This tool is specific to analysing climate change trends and their impacts at a macro level but is also useful for assessing other forms of vulnerability and risk. However, women are often more adversely impacted by climatic events, and thus the VRA tool is useful in that it takes a women-centred, bottom-up approach to assessing risks that could affect women's livelihoods and market potential, particularly in rural settings.

Furthermore, there is a risk when partnering with the private sector that businesses will be sceptical of gender inclusion. In some cases, there is concern that including or targeting women will be negative for their business model and growth, and the project is encouraging them to do something that is purely social rather than economic. When considering intervention design, scoping questions need to examine the business case, women's empowerment issues, and their nexus to posit win–win scenarios that determine how to reduce risk for the business, women clients, and the programme objectives. Some sample questions to help elicit the needed information and reduce risks around private sector uptake include:

- What is the business case for working with women in the sub-sector – that is, what is their value and contribution as customers, employees, suppliers, and service providers?
- Would engaging with women present a new business opportunity to partners? How can a programme incentivize partners to work with women?
- Is there value to the sub-sector and to women if they take on enhanced or new roles?
- What are the specific risks for business partners to engage with women? What can the programme do to mitigate the risks and create a demonstration effect?
- How will women's empowerment be impacted by involvement in the interventions? Will they have higher incomes, better jobs, improved access, increased control and decision making, greater return on labour, more manageable workloads?
- What implementation challenges is the intervention likely to face? Are there critical barriers or challenges for women that will need to be addressed?
- What implementation opportunities will the intervention be able to leverage? Are there social norms that will facilitate the intervention (e.g. women's current roles and social attitudes that support women's work in the sector)?

Programme design: developing gendered risk mitigation tools and strategies

Once the context is well understood, market systems intervention strategies can be selected and adapted to fit the context. If an intervention strategy is not adapted but simply modelled after a past example in a different sociocultural environment, then there is significant risk that the approach will be unsuccessful, as it will not be contextually appropriate. Indeed, Kabeer (2018: ii) confirms that WEE interventions that lack a contextually specific approach 'have low take-up as they lack relevance to people's lives and livelihoods'. Moreover, a contextually specific approach is conducive to enhanced tailoring of the intervention model including taking the intersectionality of women's identities into account for certain target groups. For example, low-income women who are of a certain ethnic group may be at higher risk of market exclusion than low-income women of a majority ethnic group. As indicated above, a participatory approach to intervention design can enhance understanding of the multiple barriers faced by women and enable projects to connect various aspects of women's experiences within social, economic, political, and legal environments to further reduce risk of programme failure and harm to women.

Gendering a risk register

For risk assessment to be consistent and coordinated, a tailored GE/WEE risk register for a specific context and programme can provide the framework for each stage of the intervention life cycle. The risk register should be framed according to goals and objectives and should aid information gathering during the research and analysis phase. Ongoing assessment of the risk register allows practitioners to ascertain programme bottlenecks, determine the level of likelihood that risks will occur, and devise strategies to mitigate risks.

Standard risk registers normally: 1) identify risks concerning programme stakeholders, selected activities and projected outcomes, financial and operational issues, and/or enabling environment; 2) indicate the likelihood of risk (e.g. on a scale from 1 to 4) and the level of a risk's impact; and 3) develop a risk mitigation strategy (see for example Global Affairs Canada, n.d.). However, standard risk registers need to consider gender difference, recognizing that the risks and their impacts can be either gender inclusive or gender targeted. In a risk register, a stated risk is gender inclusive if the risk has implications for both men and women, while still accounting for the fact that the implications may have differing gender impacts. If a stated risk is gender targeted, it identifies the risk as based on gender. This tool is illustrated in Table 10.1.

In WEE programming, it is possible to develop a separate risk register for women's economic empowerment dimensions within either a gender-inclusive or gender-targeted initiative. It should be noted that while developing the risk register for an MSD programme, risk analysis is not based on a separate socio-economic gender analysis. Rather, it builds on the knowledge of the market system and the inherent roles, opportunities, constraints, and risks to women's beneficial participation in and contribution to that system. Some of these risks will be based on gendered social norms, while others will relate to market dynamics and government services that may or may not be gender biased or gender blind. For example, if there are export opportunities in

Table 10.1 Sample gender-inclusive and gender-targeted risk assessment matrix

Gender-inclusive or gender-targeted risk	**Specific risk description** *'There is a risk that…'*	**Likelihood of risk** *1 low* *4 high*	**Impact on programme** *1 low* *4 high*	**Risk mitigation strategy** *'In order to mitigate this risk, the programme will…'*
Gender inclusive	There is a risk that input suppliers will not see a value of working with low-income smallholder farmers (men and women)	2	3	In order to mitigate this risk, the programme will provide evidence to input suppliers about the potential value of the smallholder market along with the roles that women and men play in buying and using inputs
Gender targeted	There is a risk that women will be excluded from government agriculture extension service training and demo plots due to standard practices of the service	3	3	In order to mitigate this risk, the programme will build awareness among extension workers about women's roles in agriculture and how to be more effective in involving women in extension activities

a specific sector, and that sector is not included in government export promotion, this may not involve a specific gender bias but simply result from a
service gap that affects the target sector.

The following WEE risk register is based on MEDA and the Economic and
Community Development Institute's (ECDI) ground-breaking WEE project in
four provinces of Pakistan – Behind the Veil (Jones and Shaikh, 2005). MEDA
and ECDI designed an MSD initiative to mainstream mobility-constrained
rural women into high-value, hand-embroidered garment markets based on
a novel woman-to-woman intermediary model. Women intermediaries could
interact directly with rural embroiderers (unlike their male counterparts), and
at the same time offer an embedded service package that included inputs,
quality control, and product design. With a total grant of US$625,000 over
three years from the United States Agency for International Development
(USAID), the programme aimed to benefit 6,000 women embroiderers (and
in fact increased incomes of approximately 9,000 – with crowding in still not
accounted for). Economies of scale and value for money were achieved by
focusing programme efforts on the 100 women intermediaries who worked
directly with groups of rural women embroiderers.

The WEE risk register used during the programme and illustrated in
Table 10.2 highlights the risks to women's empowerment based on the five
non-negotiable WEE dimensions as outlined in the Women's Empowerment
and Market Systems (WEAMS) Framework (Jones, 2016). The risk register then
elaborates the likelihood of the risk, the potential impact if the risk is realized,
and how the programme will mitigate the potential risks. Table 10.2 provides
an example for consideration.

Programme implementation: managing for gendered risks

Managing risk through partnership. An effective method of developing and managing sound risk mitigation strategies in WEE programming can be accomplished in collaboration with local partners from the public, private, and civil
society sectors. This type of partnership approach to risk mitigation bolsters
effectiveness, increases scale, and results in more sustainable outcomes. This
is because:

- Local partners understand the context, often have established networks,
  and offer invaluable contributions for project design and implementation. For example, if a financing model has been developed in a different
  context, a local partner can support the adaptation of that model to promote successful adoption and application in the given context.
- Partnerships can deliver a multiplier effect in projects, helping achieve
  scale in outreach to larger numbers of women in the selected market
  system. For example, when developing the capacity of input suppliers
  or service providers to offer fee-based services, if a few or several are
  selected at the same time, greater outreach can be achieved.

Table 10.2 Risk register framework for MEDA's Behind the Veil project in Pakistan

Dimension of women's empowerment	Specific risk description *'There is a risk that…'*	Likelihood of risk *1 low* *4 high*	Impact on programme *1 low* *4 high*	Risk mitigation strategy if score of 3 or more on either axis *'In order to mitigate this risk, the programme will…'*
Economic advancement – increased income and return on labour	There is a risk that women will be exploited by new women intermediaries	2	3	In order to mitigate this risk, women intermediaries who have relationships in target communities will be identified and supported. Monitoring with rural women will track for exploitative behaviours
Access to opportunities (e.g. training, markets, jobs)	There is a risk that women will not be able to access markets or training that are needed to flourish in the selected market system	1	4	In order to mitigate this risk, women intermediaries will deliver training and forge market linkages for women embroiderers who have limited mobility
Access to assets and services (e.g. finance, input supplies, ICTs)	There is a risk that women intermediaries will not have needed finance to offer inputs to producers and increase product volumes and quality of inputs	2	2	In order to mitigate this risk, intermediaries will both be supported to self-fund growth in line with market demand and be linked to financial institutions
Decision-making authority in different spheres including finances	There is a risk that women embroiderers and intermediaries will not have control of increased income due to gender norms and household dynamics	1	4	In order to mitigate this risk, the project will monitor for the women's assertions that men do not try to control their embroidery income as it goes against social norms and would be shameful behaviour for men
Manageable workloads	There is a risk that women embroiderers would be over-taxed with productive and reproductive labour demands	1	2	In order to mitigate this risk, women's workloads will be tracked even though women say that they already spend a lot of time embroidering for home use or low-value sales

- When an MSD intervention has run its course local business partners can continue providing products and services to women that would otherwise have ended if they had been solely subsidized by the programme. This model of sustainability is at the heart of the MSD approach. For example, if a buyer has been linked to women producers and provides both market access and quality control, if this relationship is mutually beneficial, it can be sustained in the long term beyond the life of the intervention.

When working with local partners, it may be necessary to build their capacity concerning MSD approaches and best practices. Capacity building is a critical programming strategy and is also a risk reduction technique, as it increases the abilities of local institutions to support WEE and systems change. This can involve building the capacities of local NGOs, businesses, service providers, government agencies, associations, and women's groups.

Managing risks to women's participation. During the implementation of WEE initiatives, in order to reduce the risk of a lack of participation by women, interventions can be made more responsive to women's needs, their time and mobility constraints, and prevailing sociocultural norms that could circumvent their participation. The following tips can be helpful in supporting gender-responsive intervention design:

Contents or materials can be adapted or created to be appropriate to women's educational and sociocultural background as well as their specific roles in the sector. For example, if women have lower levels of literacy, then marketing and instructional materials can use pictorial cues, and multimedia can also be a useful tool for instruction. Facilitation style should be inclusive and participatory, utilizing adult education techniques.

Location of meetings, trainings, demonstration plots, and so on need to be accessible, and in some instances relatively close, to where women live in a safe and secure environment. This will be driven by context with attention to local sociocultural norms and women's responsibilities. Facilities should also be accessible and appropriate for women, and where possible, childcare or space for childcare providers accompanying the trainees should be provided to ensure women's full participation.

Timing also needs to be convenient to women's work schedules on the farm and at home. Assess for times of day that are more convenient for women such as after lunch when children are at school and women have not yet begun the afternoon's work, all of which is contextually specific.

Invitations should be addressed to both women and men for meetings, trainings, expos, demos, and so on so that they both feel welcome. It has been found that invitations are often addressed to the head of the household (frequently men) or to the household in general but the assumption is that invitations are for men. If male permission is required or women need to be escorted by a spouse or family member, these considerations should also be addressed in planning activities.

Sensitivity to sociocultural issues is key for women's participation. In some cultures, interacting and learning in mixed gender groups is perfectly acceptable, while in others women-only or family groups are considered appropriate. The gender of the trainer or facilitator may also need to be considered, as women may be more comfortable disclosing to other women, and men with men.

Unpaid care work is a significant risk when women take on additional work outside the home. As noted elsewhere in this volume, research conducted by Institute of Development Studies (IDS) researchers Maestre and Thorpe (2016) found that solutions to address problematic aspects of care provision can create changes that: adapt market system activities based on the recognition of care responsibilities; reduce arduous and inefficient care tasks; or redistribute responsibility from women to men or from the household to the community, state, or market by using a facilitating approach.

Maestre and Thorpe found that the right solutions can reduce risks while improving women's representation and agency or influence existing norms and regulations. Table 10.3 presents a simple mapping of strategies for risk mitigation concerning the gender division of labour and women's time poverty (Maestre and Thorpe, 2016).

Implementation of these strategies involves working with a range of actors – government agencies, community organizations, cooperatives, and businesses – to identify (and unlock) the incentives for change that either accommodate unpaid care responsibilities or offer alternative solutions.

Managing community and intra-familial risk. Women may face significant risks at home and in the community when taking on greater roles within market systems through either upgrading their current status or by moving into new roles in the sector. Earlier chapters in this book (e.g. Chapter 1 on trends, Chapter 3 on enabling environments, and Chapter 4 on agricultural systems) have outlined these issues. In particular, gender-based violence is a considerable risk that has been described in detail (Hughes et al., 2015) as are social sanctions such as teasing and shunning (Markel and Miller, 2016). USAID (2014) has developed an extensive toolkit to assess and manage risks related to gender-based violence in economic growth programming. Notably, the toolkit recommends 'economic growth projects should design dual activities to build women's leadership skills while addressing resistance and backlash to their economic advancement' (USAID, 2014: 18).

An essential element of managing resistance and backlash to women's economic advancement is men's engagement. The engagement of men in gender-inclusive or gender-targeted initiatives is an important risk mitigation strategy that seeks men's support and involvement to build understanding and buy-in to support women's economic potential. As a practical application of this principle, Mayoux (2014) has developed the Gender Action Learning System (GALS) approach to women's economic development that involves male community members in gender-targeted initiatives. Such projects

Table 10.3 Risk mitigation around women's workload

Change	Adapt market system to work around care	Reduce arduous and inefficient care tasks	Redistribute some responsibility	Improve women's representation and agency (bottom-up)	Influence norms and regulations (top-down)
Examples	Change location of collection points Change timing of training Use of technology	Labour-saving equipment (e.g. laundry facilities) Village electricity Prepared foods (labour-saving product)	Redistribution of labour within the household Provision of crèche Health services (e.g. at work or in the community)	Women's social capital (e.g. support groups) Quotas for women in leadership Women's negotiating power	Influence social norms Support for women's collective action to change labour laws on work hours or maternity

contribute to changing the attitudes of men (and women) about women entrepreneurs' capacities, the choices of girls, and their education, which in turn contributes to more opportunities and greater confidence among women and girls.

A similar tool focused on gender-equitable transformation and behaviour change envisioned through a family-focused approach is the Gender Model Family methodology. Developed by SEND West Africa (2015) this methodology takes a similar participatory approach and engages men and families in transforming gender relations to be more equitable by generating greater awareness of women's unpaid contributions in the home, and under-recognized contributions on family farms, which can lead to systems change starting from the family unit. An additional useful tool that can aid in assessing men's responsiveness and resistance to women's economic engagement is the Gender-Equitable Men Scale (Singh et al., 2013). The scale can be used to assess change in social and cultural norms over time and could accompany a risk mitigation strategy to determine relative levels of impact on men stakeholders according to their perceptions of WEE and gender equality.

The importance of risk mitigation by leveraging systems change

In closing, if WEE interventions can better measure, understand, and accelerate systems change, the risks related to programme outcomes over time can be reduced, ensuring that MSD is contributing not just to sustainable change but also to dynamic adaptive change. As noted by Kabeer (2018: ii), where WEE initiatives did attempt to deliver resources to women or girls, 'the persistent structures of constraint may have prevented those resources translating into enhanced capabilities for women and girls. There is still not enough attention to the differing "initial conditions" of different groups of women and girls'. Many MSD programmes do not sufficiently target nor capture systems change, let alone gendered systems change, while also taking into consideration critical issues such as attribution and displacement.

Indeed, in a recent analysis of WEE programming implemented by OECD member countries, it was identified that 'few donors or implementing agencies address unpaid care, social norms or gender-based violence. Fewer still integrate these neglected areas through a holistic and intersectional approach' (Grantham et al., 2019: 7). Without a multi-directional, top-down/bottom-up approach that provides support in various areas of women's lives, these risks and their repercussions will continue to exist, hindering women's full socio-economic participation. Data can help tell the story, but more importantly, data can open our eyes to new ways of leveraging systems change. That is, if it is possible to observe and track dynamic and adaptive systems change, the MSD sector can be intentional about making it happen.

Risk assessment and monitoring is part of the broader task of measuring programme impact and behaviour change over time. Chapter 11, 'Measuring women's economic empowerment', will delve deeper into measurement

Table 10.4 Measuring systems change for WEE

Levels of systemic change and WEE			
Initial	*Intermediate*	*Advanced*	*Matured*
MDF partners innovate their practices to provide women with access to services, jobs, and other benefits	Partners see a vested interest in targeting women and act on this. Women continue to have access to services, jobs, and other benefits after initial partnership activities are finished. More women can access these services, jobs, and other benefits without MDF intervention	Partners expand their targeting of women due to business outcomes. Over time, more women gain access to services, jobs, and other benefits. Women see benefits (e.g. income, time saving) from their access. There are signs that women have increasing decision-making power and influence as a result	Increasingly more women gain sustained access. Women realize a sustained increased benefit from access. Other businesses adopt similar approaches to realize observed benefits. There are broader signs of increasing empowerment, particularly in areas of agency

frameworks and tools; but it should be kept in mind that all systems change has an inherent level of risk that must be managed. The Market Development Facility (MDF) funded by the Australian Department of Foreign Affairs and Trade (DFAT) in Fiji, Timor-Leste, Pakistan, Sri Lanka, and Papua New Guinea has led work on defining and suggesting a way of tracking systems change for WEE. Table 10.4 is an adaptation of a longer version available in MDF's WEE strategy/think piece (Bekkers et al., 2015), illustrating how shifts in the market system and women's empowerment can progress together, reinforcing the potential for dynamic adaptive change if risks are mitigated properly. If in the matured stage, women may have the agency to express their consumer preferences and influence the products and services that the market offers and how they are delivered, and so sustainability and dynamism will be better secured.

Useful resources

Department of Foreign Affairs and Trade (DFAT) *Operational Guidance Note: Gender Equality and Women's Economic Empowerment in Agriculture*: https://dfat.gov.au/about-us/publications/Documents/operational-guidance-note-gender-equality-and-womens-economic-empowerment-in-agriculture.pdf
Global Affairs Canada, 'Risk management': http://international.gc.ca/world-monde/funding-financement/risk_management-gestion_risques.aspx?lang=eng
Mayoux, L. Gender Action Learning System: http://www.galsatscale.net/_documents/GALSatScaleOoverviewCoffee.pdf
Morchain, D. and Kelsey, F. 'Finding ways together to build resilience: The vulnerability and risk assessment methodology', *Oxfam GB*: http://gemtoolkit.org/wp-content/uploads/2016/05/VRA-tool.pdf

References

Bekkers, H., Carter, V. and Jones, L. (2015) *Women's Economic Empowerment: How Women Contribute to and Benefit from Growth* [pdf], Market Development Facility <http://marketdevelopmentfacility.org/wp-content/uploads/2015/09/Womens-Economic-Empowerment.pdf> [accessed 20 April 2019].

Cornish, L. (2017) 'Are women entrepreneurs the key to global economic development?' [online], Devex: Inside Development – Economic Development <https://www.devex.com/news/are-women-entrepreneurs-the-key-to-global-economic-development-91010> [accessed 20 April 2019].

Department of Foreign Affairs and Trade (DFAT) (2015) *Operational Guidance Note: Gender Equality and Women's Economic Empowerment in Agriculture* [pdf] <https://dfat.gov.au/about-us/publications/Documents/operational-guidance-note-gender-equality-and-womens-economic-empowerment-in-agriculture.pdf> [accessed 20 April 2019].

Eves, R. and Crawford, J. (2014). *Do No Harm: The Relationship between Violence against Women and Women's Economic Empowerment in the Pacific* [pdf], State, Society & Governance in Melanesia, Issue Brief No. 3, Australian National University <https://iwda.org.au/assets/files/SSGM-IB-2014_3.pdf> [accessed 20 April 2019].

Gender and Development Network (2015) *Intersectionality: Reflections from the Gender and Development Network* [pdf], Thinkpieces <https://static1.squarespace.com/static/536c4ee8e4b0b60bc6ca7c74/t/5a130e9d53450a0abd9c0f8f/1511198367912/Intersectionality+GADN+thinkpiece+November+2017.pdf> [accessed 20 April 2019].

Global Affairs Canada (no date) 'Risk management' [online] <http://international.gc.ca/world-monde/funding-financement/risk_management-gestion_risques.aspx?lang=eng> [accessed 20 April 2019].

Grantham, K., Stefov, D. and Tiessen, R. (2019) *A Feminist Approach to Women's Economic Empowerment: How Canada Can Lead on the Neglected Areas of WEE* [pdf], Oxfam Canada <https://www.oxfam.ca/wp-content/uploads/2019/01/a-feminist-approach-to-womens-economic-empowerment_FINAL.pdf> [accessed 20 April 2019].

Hughes, C., Bolis, M., Fries, R. and Finigan, S. (2015) 'Women's economic inequality and domestic violence: exploring the links and empowering women', *Gender and Development* 23(2): 279–97 <https://dx.doi.org/10.1080/13552074.2015.1053216>.

International Labour Organization (ILO) (2018) *Women and Men in the Informal Economy: A Statistical Picture* [pdf] <https://www.ilo.org/wcmsp5/groups/public/---dgreports/---dcomm/documents/publication/wcms_626831.pdf> [accessed 20 April 2019].

Jones, L. (2016) *The WEAMS Framework – Women's Empowerment And Markets Systems: Concepts, Practical Guidance and Tools* [pdf], London: BEAM Exchange <https://beamexchange.org/uploads/filer_public/0d/50/0d5009be-faea-4b8c-b191-c40c6bde5394/weams_framework.pdf> [accessed 14 May 2019].

Jones, L. and Shaikh, P. (2005) *Middlemen as Agents of Change: MEDA and ECDI in Pakistan* [pdf], Washington, DC: SEEP Network <http://www.

value-chains.org/dyn/bds/docs/448/MEDA%20ECDI%20Learning%20 Paper%20Final%20PDF.pdf> [accessed 20 April 2019].

Kabeer, N. (2012) *Women's Economic Empowerment and Inclusive Growth: Labour Markets and Enterprise Development* [pdf], DFID & IDRC SIG Working Paper 1 <https://www.idrc.ca/sites/default/files/sp/Documents%20EN/NK-WEE-Concept-Paper.pdf> [accessed 20 April 2019].

Kabeer, N. (2018) *Gender, Livelihood Capabilities and Women's Economic Empowerment: Reviewing Evidence over the Life Course* [pdf], Gender & Adolescence Global Evidence (GAGE) <http://eprints.lse.ac.uk/90462/1/ Kabeer__gender-livelihood-capabilities.pdf> [accessed 20 April 2019].

Maestre, M. and Thorpe, J. (2016) 'Understanding unpaid care work to empower women in market systems approaches' [online], BEAM Exchange <https://beamexchange.org/resources/761/> [accessed 20 April 2019].

Markel, E. and Miller, E. (2016) *Gendered Social Norms for Programme Design: Sierra Leone Opportunities for Business Action (SOBA)* [pdf], London: BEAM Exchange <https://beamexchange.org/uploads/filer_public/0e/d8/0ed8ad15-535d-48ae-abd9-0cbc89946edf/soba-case_study_gender_norms.pdf> [accessed 14 May 2019].

Mayoux, L. (2014) *Gender Action Learning System* [pdf] <http://www.galsatscale. net/_documents/GALSatScale0overviewCoffee.pdf> [accessed 20 April 2019].

Mennonite Economic Development Associates (MEDA) (2019) *Land Tenure Case Study* [pdf], Greater Rural Opportunities for Women: Learning Series <https://www.meda.org/growlearning/723-land-tenure-case-study/file> [accessed 20 July 2019].

Morchain, D. and Kelsey, F. (2016) *Finding Ways Together to Build Resilience: The Vulnerability and Risk Assessment Methodology* [pdf], Oxfam GB <http:// gemtoolkit.org/wp-content/uploads/2016/05/VRA-tool.pdf>   [accessed 20 April 2019].

Oehmke, J.F. and Post, L. (2015) 'Women in agricultural & rural economies: Feed the Future program', in *UN Human Rights Council Panel on Political Will and Public Will – Fine Tuning for Gender Advocacy* [online] <https://www. researchgate.net/publication/283122344_Women_in_Agricultural_Rural_ Economies_-_Marginalized_Discriminated_-_Land_Rights_-_Feed_the_ Future_Program_-_Mutual_Accountability/download> [accessed 20 April 2019].

Puri, L. (2016) 'Gender equality is everyone's business', in *Remarks by UN Women Deputy Executive Director Lakshmi Puri at the Forbes Second Edition of the Powerful Women Summit in Mexico on 21 June* [online] <http://www. unwomen.org/en/news/stories/2016/6/lakshmi-puri-speech-at-forbes-powerful-women-summit> [accessed 20 April 2019].

SEND West Africa (2015) *Gender Model Family Manual* [online], Cordaid <https://www.cordaid.org/en/publications/gender-model-family-manual/> [accessed 20 April 2019].

Singh, A.K., Verma, R. and Barker, G. (2013) 'Measuring gender attitude: using gender-equitable men scale (GEMS) in various socio-cultural settings', Promundo   <https://promundoglobal.org/resources/measuring-gender-attitude-using-gender-equitable-men-scale-gems-in-various-socio-cultural-settings/> [accessed 20 April 2019].

United States Agency for International Development (USAID) (2014) *Toolkit for Integrating GBV Prevention and Response into Economic Growth Projects* [pdf] <https://www.usaid.gov/sites/default/files/documents/1865/USAID%20 Toolkit%20GBV%20EG%20Final%209-22-14.pdf> [accessed 20 April 2019].

UN Women (2012) 'Facts & figures' [online] <http://www.unwomen.org/ en/news/in-focus/commission-on-the-status-of-women-2012/facts-and-figures> [accessed 20 April 2019].

UN Women (2015) *Progress of the World's Women 2015–2016: Transforming Economies, Realizing Rights* [pdf] <http://www.objetivos dedesarrollodelmilenio.org.mx/Doctos/UN_Women_Summary_EN.pdf> [accessed 20 April 2019].

Value for Women (V4W) (2013) 'Infographic: investing in women-led small and growing businesses (WSGBs) in Kenya' [online], Young Female Entrepreneur Research Project <http://www.v4w.org/index.php?option=com_content&view=article&id=60> [accessed 20 July 2019].

Wood, J. (2018) '104 countries have laws that prevent women from working in some jobs' [online], World Economic Forum <https://www.weforum. org/agenda/2018/08/104-countries-have-laws-that-prevent-women-from-working-in-some-jobs/> [accessed 20 April 2019].

World Bank Group (2017) *Doing Business 2017: Equal Opportunity For All – Comparing Business Regulation for Domestic Firms in 190 Economies*, 14th edn [pdf] <http://www.doingbusiness.org/content/dam/doingBusiness/media/ Annual-Reports/English/DB17-Report.pdf> [accessed 20 April 2019].

World Bank Independent Evaluation Group (2010) *An Evaluation of World Bank Support, 2002–08: Gender and Development Evaluation Summary* [pdf], Washington, DC: World Bank <http://siteresources.worldbank.org/ GENDERINT/Resources/GenderEvalSumm.pdf> [accessed 20 April 2019].

World Economic Forum (2015) *The Global Gender Gap Report 2015* [online] <http://reports.weforum.org/global-gender-gap-report-2015/> [accessed 20 April 2019].

CHAPTER 11

Measuring women's economic empowerment

Yasir Dildar

Abstract

The chapter discusses the importance of developing measurement systems for wom-en's economic empowerment and provides a broad review of the various indicators, frameworks, and indices for identifying change in gender equality and women's eco-nomic empowerment in market systems.

Keywords: gender equality, women's economic empowerment, monitoring and evaluation, gender equality mainstreaming, indicators, frameworks

Introduction

The measurement of women's economic empowerment (WEE) is integral to international development, both at the practice and policy levels. Measurement systems are important since they provide information and data that can highlight WEE gaps so that remedial actions can be taken at the project or macro levels; hold organizations and countries accountable in meeting WEE commitments; and demonstrate how WEE contributes to meeting other development outcomes, including household well-being. For instance, measuring WEE has revealed that women's economic advancement leads to increased investments in children's education and health and reduces household poverty (for example: Malapit et al., 2018; World Bank, 2012). Other data collection and analysis suggest that 'national economies lose out when a substantial part of the population cannot compete equitably or realize its full potential' (Golla et al., 2011: 3, cited in Hunt and Samman, 2016).

This chapter provides information about various WEE measurement approaches, frameworks, tools, and indicators that are widely used in market systems development (MSD) programming. The chapter is neither an attempt to offer a particular definition of WEE nor to recommend one WEE measurement approach over others. Rather, the chapter describes various WEE measurement systems to enable practitioners, researchers, and policy makers to choose whichever approach or tool is appropriate for their initiative.

http://dx.doi.org/10.3362/9781780447506.011

The remainder of the chapter is organized into three sections. The next section discusses major WEE measurement frameworks. This is followed by a menu of indicators and tools, including indices, that are commonly used to measure WEE. The final section concludes with a reflection on challenges and key principles in measuring WEE in MSD.

WEE frameworks

To date, there is no single measurement framework or approach that can fully capture all dimensions of WEE resulting from MSD programming. Various approaches have been developed or co-opted to meet the specific needs of an organization or their market systems initiative. Most frameworks measure WEE at the individual level, a few consider household well-being, and some attempt to assess system-level change. It is important for the measurement of WEE to understand the level of measurement so as not to obscure the impact of the intervention on women.

This section describes the most widely used frameworks that have informed major international development agencies and institutional donors in the design and implementation of gender-inclusive or gender-targeted pro-grammes in MSD. The frameworks have many common aspects but also differ in what and how they measure the change in status for women. For example, the Women's Empowerment in Agriculture Index (WEAI) includes 'commu-nity leadership' as a measurement dimension, while the Making Markets Work for the Poor (M4P) WEE framework measures change in women's 'access to opportunities', and the Donor Committee for Enterprise Development (DCED) places more emphasis on institutional environments and their effect on WEE. An organization's approach to WEE will determine what dimen-sions, or domains of change, the organization will want to measure in order to ascertain if the intervention is having the desired effect. The selection of a framework will depend on the local context, type of programme, and desired outcomes (DFAT, 2015).

International Centre for Research on Women (ICRW) Framework

This is an early framework (Golla et al., 2011) that captured the concepts of 'access' and 'agency', which have been widely adopted in MSD programming. ICRW's framework includes measures for economic advancement and wom-en's power and agency, while also stressing the importance of resources (finan-cial, human, social, physical) and norms and institutions to address women's economic empowerment. The ICRW framework defines power and agency as the ability to make and act on decisions and control resources and profits, and defines economic advancement as skills and resources to compete in markets, as well as fair and equal access to economic institutions (Golla et al., 2011), which have been important contributions to WEE in market systems.

The Making Markets Work for the Poor (M4P) Women's Economic Empowerment (WEE) Framework

The M4P WEE Framework (Jones, 2012) was a seminal paper that brought a WEE perspective to MSD. It builds on the M4P approach to develop market systems so that they function more effectively, sustainably, and beneficially for low-income people, building capacities of the poor and facilitating opportunities to enhance their lives. The M4P WEE Framework examines the following domains of change or empowerment:

- Poverty reduction, income, and return on labour.
- Access to opportunities and life chances such as skills development or job openings.
- Access to assets, services, and needed supports to advance economically.
- Decision-making authority in different spheres including household finances.
- Manageable workload.

The Women's Empowerment and Market Systems Framework (WEAMS)

The WEAMS Framework (Jones, 2016) builds on the earlier M4P WEE Framework, highlighting the paradigm shift that must take place for MSD initiatives to fully embed women's empowerment and to create sustainable and equitable systems change. The framework provides detailed guidance on measurement and related concepts such as access and agency. The framework recommends the use of the DCED Standard for Results Measurement. This is compatible with MSD approaches with its: 1) articulation of logic models (results chains) that track the changes from programme activities to ultimate impact; and 2) identification of indicators that capture the changes at both the individual and business level as well as wider changes in the market system.

The Donor Committee for Enterprise Development (DCED) Framework

This framework is developed by DCED's women's entrepreneurship development working group to support DCED member projects in integrating gender considerations more fully into private sector development measurement systems. DCED (2016) provides examples of specific indicators to measure WEE changes at different levels as they relate to the dimensions defined earlier by Wu (2013):

- *Agency.* Capabilities, knowledge, individual will, skills, and confidence to pursue one's own interests, and access assets, services, and needed support. This may include power of decision making and control to adopt new strategies and technologies to enhance productivity and income.
- *Institutional environment, norms, recognition, and status.* Systems of values, norms, institutions, and policies that shape the economic and social environment and condition one's choices. This includes access issues

in the social and physical environment, in relation to rights and use of assets and services, opportunities, and expectations.
- *Social relations, accountability, networks, influence.* Power and networks that help women achieve their potential and negotiate for their rights and interests. This may involve processes of bargaining, negotiation, decision making, collaboration, and collective action.
- *Economic advancement.* Income, assets, resilience, and return on labour.

Typology of Power Framework

Another commonly used framework that measures power dynamics is the Overseas Development Institute approach to defining and measuring WEE, identifying four power domains as 'power within', 'power to', 'power over', and 'power with' (Hunt and Samman, 2016).

- *Power within.* The knowledge, individual capabilities, sense of entitlement, self-esteem, and self-belief to make changes in their lives, including learning skills for jobs or to start an enterprise.
- *Power to.* Economic decision-making power within their household, community, and local economy (including markets) not just in areas that are traditionally regarded as women's realm but extending to areas that are traditionally regarded as men's realm.
- *Power over.* Access to and control over financial, physical, and knowledge-based assets, including access to employment and income generation activities.
- *Power with.* The ability to organize with others to enhance economic activity and rights.

Gender Change Matrix

The Change Matrix was originally produced by Aruna Rao and David Kelleher at Gender at Work in 2002 and adapted by Srilatha Batliwala in 2008. The matrix classifies the following four domains in which gender power structures operate (DME for Peace, 2014): beliefs, attitudes, and values; access to and control over resources; informal cultural norms and practices; and formal institutions, laws, and policies.

These four areas align with MSD, and provide in-depth insights, particularly when assessing power structures through the lens of formal and informal rules and norms and their effect on WEE in market systems.

Gender Equality Mainstreaming (GEM) Framework

In partnership with the United States Agency for International Development (USAID) and Chemonics, Mennonite Economic Development Associates (MEDA) developed the Gender Equality Mainstreaming (GEM) Framework that supports small and medium enterprises (SMEs) and investors to improve women's empowerment within business operations. Through mainstreaming gender across environmental, social, and governance (ESG) standards, the GEM Framework offers a suite of tools to assess SMEs' level of gender inclusion, develop gender strategies, build capacity, and measure impact of businesses striving towards greater gender equality. The GEM Framework includes a series of gendered ESG indicators to measure a company's performance in gender-inclusive business practices and policies. By analysing each ESG factor from a gender perspective, the assessment tool aligns and enhances existing ESG standards used in the investment ecosystems (MEDA, 2018).

WEE indicators, tools, and indices

WEE indicators along with supporting tools and indices allow us to measure and benchmark the achievement of greater equality and empowerment. WEE indicators highlight if and how interventions have been successful in achieving desired results, while aggregate indices assess policies and trends, holding institutions and countries accountable by exposing gaps between commitments or targets and actual results. However, as with frameworks, there is no universal set of indicators that is appropriate for all MSD interventions.

Quantitative and qualitative indicators

The most common distinction among indicators is that between quantitative and qualitative indicators. In MSD programme measurement, it is common to combine quantitative and qualitative indicators – while quantitative indicators and surveys deliver statistics on outreach and impact, qualitative indicators and tools allow us to drill down on the nuances of motivations, challenges, and so on, which are especially helpful in assessing and understanding women's empowerment.

Quantitative indicators. Quantitative indicators are data points, and are therefore represented by numbers, ratios, percentages, and so on. For example, MSD programmes might measure the percentage of women entering the labour force following a targeted campaign, the number of women who take on new roles in a market system (e.g. from producer to trader) after receiving training, or the ratio of women to men who are active in a particular sector. One of the main advantages of quantitative indicators, in particular standard indicators, is that they allow for comparison over time and across contexts (Demetriades, 2007). Data for quantitative indicators are usually collected through censuses or surveys that include structured questions often with numeric or 'yes/no' answers.

Qualitative indicators. Qualitative indicators present perspectives, views, and opinions that are difficult to describe in numbers. An example could be a woman's opinion about the factors that enable or prevent her from participating in a market system. Qualitative indicators permit an in-depth examination of WEE that is not possible through quantitative indicators, leading to a nuanced understanding of women's empowerment in a market system (Jones, 2016). Data for qualitative indicators are usually collected through open-ended interviews and focus group discussions.

Indicator bank

There are a multitude of indicators that are used by various organizations to measure WEE. Table 11.1 offers a bank of indicators consolidated from multiple sources from which practitioners draw, keeping in view the context and objectives of their target intervention. These indicators are organized according to commonly used WEE categories; however, this categorization is not mutually exclusive. For example, Autonomy and some aspects of Economic Advancement could be considered part of Agency.

Aggregate indices

An aggregate index combines different measurements of WEE and gender equality into a single score by assigning mathematical or statistical weighting to different empowerment elements. These composite or aggregate indices are used to measure progress of institutions and/or countries in terms of advancement made in WEE. There are many aggregate indices available for the measurement of WEE; therefore, the ones that are most relevant to MSD programming are included here.

It should be noted that aggregate indices are subject to criticism because the information they convey can be misconstrued. That is, they provide averages without any information regarding age, location, regional, or context specificity of the nature of economic empowerment. Additionally, because indices aggregate multiple indicators, the scope of a measurement can be broad, making it difficult to draw meaningful conclusions or recommend specific policy. Further, indices that include some gender-sensitive indicators can cause the overall gender score to be ambiguous since the weight that these indicators are given in the overall calculation is often unknown (Aggarwal and Chakraborty, 2016). In addition, indices are often criticized for the choice of indicators used to measure WEE (Bartusková and Kubelková, 2014).

Women's Empowerment in Agriculture Index (WEAI)

The Women's Empowerment in Agriculture Index (WEAI) was a ground-breaking, survey-based measure that gathers data at individual and household levels to assess several different dimensions of empowerment within agricultural sectors (IFPRI, 2012). The WEAI gathered data across the following dimensions: production decision making; access to productive resources; control over use of income; community leadership; and time allocation. In addition,

Table 11.1 Indicator bank for WEE in MSD

Domain or change	Indicators	
	Individual/Household	*Institutional analysis questions*
Outreach	Number of women selected for the intervention Number/percentage of women selected but did not participate in the intervention Number/percentage of women selected and are participating in the intervention	How did the community respond to the activities? How did the community respond to women's participation?
Access to resources/ assets	Percentage share of women's ownership in productive assets (e.g. land, animals, machinery) Money value of productive assets owned by women Number/percentage of women with access to information and technology Number/percentage of women reporting increased access to financial services and products (e.g. loans, credit, insurance) Number/percentage of women reporting increased market opportunities Number/percentage of women reporting increased business skills/knowledge Number/percentage of women using modern technology (e.g. phone, computer)	What are the formal/informal laws/norms that regulate access to and control over resources/assets? How do these laws support/impede WEE?
Agency/ decision making	Number/percentage of women making major household decisions (e.g. large purchases such as house, car) Percentage of women's income spent on herself and children Percentage of household expenditure decided by women (and/or jointly) Percentage of non-household expenditure decided by women (and/or jointly)	What is women's representation in community groups? To what extent and how are women involved in decision making? How many community groups are led by women? To what extent does the community recognize women's contribution to ?? household and community well-being?
Autonomy and mobility	Number/percentage of women visiting public spaces (e.g. market, banks) independently Number/percentage of women independently using public transport Number/percentage of women independently visiting friends and families Number/percentage of men/women exhibiting changes in attitudes towards women and their mobility Number/percentage of men/women exhibiting changes towards women and work in specified sub-sectors	What are men's/women's attitudes about women and their mobility? What are the rates of abuse, assault, and harassment against women in public places? What are the informal/ formal rules about women's mobility?

(Continued)

Table 11.1 *Continued*

Domain or change	Indicators	
	Individual/Household	*Institutional analysis questions*
Self-confidence	Number/percentage of women reporting increased self-confidence Number/percentage of women reporting future life goals Perspective of women about making contribution to household and community well-being	How many community groups are led by women? To what extent does the community recognize women's contribution to household and community well-being?
Gender division of labour	Number of hours women and men spend on housework Number of hours women and men spend on community work Number of hours women and men spend on productive work (e.g. job, farming)	What are community members' attitudes on what work women should do? What are sex-disaggregated employment rates by sector in the community?
Economic advancement	Average weekly earnings/wages of women Percentage share of household income provided by women Number of new jobs or enterprises started by women Number of new and/or growing market opportunities to which women are connected Percentage increase in women's income (wages or profit) Percentage of women reporting enhanced ability to respond to market demand	What is the labour force participation of women in the community? Do working hours, conditions, and remuneration meet international labour standards? Is the business environment conducive to women entrepreneurs? Why or why not?

Sources: DCED (2014, 2016), Said Business School (2016), Wu (2013), Aggarwal and Chakraborty (2016), DFAT (2015), Golla et al. (2011), Chung et al. (2013), Wales (2016), Peterman et al. (2015), Buvinic (2017), and Jones (2016)

the index allows users to compare women's and men's level of empowerment across dimensions, and to track empowerment trends over time. The WEAI has spawned a significant body of literature on women's empowerment in agricultural systems and is available on the International Food Policy Research Institute (IFPRI) WEAI Resource Center website (IFPRI, 2018).

Katalyst's Women's Economic Empowerment (WEE) Index

The Katalyst WEE Index (Jones et al., 2018) allows for the scoring and ranking of productive activities (e.g. unpaid labour, family member in maize versus maize contract farmer) across agricultural sectors in order to assess and compare the impact of a specified productive activity on WEE. It utilizes statistical analysis of treatment and control groups to determine findings, understand empowerment outcomes, test the validity of the index, and rule out attribution. Specifically, the index sought to determine the influence that Katalyst programming had on its target outcomes (adapted from the M4P WEE

Framework; Jones, 2012). A pilot approach was successfully tested and scaled up. Even in the early stages of interventions, significant differences between treatment and control groups were found in greater decision-making authority and improved access to skills development opportunities for women targeted by Katalyst. In particular, the Katalyst WEE Index proved statistically valid and the findings can serve as a baseline benchmark for future applications of the Katalyst WEE Index (Jones and Weber, 2015).

Oxfam Women's Empowerment Framework

Oxfam Women's Empowerment Framework provides a context-specific composite index. While the framework itself remains constant, the specific characteristics and relevant indicators of empowerment are defined differently to enable users to build a context-specific measurement system. This framework recognizes three levels at which change can take place: personal, relational, and environmental (Oxfam, n.d). *Personal changes* refer to changes in how a woman sees herself, how she considers her role in society and that of other women, how she sees her economic role, and her confidence in deciding and taking actions that concern herself and other women. *Relational changes* take place in the relationships and power relations within a woman's surrounding network. This includes changes both within the household and within the community, and encompasses markets, local authorities, and decision makers. *Environmental changes* take place in the broader context. These can be informal changes, such as in social norms and attitudes and the beliefs of wider society, or they can be formal changes in the political and legislative framework. Although not specifically designed for an MSD programme, the index can be applied to examine systems change, particularly in enabling environment change including both regulatory and sociocultural contexts.

Women's Economic Opportunity Index (WEOI)

WEOI was developed by the Economist Intelligence Unit and builds on the Gender-Related Development Index and the World Economic Forum's Global Gender Gap Index. Women's economic opportunity is defined as a set of laws, regulations, practices, customs, and attitudes that allow women to participate in the workforce under conditions roughly equal to those of men, whether as wage-earning employees or as owners of a business. The index includes the following aspects (Economist Intelligence Unit, 2010): labour policy and practice (e.g. restriction of job types for women, maternity/paternity leave provisions, equal pay for equal work, affordability and availability of childcare); access to finance (e.g. availability of private sector credit, access to finance programmes); education and training (e.g. literacy rate, school life expectancy, training opportunities); women's legal and social status (laws protecting women against violence, freedom of movement, ownership rights); and general business environment (e.g. regulatory environment, infrastructure risk, mobile phone penetration). Like the Oxfam Women's Empowerment Framework, the WEOI was not developed for MSD programming, although it is used for assessing systems change in labour force participation initiatives.

Conclusion

There is no common approach to defining or measuring women's economic empowerment. While the M4P WEE Framework (Jones, 2012) and the WEAMS Framework (Jones, 2016) have been used widely in MSD programmes, they require adaptation to the project and context, and are often expanded upon and combined with other frameworks to inform measurement decisions. Some argue whether it is even possible to measure empowerment across different contexts, and, since changes in WEE can take a considerable amount of time to occur, short-term initiatives or projects therefore cannot fully comprehend longer-term results associated with WEE (Triple Line, n.d.).

Another major challenge in measuring WEE is related to non-availability of data or poor data quality, which is particularly true for aggregate indices and standardized indicators. First, for conducting longitudinal analysis and trends of WEE, it is very important that data is gathered in a consistent manner (i.e. using the same tools, methods, etc.), which is not usually the case. Also, perspectives of the community, including those of women, may change over time as 'women's expectations and perceptions of their own empowerment may shift over time and so can also create challenges when relying on self-defined empowerment indicators or self-reported empowerment levels' (Wales, 2016: 6). In addition, comparison across contexts requires consistency in terms of data gathering.

Generally, there is a lack of standardization in collecting data within an organization and among countries. In many household surveys, collection of WEE data may be problematic as men often respond on behalf of women (Chung et al., 2013). WEE indicators may vary in terms of their importance across contexts. For instance, the female literacy rate may be a significant measure of WEE in Nepal and is less important in Sri Lanka where the overall literacy rate is the highest in South Asia and the gap between female and male literacy rates is rapidly closing. In many developing economies, obtaining representative data on the informal economy, where women entrepreneurs are mostly concentrated, is extremely challenging. In addition, there is a general lack of sex-disaggregated data when it comes to recognizing the different experiences of girls and women during different stages of their lives (Pereznieto and Taylor, 2014).

As noted earlier, most project-level WEE frameworks measure economic empowerment at the individual level, while a few consider household well-being. However, household members, particularly women, are interdependent on each other and a 'change in the income of a single household member is not only difficult in itself, but such measurement may neglect possible positive or negative "spillover" effects of the individual's activities on income-earning activities of other household members' (Buvinic and Furst-Nichols, 2015). Household economic surveys, on the other hand, do not generally disaggregate data by sex and information on what happens within the household is sorely missing (CARE, 2014).

In conclusion, there is no 'right' WEE measurement system or set of indicators that is relevant for every intervention, sector, or context. Multiple measures may be helpful depending on the objective(s) of the intervention, context, and available human and financial resources. The following outlines general principles that may help in designing appropriate WEE measures for MSD interventions.

- A WEE measurement system should go beyond simply counting women or capturing sex-disaggregated data (DFAT, 2015).
- Develop a logic model or results chain demonstrating how intervention activities will promote WEE and identify gender-responsive indicators measuring various categories of results (DFAT, 2015; CARE, 2014). In doing so, determine the following (Jones, 2012, 2016; Markel, 2014):
  - Is there a need to develop separate logic models (or branching logic models) for women and men?
  - Are key indicators appropriate for women's mainstreaming (not just disaggregated)?
  - Does the choice of indicator provide the right targets for the interventions? Have indicators for women's advancement been differentiated from men's?
  - Has quantitative data collection been augmented by indicators that capture women-specific access and agency outcomes?
  - Has the project committed to gathering qualitative information to gain a more nuanced understanding of women's empowerment?
  - Is there an adequate approach to estimating attribution and to assessing wider change?
- Measure changes in different units of analysis: the individual, household, and, if possible, community. It is important to measure effects at both the individual and household levels, considering the broader context of women's well-being within the household (CARE, 2014; Buvinic and Furst-Nichols, 2015).
- Given the interdependence of women's economic and social roles, measure both economic and social outcomes to understand women's economic empowerment (Buvinic and Furst-Nichols, 2015).
- Capture both breadth (scale) and depth of WEE results. Measure not only how many women benefited but also how much improvement at various levels of empowerment has been made. Quantitative indicators can help measure the scale or breadth of change; however, qualitative indicators will prove useful in capturing the depth of an impact.
- Use simple indicators that are feasible, reliable, and relevant to WEE.
- Explore what information/data already exists that could be utilized to measure WEE (Demetriades, 2007).

Useful resources

BEAM Exchange's WEAMS Framework: Women's Empowerment and Markets Systems Concepts: Practical Guidance and Tools: https://beamexchange. org/resources/794/

Data2X's review of WEE Measurement: Measuring Women's Economic Empowerment: Overview: https://pdfs.semanticscholar.org/6be0/ 35faa95a4ec4d553a785e7c9b546dcb6c656.pdf_ga=2.158128954. 1294682797.1563733200-1974881838.1563733200

MEDA's Gender Equality Mainstreaming (GEM) Framework: Gender Equality Mainstreaming for Business Growth and Impact: https://www.meda.org/gem

Poverty Action Lab's Research Workshop: IPA J-PAL Measuring Women's Empowerment Researcher Gathering: https://www.povertyactionlab.org/ event/ipa-j-pal-measuring-women%E2%80%99s-empowerment-research-er-gathering

The SEEP Network's Webinar: Women's Economic Empowerment: Practical Tools for Gender-Responsive Poverty Measurement: https://seepnetwork. org/Webinar-Post/Women-s-Economic-Empowerment-Practical-Tools-for-Gender-responsive-Poverty-Measurement-Webinar

United Nations Foundation and the ExxonMobil Foundation's Resource: Monitoring and Evaluation Guidelines for Women's Economic Empowerment Programs: http://www.womeneconroadmap.org/sites/ default/files/Monitoring%20and%20Evaluation%20Guidelines.pdf

References

Aggarwal, B. and Chakraborty, L. (2016) *The 2030 Sustainable Development Goals and Measuring Gender Inequality: A Technical Articulation for Asia-Pacific* [pdf], Working Paper No. 859, New York: Levy Economics Institute <http:// www.levyinstitute.org/pubs/wp_859.pdf> [accessed 20 May 2017].

Bartusková, L. and Kubelková, K. (2014) 'Main challenges in measuring gender inequality', in *Proceedings of FIKUSZ'14 Symposium for Young Researchers, 2014*, pp. 19–28 [pdf], Obuda University <https://kgk.uni-obuda.hu/ sites/default/files/02-Lucia-Bartuskova-Karina-Kubelkova.pdf> [accessed 15 September 2017].

Buvinic, M. and Furst-Nichols, R. (2015) *Measuring Women's Economic Empowerment* [pdf], United Nations Foundation <http://www.women econroadmap.org/sites/default/files/Measuring%20Womens%20Econ%20 Emp_FINAL_06_09_15.pdf> [accessed 16 August 2017].

CARE (2014) 'Strategic impact inquiry: women's empowerment' [online] <http://www.care.org/our-work/womens-empowerment/gender-inte-gration/strategic-impact-inquiry-womens-empowerment> [accessed 10 September 2017].

Chung, B., Kantachote, K., Mallick, A., Polster, R., and Roets, K. (2013) *Indicators of Women's Empowerment in Developing Nations* [pdf], University of Wisconsin-Madison <https://www.lafollette.wisc.edu/images/publications/ workshops/2013-women.pdf> [accessed 10 June 2017].

Demetriades, J. (2007) *Gender Indicators: What, Why, and How?* [pdf], BRIDGE <http://www.oecd.org/dac/gender-development/43041409.pdf> [accessed 3 July 2017].

Department of Foreign Affairs and Trade (DFAT) (2015) *Gender Equality and Women's Economic Empowerment in Agriculture* [pdf] <https://dfat.gov.au/about-us/publications/Documents/operational-guidance-note-gender-equality-and-womens-economic-empowerment-in-agriculture.pdf> [accessed 10 August 2017].

DME for Peace (2014) *The Change Matrix* [pdf] <http://www.dmeforpeace.org/educateforpeace/wp-content/uploads/2014/07/The-Change-Matrix.pdf> [accessed 12 July 2017].

Donor Committee for Enterprise Development (DCED) (2014) *Measuring the Results of Women's Economic Empowerment in Private Sector Development* [pdf] <https://www.enterprise-development.org/wp-content/uploads/WEE_Measuring_Womens_Economic_Empowerment_Overview.pdf ? [accessed 15 June 2017].

DCED (2016) *Practitioner Brief: Rapid Qualitative Assessment Tool for Understanding Women's Economic Empowerment Results* [pdf] <https://www.enterprise-development.org/wp-content/uploads/WEE-Rapid-Qualitative-Assessment_Practicioner-Tools-Brief_Formatted.pdf> [accessed 20 June 2017].

Economist Intelligence Unit (2010) *Women's Economic Opportunity* [pdf] <http://graphics.eiu.com/upload/weo_report_June_2010.pdf> [accessed 12 July 2017].

Golla, A., Malhotra, A., Nanda, P. and Mehra, R. (2011) *Understanding and Measuring Women's Economic Empowerment: Definition, Framework and Indicators* [pdf], International Centre for Research on Women (ICRW) <https://www.icrw.org/wp-content/uploads/2016/10/Understanding-measuring-womens-economic-empowerment.pdf> [accessed 2 February 2017].

Hunt, A. and Samman, E. (2016) *Women's Economic Empowerment: Navigating Enablers and Constraints* [pdf], London: Overseas Development Institute <https://www.odi.org/sites/odi.org.uk/files/resource-documents/10683.pdf> [accessed 7 March 2017].

International Food Policy Research Institute (IFPRI) (2012) *Women's Empowerment in Agriculture Index* [online] <http://www.ifpri.org/publication/womens-empowerment-agriculture-index> [accessed 10 May 2017].

IFPRI (2018) 'IFPRI WEAI Resource Center' [online] <http://weai.ifpri.info/> [accessed 29 April 2019].

Jones, L. (2012) *Discussion Paper for an M4P WEE Framework: How can the Making Markets Work for the Poor Framework Work for Poor Women and for Poor Men?* [pdf], Durham, UK: The Springfield Centre <https://beamexchange.org/uploads/filer_public/0e/c6/0ec60255-beb7-4614-a6c9-920826ed1f3c/wee_m4p_framework_discussion.pdf> [accessed 10 March 2017].

Jones, L. (2016) The *WEAMS Framework: Women's Empowerment and Markets Systems: Concepts, Practical Guidance and Tools* [pdf], London: BEAM Exchange <https://beamexchange.org/uploads/filer_public/0d/50/0d-5009be-faea-4b8c-b191-c40c6bde5394/weams_framework.pdf> [accessed 5 July 2017].

Jones, L. and Weber, O. (2015) *Report on Katalyst's WEE Index Pilot Study*, Bangladesh: Katalyst.

Jones, L., Weber, O. and Khan, B. (2018) *Katalyst – Innovation in Women's Economic Empowerment Measurement: Learning from the Application of the WEE Index* [pdf], Katalyst <http://katalyst.com.bd/archive/

wp-content/uploads/2018/03/INNOVATION_IN_WOMEN_-ECONOMIC_ EMPOWERMENT_MEASUREMENT.pdf> [accessed 21 July 2019]

Malapit, H., Sraboni, E., Quisumbing, A. and Ahmed, A. (2018) 'Intrahousehold empowerment gaps in agriculture and children's well-being in Bangladesh', *Development Policy Review* 37(2): 176–203 <https://doi.org/10.1111/ dpr.12374>.

Markel, E. (2014) *Measuring Women's Economic Empowerment in Private Sector Development: Guidelines for Practitioners* [pdf], Donor Committee for Enterprise Development (DCED) <https://www.enterprise-development. org/wp-content/uploads/Measuring_Womens_Economic_Empowerment_ Guidance.pdf> [accessed 10 June 2017].

Mennonite Economic Development Associates (MEDA) (2018) *The GEM Framework: Gender Equality Mainstreaming for Business Growth and Impact*, Waterloo, ON: MEDA.

Oxfam (no date) *A 'How To' Guide to Measuring Women's Empowerment: Sharing Experience from Oxfam's Impact Evaluations* [online] <http://policy-practice. oxfam.org.uk/publications/a-how-to-guide-to-measuring-womens-em- powerment-sharing-experience-from-oxfams-i-620271> [accessed 15 May 2017].

Pereznieto, P. and Taylor, G. (2014) 'A review of approaches and meth- ods to measure economic empowerment of women and girls', *Gender & Development* 22(2): 233–51 <http://dx.doi.org/10.1080/13552074.2014.920 976>.

Peterman, A., Schwab, B., Roy, S., Hidrobo, M. and Gilligan, D. (2015) *Measuring Women's Decision Making: Indicator Choice and Survey Design Experiments from Cash and Food Transfer Evaluations in Ecuador, Uganda, and Yemen* [pdf], IFPRI Discussion Paper no. 1543 <https://papers.ssrn.com/sol3/papers. cfm?abstract_id=2685232> [accessed 30 May 2019].

Said Business School (2016) *Advisory Note on Measures: Women's Economic Empowerment*, Said Business School Research Paper, Oxford: University of Oxford.

Triple Line (no date) *Women's Economic Empowerment (W.E.E): Trends and Debates* [pdf] <http://www.tripleline.com/wp-content/uploads/2014/10/ Womens-Economic-Empowerment-Triple-Line-Note.pdf> [accessed 15 August 2017].

Wales, J. (2016) *Women and Power: What Can the Numbers Tell Us About Women's Voice, Leadership and Decision-Making* [pdf], London: ODI <https://www.odi. org/sites/odi.org.uk/files/odi-assets/publications-opinion-files/10276.pdf> [accessed 25 May 2017].

World Bank (2012) *World Development Report 2012: Gender Equality and Development* [online] <https://openknowledge.worldbank.org/han- dle/10986/4391> [accessed 5 May 2019]

Wu, D. (2013) *Measuring Change in Women Entrepreneur's Economic Empowerment: A Literature Review* [pdf], Working Paper, DCED <https://www.enterprise- development.org/wp-content/uploads/Measuring_Change_in_Women_ Entrepreneurs_Economic_Empowerment.pdf> [accessed 16 June 2017].

PART 4

In conclusion

As we finalize this book, the year is 2019, and we are amid unprecedented change in social, political, economic, and physical realms. There are days when we wonder if the world could, quite frankly, get more crazy, sad, and dysfunctional. But there is a glimmer of hope. Despite the disparities in wealth, growing tribalism within and among nations, tragic wars, and the degradation of our planet Earth, we may be seeing the death throes of an old way of being. That is, most of us – from Timbuktu to Parkland, from Caracas to Damascus, from Maungdaw to Mazar – do prefer equality, acceptance, peace, and stewardship. And, practically speaking, there are not just cracks but chasms in the armour of the old guard with changing demographics, intergenerational wealth transfers, new communication technologies, innovation in social business models, and energy capture from the wind, sun, and rain.

As market development practitioners and policy makers, we are contributing to redressing imbalances, creating new partnerships, and building a greener, more peaceful world. We are driven by our vision and our mission, each doing our best in our imperfect earthly frame, to be agents of change in this beautiful, broken world.

In the midst of global change, part 4 focuses on two sets of emerging trends: innovative finance – especially gender lens investing (GLI) – and information and communications technologies (ICTs). These are two areas that hold significant potential for gender equality and women's economic empowerment.

CHAPTER 12

Emerging trends in innovative finance and technology innovation

Abstract

This chapter discusses new and emerging trends in market systems development, namely the advent and popularity of gender lens impact investing and blended finance models, and the application of rapidly developing information and communications technologies for international development initiatives.

Keywords: blended finance, gender lens investing, impact investing, information and communications technology, digital development, blockchain

Innovative financing for development

Carolyn Burns

With the launch of the Sustainable Development Goals (SDGs), it soon became apparent that Official Development Assistance (ODA) falls far short of the funding required to achieve these ambitious goals. According to the UN, 'at today's level of public and private investments in SDG-related sectors, developing countries face an average annual funding gap of USD 2.5 trillion' (UN Development Operations Coordination Office, 2018: 3). All eyes turned to the private sector as a partner and funder of change. For many in the development arena, this is not a comfortable fit, and many government donors are working hard to figure out how to support these partnerships, offer blended finance solutions, and not enrich some at the expense of others.

But change is happening. For example, in two large global blended finance programmes (INFRONT and Trading Up), Mennonite Economic Development Associates (MEDA), in partnership with Global Affairs Canada, is piloting the use of government funds to leverage private investment that should ultimately achieve poverty reduction, gender inclusion, and other development outcomes (MEDA, 2018). Other initiatives are piloting similar schemes, such as development impact bonds and other forms of outcome payments, challenge grants, public–private partnerships, and more.

Gender lens investing (GLI) is an exciting area that is gaining traction among development funders and practitioners alike. The following reports on some exciting new developments.

http://dx.doi.org/10.3362/9781780447506.012

Gender lens investing

As a subset of impact investing, GLI initiatives have coalesced to form a stand-alone, material investment strategy that recognizes women as a powerhouse market. GLI now sits at the intersection of a cultural evolution in which women are mainstreamed across economic, social, and political life. Gender's cross-cutting influence means that GLI is well-positioned to see continued growth in both public and private markets, as well as across asset classes. High investor demand for the supply of more GLI products and greater experimentation in GLI strategies is reinforcing the application of finance in breaking down sociocultural barriers. Asset managers are now in a race to capitalize on this positive investor sentiment and 'up their gender game'. Likewise, the push for greater corporate disclosures on gender themes has given rise to a larger composition of GLI data. This has reinforced the merit of GLI strategies, created new GLI markets, and expanded GLI's circle of influence. For instance, SheTrades is a mobile and website platform that has recently launched with the intention of connecting 1 million women entrepreneurs to markets by 2020 (SheTrades, n.d.). It aims to provide women entrepreneurs with access to the same capital markets as men and advocate for women's rights to invest their money as freely as men (SheTrades, n.d.). 2018 was named the year of GLI and the Criterion Institute's campaign to aggregate US$1 tn in investment capital to address gender-based violence symbolizes GLI's increasing visibility and higher capital flow. The Educate Girls Development Impact Bond (DIB) and Grand Challenges Canada menstrual hygiene management (MHM) portfolio also represent the growing diversity of interest in GLI and the sophistication of the GLI market. Despite its heightened progression, the GLI movement ultimately remains committed to redefining the value of girls and women and creating a more inclusive society.

The Educate Girls DIB represents a shift in GLI becoming less of an output-oriented practice (i.e. focusing on higher counts of women and women-linked items) towards an outcome-based financing model (i.e. recognizing an increased uptake in positive women-linked systems). The Educate Girls DIB's objective is to achieve better educated girls (Instiglio, 2015). To achieve this objective, the UBS Optimus Foundation has provided $238,000 to fund the delivery of the development intervention, while ID Insights will evaluate the efficacy of the development intervention. For each validated unit of improved learning, Children's Investment has agreed to pay UBS Optimus Foundation $44.37 (Instiglio, 2015). The UBS Optimus Foundation aims to earn 10 per cent internal rate of return on their investment should the development intervention reach targeted outcome levels (Instiglio, 2015). The Educate Girls DIB represents an evolution in GLI because it has effectively set the market rate for funding girls' educational gains and reducing gender-based educational disparities (Instiglio, 2015). The Educate Girls DIB model has also shifted the onus onto Educate Girls to demonstrate the financial merit of their education programme and incentivized the UBS Optimus Foundation to put pressure on Educate Girls to scale their education programme in an effective manner.

Grand Challenges Canada's creation of an MHM portfolio illustrates GLI's maturation from a singular deal, industry-agnostic approach towards a port-folio-wide, industry-intensive strategy. Investments were made in a series of deals involving the manufacturing of disposable and reusable MHM products, provision of logistical support, and menstrual and reproductive health edu-cational activities (Gellis, 2016) to rectify the sector's fragmentation. Grand Challenges Canada's market-building approach ensured that its financial mediation reinforced the MHM market through greater horizontal (e.g. invest-ment in MHM product and service competitors) and vertical (e.g. investment in different levels of the same MHM product and service value chain) linkages (Gellis, 2016).

Reflections on ICT4WEE

Adam Bramm

> The true digital disruptors in development are not those who finally get the latest digital gadget to the last mile and stop. They are the devel-opment organizations that act with a sense of urgency to mainstream digital tools and technologies beyond the program into the traditional economy – a rising tide that lifts all boats (Ford and Lobo, 2017: 7).

In Chapter 9 on information and communications technology for women's economic empowerment (ICT4WEE) we illustrated the potential impact of ICTs and digital disruption on economic, political, and sociocultural systems, espe-cially as they relate to WEE. A 2017 report by Accenture illustrates how ICTs are disrupting the international development sector itself by introducing not just new technologies, but also new stakeholders, market actors, donors, and business and funding models (Ford and Lobo, 2017). Drawing parallels with private sector innovators, the report aptly demonstrates the need for interna-tional development practitioners to also adapt to the rapid developments in the digital ecosystem. One of the most important points raised by the report is the need to remember that technology can only support solutions to complex human problems, technology cannot be the solution itself. To do this, develop-ment efforts must put people at the centre of the design process (an approach already known as human-centred design), something that digital development lends itself readily to doing with fast and efficient feedback loops, data analysis, and compressed innovation cycles. This is particularly applicable with regard to women, who are often excluded not only from the intervention, but also from the central design element; ICT can very easily incorporate women into digital design processes that can then better address women's needs. Thus, a future trend in international development will be a greater use of ICTs for development purposes based on human-centred design principles.

A closely related trend will be the decentralization of ICTs and digital solutions within the development context. As the digital ecosystem rapidly expands, development organizations based in developed countries will lose the monopoly over technologies and innovation processes. In fact, digital solutions to developing world problems will increasingly come from the developing world itself. According to Caesar Sengupta, Google's VP, Next Billion Users Team, 'The next generation of global tech companies are just as likely to come out of a local coffee shop in Bangalore or Ho Chi Minh City as they are from Silicon Valley' (Bellman, 2017). This is particularly promising for women as locally developed solutions will have a more intimate understanding of the complex environment in which they are developed and, because they are 'homegrown', they are potentially more sustainable. But if the development community can facilitate women's greater education in ICTs (perhaps using ICTs), then women themselves could create digital solutions to their most pressing needs. Speaking at the Tech4Women programme at the GSMA Mobile World Congress, Aline Santos made a case for adding entrepreneurship as a fundamental skill that all women and girls should be taught, in addition to the push for more female representation in the science, technology, engineering, and maths (STEM) areas. In Santos' opinion, STEM should be changed to STEEM, with the additional 'E' standing for entrepreneurship (Santos, 2018). Women creating digital solutions for women is a true state of empowerment.

The development of a digital ecosystem, with local, women-owned tech companies will require the international development industry to think more in systems terms. The roadmap for greater development in ICTs will require strong partnerships, particularly between the public and private sectors, which the international development community could facilitate. Such a state could harness private sector innovation and release new funding models, while at the same time address the negatives to ICT use such as privacy and cyber security. This kind of digital disruption could challenge negative gender norms and change power dynamics for women, opening new opportunities not just for economic empowerment. As the Accenture report succinctly states:

> Today, there is an opportunity to move beyond digital point solutions to an interwoven market of digital solutions and economies. This can accelerate the impact of interventions and sustain economic growth long after they end. Because digital for development is not about the innovation of solutions themselves. It is about how they reimagine the way people live and work in developing countries (Ford and Lobo, 2017: 2).

In addition to the above-mentioned trends, below are a few up-and-coming technologies that show potential for ICT4WEE initiatives.

Artificial intelligence (AI)

> AI is probably the most important thing humanity has ever worked on. I think of it as something more profound than electricity or fire (Sundar Pichai, CEO, Google, quoted in Ibaraki, 2018).

Artificial intelligence (AI) has gained a lot of attention in recent years. For those working on AI, the technology opens limitless possibilities for human advancement. Yet for others, the mention of AI conjures images of Terminator-style end of days scenarios. This has sprouted the AI for Good movement to combat these negative stereotypes, and to explore ways that AI could be used to solve societal problems, especially within an international development context.

A coalition of partners have come together to launch the Partnership on AI to Benefit People and Society, with the stated mission 'to study and formulate best practices on AI technologies, to advance the public's understanding of AI, and to serve as an open platform for discussion and engagement about AI and its influences on people and society' (Partnership on Artificial Intelligence, n.d.). There are several AI applications, but one that is gaining considerable attention is how AI can transform the education sector, especially for marginalized populations such as women and girls. Much has been written about the potential for ICTs to better deliver educational services in developing economies; what AI adds to this initiative is a methodology that can adapt to individual learning styles and informational needs. This can level the educational playing field for women and girls, who may be excluded from formal educational systems and/or do not have the confidence to pursue certain subjects due to societal pressures. The proportion of women entering STEM education remains low at less than 20 per cent worldwide (Porter, 2018), due, in part, to the perceived dominance of males within these subjects. AI could provide women with virtual personal teachers, capable of teaching any subject, thus fundamentally changing the system for women's education, not to mention the ways that increases in education could affect economic, political, and sociocultural systems.

Increasing educational opportunities for women is just one way that AI could play out in an international development context. While specific applications of AI are still being explored, it's clear that AI will be the next big digital disruption. As Stephen Ibaraki, a renowned social entrepreneur and futurist, states, 'AI has the potential to yield exponential overlapping amplification of value to government, industry, and education. But wariness of unintended consequences for society, economic development, and our paths to prosperity will increase' (Ibaraki, 2017).

Blockchain

Blockchain in international development is a nascent technology, and perhaps the least understood. At the mention of blockchain, most people think of bitcoin; bitcoin and other cryptocurrencies are a good example of the application of blockchain technology, but there are other applications that show promise, particularly within an international development context. The GSMA report *Blockchain for Development: Emerging Opportunities for Mobile,*

Identity, and Aid provides a good overview of how blockchain technology works and highlights three areas of interest for development: self-sovereign identity; aid transparency; and humanitarian cash payments (GSMA, 2017). Of these, the first shows exciting potential for women. The World Bank estimates that 1.5 million people lack identification; half of those are women (World Bank Group and Global Development Group, 2017). Without official identification, women are excluded from many economic and political systems, including opening bank accounts and accessing capital, owning land, and registering to vote. The mobile industry is increasingly requiring formal identification for SIM card ownership, which would exclude undocumented women from owning, and benefiting from, mobile phones. Women displaced by violence or environmental catastrophes are even more vulnerable if they are undocumented; they cannot prove citizenship, asset ownership, and are often unable to access support services.

Blockchain technology is showing potential in creating digital identities for these women. A United States Agency for International Development (USAID) report on blockchain for development (USAID, 2018) lists a few areas where a blockchain-backed ID could prove beneficial for women:

- An accretionary ID, where a woman's identity is built up over time through a series of transactions stored on a blockchain and verified by others.
- Use of a blockchain-based distributed ledger platform as the back-end database for a more traditional ID system.
- Use of a blockchain-based distributed ledger platform to log transactions linked to a previously established identity.

Of course, for women to build blockchain-backed identifications they need to be able to have some kind of digital footprint. This is where international development efforts could support women's ICT skills and facilitate greater access to and use of ICTs. Over time, women could build blockchain IDs that are more persistent and resilient than traditional ID systems.

Big data

As was discussed in Chapter 9 on ICT4WEE, the advent of big data for international development, or data-intensive development (Heeks, 2015), has changed international development by providing more and better information to direct national policies and international development efforts to better serve the intended populations. It is now possible to analyse enormous data sets from multiple disparate sources to form a clearer picture of development issues. Moreover, big data is supporting the achievement of the SDGs by providing country-level data mapped to specific indicators.

For women, big data carries the potential to elucidate the barriers women face for greater economic empowerment and, thereby, better support initiatives that target those barriers. The importance of sex-disaggregated data has become a given with practitioners of WEE and has gained momentum in international development monitoring and evaluation systems; the next step is for big data to recognize the impact that sex-disaggregated data can have not only on the lives of women, but on economic, sociocultural, and political systems.

However, big data also carries inherent fallacies. First, as was explained in Chapter 9, big data reflects societal biases; this can reveal itself in the kind of information generated pertaining to women, or the lack thereof. Data from mobile phones, for example, is perhaps the largest data set; however, as many women globally cannot or do not have access to mobile phones, the mobile phone data set masks women's behaviour. Moreover, as many women occupy liminal or informal sectors within society, capturing data that accurately represents their circumstances is difficult. Second, big data cannot factually determine cause and effect; it can only show historical data and patterns. Extrapolations from that data and predictive modelling is the purview of other disciplines and development practitioners should be careful not to extrapolate beyond what big data can explain. Lastly, there is already growing disparity between who controls, uses, and has access to big data, a phenomenon that Hilbert (2016) calls a 'new kind of digital divide'. Just as the digital divide shows disparity in the access to and use of ICTs, the information divide can reinforce power disparities between those who have control over the information value chain and those who do not (Heeks, 2015), and, once again, the situation of women can fall through the divide.

Big data represents a trend in international development that is here to stay. The work of development practitioners, especially those working on WEE, is therefore to ensure that data accurately captures the circumstances of women and that this data is open and accessible to those who need it – even entrenched in big data sets – so that the situation of women is neither invisible nor avoidable.

Messaging applications

The *communications* component of ICT is its defining feature. The ability to quickly and easily communicate via ICTs was what spurred the 2011 Arab Spring (Stepanova, 2011). In fact, messaging applications such as Messenger, WhatsApp, and Viber have surpassed social networking platforms such as Facebook and Twitter in terms of users (BI Intelligence, 2016).

Messaging apps have grown exponentially, particularly in the developing world, because they provide a fast, low-tech, and cost-effective means of communicating globally. As they are a mobile application, often users do not realize they are using the internet, in the same way as other popular mobile applications such as Facebook (Mirani, 2015). Likewise, more and more technologies are incorporating image and voice recognition services (Fischer, 2017), which will make it easier for illiterate and semi-literate populations to use these services.

As was described in Chapter 9 on ICT4WEE, the ability to network has provided immense benefits to women entrepreneurs and messaging apps could facilitate that networking and communication to a greater degree. As companies and service providers continue to evolve messaging apps, including flowing-out and bundling services, these apps will increasingly integrate with other services, providing a safe, easy, and inexpensive way for women to communicate.

References

Bellman, E. (2017) 'The end of typing: the next billion mobile users will rely on video and voice', *The Wall Street Journal*, 7 August 2017.

BI Intelligence (2016) 'Messaging apps are now bigger than social networks', [online], 20 September 2016 <http://www.businessinsider.com/the-messaging-app-report-2015-11> [accessed 17 August 2017].

Fischer, S. (2017) 'The end of typing' [online], Axios <https://www.axios.com/the-end-of-typing-1513302676-e00da61a-630a-4715-847f-90ec9df073f4.html> [accessed 14 May 2018].

Ford, F.R. and Lobo, I. (2017) *Digital Disruption: Development Unleashed – Multiply Innovation, Collaboration and Impact through Digital in International Development* [pdf], Accenture <https://www.accenture.com/t20170601T083538Z__w__/us-en/_acnmedia/PDF-40/Accenture-Digital-Disruption-Development-Unleashed.pdf> [accessed 15 May 2019].

Gellis, L. (2016) 'Empowering women and girls by investing in menstrual health', [online], 27 May 2016, Grand Challenges Canada <http://www.grandchallenges.ca/2016/empowering-women-girls-investing-menstrual-health/> [14 May 2018].

GSM Association (GSMA) (2017) *Blockchain for Development: Emerging Opportunities for Mobile, Identity, and Aid* [pdf], London: GSMA Association <https://www.gsma.com/mobilefordevelopment/wp-content/uploads/2017/12/Blockchain-for-Development.pdf> [accessed 15 May 2019].

Heeks, R. (2015) 'Data-X development: what's in a name?' [online], ICTs for Development <https://ict4dblog.wordpress.com/2015/11/16/data-x-development-whats-in-a-name/> [accessed 14 May 2018].

Hilbert, M. (2016) 'Big data for development: a review of promises and challenges', *Development Policy Review* 34(1): 135–74 <http://dx.doi.org/10.1111/dpr.12142>.

Ibaraki, S. (2017) '2017's top 5 AI trends are about far more than technology: Stephen Ibaraki' [online], 16 January 2017, ITU News <http://news.itu.int/2017s-top-5-ai-trends-are-about-far-more-than-technology-stephen-ibaraki/> [accessed 3 May 2018].

Ibaraki, S. (2018) 'Why "AI for Good" is gaining ground', [online], 22 March 2018, ITU News <https://news.itu.int/why-ai-for-good-is-gaining-ground/> [accessed 3 May 2018].

Instiglio (2015) *Educate Girls Development Impact Bond: Improving Education for 18,000 Children in Rajasthan* [pdf] <http://instiglio.org/educategirlsdib/

wp-content/uploads/2016/03/EG-DIB-Design-1.pdf> [accessed 14 May 2018].

Mennonite Economic Development Associates (MEDA) (2018) 'Investment' [online] https://www.meda.org/expertise/investment [accessed 20 July 2019].

Mirani, L. (2015) 'Millions of Facebook users have no idea they're using the internet', [online], 9 February 2015, Quartz <https://qz.com/333313/milliions-of-facebook-users-have-no-idea-theyre-using-the-internet/> [accessed 2 April 2018].

Partnership on Artificial Intelligence (no date) 'Homepage' [online] <https://www.partnershiponai.org/> [accessed 10 May 2018].

Porter, S. (2018) 'Empowering girls and women all over the world for AI for good', [online], 30 April 2018, ITU News <https://news.itu.int/empowering-women-and-girls-all-over-the-world-to-promote-ai-for-good/> [accessed 3 May 2018].

Santos, A. (2018) 'Accelerating digital inclusion for women', presented at the GSMA Mobile World Congress, Barcelona.

SheTrades (no date) 'Homepage' [online] [accessed 14 May 2018].

Stepanova, E. (2011) 'The role of information communication technologies in the "Arab Spring": implications beyond the region', *PONARS Eurasia Policy Memo No. 159* [pdf] <http://pircenter.org/kosdata/page_doc/p2594_2.pdf> [accessed 30 April 2019].

UN Development Operations Coordination Office (2018) *Local Insights, Global Ambition: Unlocking SDG Financing: Good Practices from Early Adopters* [pdf], United Nations Sustainable Development Group <https://undg.org/wp-content/uploads/2018/07/Unlocking-SDG-Financing-Good-Practices-Early-Adopters.pdf> [accessed 30 April 2019].

United States Agency for International Development (USAID) (2018) *Identity in a Digital Age: Infrastructure for Inclusive Development* [pdf] <https://www.usaid.gov/sites/default/files/documents/15396/IDENTITY_IN_A_DIGITAL_AGE.pdf> [accessed 30 April 2019].

World Bank Group and Global Development Group (2017) *Principles on Identification for Sustainable Development: Towards the Digital Age*, Washington, DC: World Bank Group.

Index

Page numbers in *italics* indicate figures and tables, those in **bold** refer to case studies.

www.ingramcontent.com/pod-product-compliance
Lightning Source LLC
Chambersburg PA
CBHW070924030426
42336CB00014BA/2523